Gerald Butt

LIFE AT THE CROSSROADS
A History of Gaza

Rimal Publications

© Gerald Butt 1995, 2009

The right of Gerald Butt to be identified as the author of this work has been asserted by him in accordance with the Copyright, Designs and Patents Act 1988.

All rights reserved

No part of this publication may be reproduced or utilized in any form or by any means electronic or mechanical, including photocopying, recording or any information storage and retrieval system, without permission in writing from publisher.

First published 1995
by Rimal Publications and Scorpion Publishing Ltd.

This second edition published in 2009
by Rimal Publications
Nicosia - Cyprus

ISBN 978-9963-610-38-9

Photographs courtesy of Ramattan News Agency and Media Services, Gaza unless otherwise indicated.

Rimal Publications, Nicosia
and
Melisende Publishing, London

For information on our publications, visit our website
www.rimalbooks.com
and for
Melisende Publishing, UK, www.melisende.com

Designed by Myriam Misk Saikaly

Printed and bound by Calligraph
Beirut - Lebanon

Contents

Foreword	5
1. 'A Long Experience of War'	9
2. A City on the Border	25
3. The Roots of Palestine	39
4. Assyrians, Babylonians and Persians	53
5. The Rule of Greece and Rome	65
6. Under the Byzantine Cross	83
7. The Arrival of Islam	95
8. The Crusades: A Bruising Encounter	109
9. Ottoman Domination	129
10. The First World War: 'A Scene of Sad Desolation'	143
11. The British Road to Disaster	163
12. Egyptian Rule and the First Israeli Occupation	179
13. Arab Defeat and Israeli Military Rule	197

14. *Intifada*: 'A Mass Expression of Outrage'	213
15. Optimism and Countdown to War	229
Bibliography	253
Index	259

Maps

Gaza at the Crossroads	7
Gaza - A Philistine City	41
Gaza 1967 - The Final Occupation	199
The Gaza Strip in the 1990s	231

Foreword

The first edition of *Life at the Crossroads*, published in 1995, ended on a positive note. The final chapter was entitled 'The End of the Wilderness Years?'. Despite obstacles delaying the implementation of agreements between the Palestinian leadership and Israel, the momentum seemed to be in the right direction – towards the ending of Israeli occupation and eventually, perhaps, the creation of an independent Palestinian state consisting of the Gaza Strip and the West Bank.

This edition concludes with one of the most brutal wars that the Middle East has experienced, waged on the Gaza Strip. So, sadly, the wilderness years have not ended. Thousands more Gazans have been killed since those days of cautious optimism in the 1990s. Life in the Gaza Strip has also become immeasurably more difficult. It would be good to look forward to a day when a third edition of this book was required to chronicle a happier era in Gaza's very long and distinguished history.

The biography of Gaza that is related in the following pages has been drawn from a wide range of published source material, as well as from my own interviews and observations. In transcribing Arabic names and words into English I have made every effort to remove inconsistencies; but at the same time I have tried to use spellings which will be most familiar to general readers and cause as little puzzlement as possible. My apologies are offered in advance to the purists who find this irritating.

My thanks again to the people of Gaza who told me their stories, and to Elizabeth Woonton for invaluable research which formed the foundation for the early chapters.

Gerald Butt, Nicosia
February 2009

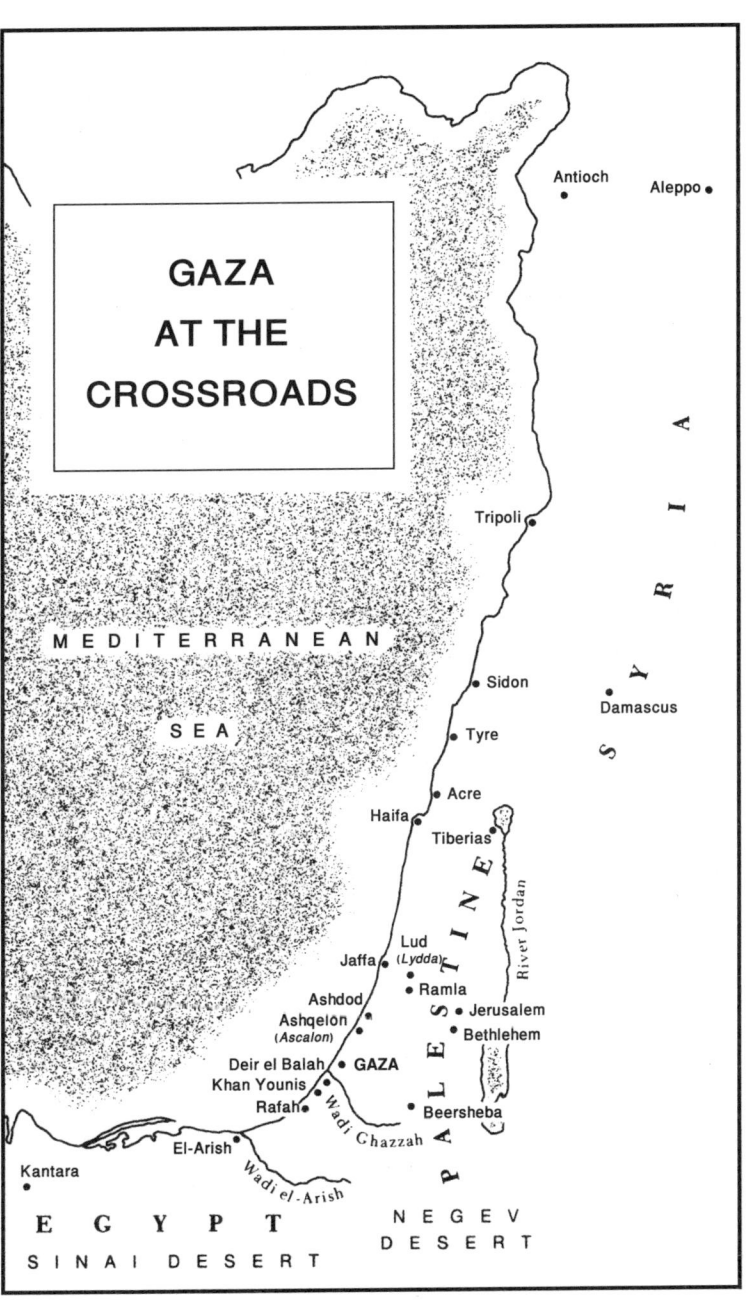

CHAPTER 1

'A Long Experience of War'

The story of Gaza is one that is interspersed, from the very earliest years of recorded history until today, with war and conflict.
'Gaza has a long experience of war,' wrote a British priest who visited the city in 1918. He went on to list some of the peoples and military leaders who were associated with its history: 'the Philistines, the Pharaohs, Nebuchadnezzar, Cambyses and Alexander the Great were all there; Antigonus and Ptolemy, Judas Maccabee and Alexander Janneus took toll of its wealth and life. Pompey restored it, Augustus gave it to Herod, and Baldwin to the Templars, and Arabs, Turks and Mamluks rode over it; Ali held it in 1771 and Napoleon in 1799. After the battles of this war [World War I], Gaza was a very lamentable spectacle.'[1]

The British priest, the Reverend Father Waggett, was in Gaza just after the Ottoman army had been defeated by the British and Allied forces commanded by General Edmund Allenby. Gaza had suffered three onslaughts in a matter of months. The city was in ruins – most of its inhabitants had fled for safety. Gaza, the priest continued, through its rich historical associations, promised much; but the newcomer was bound to be disappointed by what he found. It is easy to see why. Gaza's true face and identity – reflecting long periods when the city was a flourishing centre of learning and commerce – have been ravaged by occupation and war, and the physical traces of its past buried under the detritus of conflict, to an extent that its rich historical associations have been largely forgotten.

The Israeli war on Gaza that began at the end of December 2008 was probably the most sustained bombardment, creating the highest number of civilian casualties, in the territory's long history, perhaps an inevitable consequence of the destructive capability of modern weaponry. But for those familiar with the history of the region the Israeli bombardment evoked echoes of previous ones – the two-month-long siege of Gaza and its ultimate destruction by Alexander the Great in 332 BC, to mention just one example.

Images of the 2008-09 war and in particular the gruesome television pictures of civilian casualties are likely to influence the world's impression of the territory for many years. But the events of those horrifying weeks did not occur in isolation. Rather, they were part of a protracted campaign between the Palestinians of Gaza on the one side, and Israel on the other. The campaign began in earnest in the aftermath of the Arab-Israeli war of June 1967 in which the Gaza Strip came under Israeli occupation. The closing decades of the 20th century were marked by the battles of a people to liberate their land from occupation and to achieve independence, and that struggle has continued into the present century. The Palestinians' militant campaign began with sporadic guerrilla actions observed by a passive population. But it later developed into mass popular uprisings, or *intifadas*, the first beginning in 1987 and the second in 2000. The people of Gaza have fought many occupying forces over the

'A Long Experience of War'

centuries, and it was no surprise that Gazans led the way in the struggle against the occupying Israeli army. The first *intifada* began in the Gaza Strip and in subsequent years the flame of Palestinian resistance has continued to burn more fiercely there than in the West Bank.

The first *intifada* put Gaza on the world map, focussing international attention on the plight of the Palestinian people who had been living under Israeli occupation since 1967; and it reminded the world that no pressure had been put on Israel to abide by UN Security Council resolutions requiring it to withdraw its army from occupied Arab land. But at the same time both *intifadas* reinforced Gaza's association in the public mind with violence and conflict. Gaza has become one of the names on the map of the Middle East which is familiar to millions of people around the world. The shocking images of December 2008 and January 2009 have now superseded all others. But even in the 1980s and 90s Gaza's very name conjured up a clear image of turmoil and despair, of tear-gas, of Israeli troops firing into crowds of Palestinians, of young Palestinian youths – their faces covered by *keffiyehs* – throwing rocks or petrol bombs at the occupying forces, of refugees living in squalor, of house demolitions, of land confiscation. The relentless violence, against a backdrop of widespread poverty, inevitably pushed Gaza's long and rich history further into obscurity.

In 1994, Gaza was in the news for more positive reasons. Along with Jericho in the West Bank it was one of the first areas to be granted autonomy as Israeli troops pulled out of some of their positions in the centre of the territory – even though Israeli settlers remained and a sizeable Israeli military force continued to be deployed on Palestinian soil to protect them. On 1 July 1994 television screens around the world showed emotional scenes in Gaza as the chairman of the Palestine Liberation Organization (PLO), the late Yasser Arafat, set foot again on Palestinian soil after 27 years in exile. As one newspaper correspondent described the event, 'he was whisked through the Rafah border to a tumultuous reception in the Gaza Strip and a spectacular 30 minute motorcade past thousands of adoring supporters to Gaza city. It was a day which every Gazan had decided to call historical.' The Palestinian leader saw his arrival in Gaza as a symbolic move in the direction of the establishment of a Palestinian state. Gaza in 1994, as in the many decades and centuries before, appeared to be serving as a crossroads – this time it was traversed by Palestinian people en route from a life in diaspora or under Israeli occupation towards statehood. That, at least, was the dream.

There were a few years of hope when it seemed that Gazans, and Palestinians as a whole, might be able to achieve peace with honour, leading eventually to statehood. In December 1996, US President Bill Clinton visited the territory. Peace talks were held in the Middle East, in Europe and the United States. But the wheels turned slowly and there were many setbacks. Expectations that the granting of autonomy to Gaza would set in motion a speedy mechanism to create a Palestinian state proved unfounded. The images of violence began to appear again on television screens. The Gaza Strip was frequently sealed off by Israel, soldiers and civilians were shot at the Erez crossing point between Gaza and Israel, Palestinian suicide bombers targeted Israeli civilians, militant Islamic leaders were assassinated, angry Palestinians from Gaza took to the streets to accuse Yasser Arafat of having betrayed their cause, and Palestinian police fired into crowds of Palestinian protesters. The years of hope gave way to years of more despair.

The 2000 *intifada* was far more brutal than the first uprising, and the Israeli response was proportionately stronger. Many people, Israelis as well as Palestinians, were killed in the years of violence that began in 1987 and continued with greater or lesser intensity into the opening decade of the new century.

'A Long Experience of War'

But the 2008-09 war inflicted death and devastation on a scale that was different from anything experienced by Gazans in recent history. Around 1,300 Gazans were killed in that three-week war.

A number of factors combined to trigger the conflict. The Palestinian National Authority (PNA) proved incapable of stopping the suicide attacks carried out by militant Islamic groups, particularly those based in Gaza. The people of Gaza accused the PNA of corruption and of failing to implement policies to end economic hardship in the territory. The Islamic movement, Hamas, denounced the PNA for seeking peace with Israel. The PNA accused Hamas of derailing peace hopes. The split within the Palestinian community was complete. Ever since Hamas came to power in Gaza in January 2006, the territory had been subject to a blockade by Israel, supported by the United States and the European Union. As Palestinian academic Rashid Khalidi pointed out in a *New York Times* article in January 2009, 'fuel, electricity, imports, exports and the movement of people in and out of the Strip have been slowly choked off, leading to life-threatening problems of sanitation, health, water supply and transportation.' Hamas responded to the blockade and Israeli military incursions by launching rockets into Israeli towns, killing and injuring a number of civilians there. This chain of events ignited the war. Palestinian civilians were once again victims of a catastrophic failure of their community to remain united and of the failure of the rest of the world to exert the effort necessary to reach an honourable and comprehensive peace between the Arabs and Israelis.

Against this background it is a challenge to try to portray Gaza as anything other than a scene of conflict and devastation. It is hard to comprehend that the city and the land round it have a continuous history of human habitation stretching back more than 3,000 years. Ala-Eddine al-Shawa is a Gazan married to an American. 'At one level,' he says, 'people in the United States know a remarkable amount about Gaza – they know there's an Islamic group called Hamas, that there are refugee camps, that there's been a lot of trouble with the Israelis, and so on. But they also think it's very confusing and complex – it seems to be a case of everyone hating and killing everyone else. They wonder how I can want to go there and stay there.'[2]

Gaza, therefore, might appear to be an unpromising subject for a biography and an unlikely place to claim the significance of having been a crossroads of the Middle East. Distinguished cities with much better chronicled histories have claimed this role – Cairo, Beirut, Damascus and Istanbul amongst them. Gaza is not in the same league; it has no great pyramids, it has never been a magnet for tourists or businessmen, nor has it ever been a great military power in its own right. Everyone knows at least a little about Cairo and the other cities: about Gaza's past, few people can tell one very much. 'Even Gazans know very little about their own history,' a school teacher said. 'We have the excuse that we have been too preoccupied with trying to survive to have the luxury to sit back and look at the past.'

The way Gaza has escaped serious attention in the history books is remarkable. Because, in its way, it has been tied up closely with the history of all the major cities in the eastern Mediterranean, as well as with Cairo and with urban centres in the Arabian peninsula and beyond. Precisely because of its geographical position, most of the major players in the history of the Near and Middle East have had to take the status of Gaza into account in order to pursue their political, military or commercial ambitions. This remains as true in the 21st century as it was in the 2nd century BC. Gaza is, quite simply, one of the oldest living cities, sited at one of the oldest crossroads.

The ignorance and misunderstanding of Gaza's role in the past relate to the question of image. One of the oldest cities in the world, it may be. But visiting it today, one would hardly

'A Long Experience of War'

think that this was the case. Arriving in the Gaza Strip from the north and travelling, as countless thousands have done over the past 3,000 years, down one of the oldest highways in the world, one eagerly anticipates the first glimpse of this ancient city. But one must be ready to be disappointed. The prospect is far from promising. A tall bank of sand dunes with small shrubs growing among them on the right-hand side of the road obscures the view of the Mediterranean; on the left, interspersed with small and insignificant buildings and date palms, lie citrus groves. But as the road, busy with horse and donkey carts as well as cars and trucks, curves southwards there is no clear view of an ancient city. Instead of a neat conglomeration of buildings fringed by orchards and fields, as one might have expected, with Gaza port somewhere over to the right, the view is one of chaotic urban sprawl on a huge scale. It extends from a considerable distance to the left (eastern) side of the main road all the way to the sea on the right.

On closer inspection the visitor sees that the urban landscape bears some resemblance to that of other Middle Eastern cities with its modern apartment and office blocks, built mostly in Gaza's case during the brief period of optimism in the 1990s. Many of these have subsequently been wrecked or even flattened by successive Israeli bombardments – and most of all by the 2008-09 war. Gaza consists largely of dusty and crumbling buildings, ill-constructed and badly finished concrete structures and the shanty accommodation of eight refugee camps, squeezing out the remaining areas of agricultural land. The visitor might well dismiss Gaza as an insignificant corner of the Middle East. Many people have done just that. Gazans had grown used to the idea that their city was perceived by the world in the decades before the outbreak of the 1987 *intifada* as a forgotten and unwanted backwater.

But appearances are misleading and have done Gaza a gross disservice. The violence and destruction of the past two decades and more have been played out on land that is steeped in history. The great highway which crosses the territory from north to south, 'the way of the sea, the land beyond the Jordan, Galilee or all nations' as it is described in the Book of Isaiah in the Old Testament of the Bible, has been tramped by scores of conquering and defeated armies. In the same way, the walls and ancient buildings of the city have been destroyed and rebuilt on countless occasions. This strategically important crossroads has witnessed spectacular developments of history. But equally it has been subject to the whims of the powerful forces seeking to control the junction. The latest war and the earlier uprisings of the Palestinian people against Israeli occupation were but the latest chapter in a long saga of attempts by the people of Gaza to resist and remove foreign domination.

While archaeological remains from the past are few by comparison with other significant Middle East sites, a visit to Gaza is valuable in attempting to understand why this territory had such an important role to play in history. In the absence of major historical structures to act as landmarks the landscape itself – the geography and topography – helps a visitor to get a sense of location. For a start, it is possible to see – through the density of modern buildings – why Gaza city was built where it was. Heading south, one turns right up a slope to reach the centre of Gaza. In other words, the city was built on a small hill just to the west of the road that afforded it natural protection. This hill, once protected by city walls, provided unrivalled control of the land route along the coastal plain connecting Syria with Egypt and Arabia. The walls have gone, but there is still a clear sense of climbing into a compact city centre; and this sense is compounded by the sight of crumbling tombstones in the cemeteries at several spots on the slopes of the hill – areas which would have lain outside the walls.

Most of the old buildings of Gaza city are made of sandstone, while in the villages round about there are still many made from mud-bricks mixed with straw. The more affluent of Gazans built with stone and marble imported from distant parts of Palestine, Egypt, Syria or even Greece. The Mosque of Umar, the Grand Mosque, is the dominant feature of the city centre today, sited close to Palestine Square.

The whole focus of life in the historic city was on movement along a north-south axis, in parallel with the highway which gave the city its *raison d'etre*. Gaza port, in ancient times called Maioumas, was a separate city. Only in the early part of this century was a route opened up from Gaza westwards to the sea – the boulevard called today Umar al-Mukhtar Street – cutting across the traditional north-south axis. In the 1950s another east-west route was cut – the contemporary al-Wihda Street. Where this heads down the slope from the old city centre to the sea one can see scars of Mamluk and Ottoman buildings in the Daraj district which have been sliced through to allow the passage of the road. Today the city sweeps all the way from the centre down to the sea. But in the living memory of some Gazans this area was, as one described it, 'a jungle of trees and shrubs growing in the sand, with only a few ways where one could pass safely on foot to reach the coast.'

Today the city is inclining more and more towards the sea. In the 1990s, when it seemed Gaza might soon become part of an independent Palestine, a new port and free trade zone were planned, sited close to where the original port once stood in the Roman period and early times. It is also close to the spot where for centuries Gazan fishermen have anchored their small wooden craft. Yasser Arafat chose a building right on the coast for his own headquarters in Gaza, and new hotels, apartment blocks and other high-rise buildings – the design of which did nothing either to enhance the landscape or evoke memories of Gaza's history – appeared out of the sand dunes in this western edge of the city. The district is known as Rimal – from the Arabic word for sand.

Life at the Crossroads

Today the city is made up of eight districts. Shuja'iya and Zaitoun, poor and densely packed areas, straddle the main highway (known locally as the Rafah-Jaffa road). The other districts are Tuffah, Sabra, Daraj, Nasir, Sheikh Radwan and Rimal. There was a time when different areas of the city specialized in particular crafts and skills. On the western edge of the old walled city, for example, it was possible to find potters at work. And some pottery is still manufactured in this district.

The production of pottery was still an important local industry and a source of livelihood as late as the period immediately after the First World War. Father Waggett, who visited the city in the wake of the devastation caused by three battles for Gaza in 1917, emphasized the importance of re-establishing pottery and other crafts 'to rebuild the city and bring her children home. The manufacture of the very jolly black jugs and bowls is growing well under the impulse of a contract for hospital furnishings with the Red Cross Society.'[3]

Today the focus of daily trading in everyday commodities is the Feras market, on Umar al-Mukhtar Street just to the West of Palestine Square. It is the kind of informal free-for-all market that you find in every ancient Arab city. On the pavements and in every empty space people hang out clothes they hope to sell – a feast of brilliant colours – reds and pinks predominating among the clothes for ladies and children. But there is everything there, including CDs, kitchen ware and jewellery.

Close by is the Suq al-Imla, where the money-changers work – the official ones behind counters in tiny shops, the unofficial ones trying their luck, amid much chatter and waving of arms, on the street.

By the side of the Umari mosque is the gold *souq*, the Qaisariya – a small covered area with a vaulted roof that could have been lifted from one of a dozen old markets of its kind in Damascus, Aleppo, Amman, Baghdad or any other old Arab city.

But the overcrowding of Gaza city and its repeated destruction over the centuries have led to haphazard development. The result is that districts of the city have generally lost their individual character. Commercial and residential property are intertwined, so that in a small stretch of any street one is likely to find small mechanical workshops, furniture manufacturers, fruit and vegetable sellers, and hairdressers dotted among crumbling buildings housing Gazan families.

An assortment of traffic passes through these streets. Along with all the mechanical vehicles, ancient and modern, donkey and horse carts still carry goods between businesses, and bring families and their produce into Gaza from the villages nearby. In the early mornings, with smoke and mist drifting through the narrow streets and alleys of the towns and refugee camps you can hear a voice calling 'Bai'i Halib' – Milk Seller. The cry usually comes from an old man from one of the villages or from a bedouin family, and he travels slowly round the town by donkey cart. And many people still prefer to trust the freshness and unwatered purity of his milk to that bought in packets at the shops.

But it is poverty that keeps the donkey and horse carts in use in Gaza, just as it is poverty that forces children to play around in the dusty, rubbish-strewn alleys in the refugee camps and between the old houses, wearing slip-on shoes, or as often as not, without shoes. After the winter rains the streets fill with water and the alleyways become mud paths

The main roads also become coated with mud in winter, as cars pull out of the unmade tracks and side streets. The arterial Rafah-Jaffa highway in and out of Gaza is like a road in a suburb of any Arab city. Most of the businesses crowded along its edges make a living by servicing the cars and other vehicles that use the highway. In Gaza's case the main custom comes from work on the Peugeot taxis which, when the crossings are open, take workers each day from the territory into Israel in search of work. These vehicles are so common that Peugeot has become a synonym for taxi.

The highway today, then, because of the complexities of international borders, does not serve as a link between Egypt and greater Syria as it did for centuries. Its role is mainly to provide a link between the Gaza Strip and Israel, and in this respect the road serves as an umbilical cord. Gaza is dependant for its economic survival on this link through which most of its imports and exports must pass. And with more than half the Gazan workforce unemployed, the territory is dependent on Israel as a source of employment. For the same reasons it is uniquely vulnerable to Israeli blockades, of the kind that strangled life there in the latter part of 2008. Gaza is a reluctant recipient of nutrients through the umbilical cord. Breaking that link – as the Gazans have sought to do with earlier enforced attachments to other superior military powers to the north and south over the centuries – remains the dominant aim of its people in the 21st century.

The physical pressures on Gaza and its people in recent years have come from a number of sources, not least from the Israeli military occupation; but among the most serious of these is overcrowding. The Gaza Strip is tiny and claustrophobic; and the pressure on its meagre resources increased dramatically in 1948 with the arrival of 200,000 Palestinian refugees. Today, around 480,000 refugees still live in eight refugee camps around the Gaza Strip. Not all refugees live in camps. According to United Nations figures, more than three-quarters (1.1 million) of Gaza's total population of 1.5 million are registered as refugees. The refugee camps, which have the appearance of small and chronically overcrowded squatter towns, dominate the character and political outlook of contemporary Gaza. They are symbols of the conflict which have given Gaza its current character; and it was that character in turn which spawned the reaction to the Israeli military occupation of the territory, creating the image of

'A Long Experience of War'

violence that it has subsequently acquired in the world at large.

The 1.5 million-strong population of Gaza (80 per cent of whom are refugees from 1948) are crammed into 360 square kilometres of flat land on the coastal plain, and the population is increasing by around 40,000 a year. Some 400,000 people live in Gaza city (which includes 80,000 in the Beach refugee camp). The rest of the population is distributed among the other three towns in the Strip (Khan Younis, Deir al-Balah and Rafah) along with the nine villages and the remaining seven refugee camps.

Geographical studies speak of Gaza lying in a very fertile part of the eastern Mediterranean region which is rich in wells of sweet water. You can still see evidence of this – not only in the fields, but also in the fruit and vegetable markets which operate every morning in Gaza and in all the towns and villages in the strip. But such are the dimensions of this little wedge of territory – 45 kilometres in length and varying in width between four and 10 kilometres – that the demand on agricultural land for urban development is irresistible. Compounding this problem, too, is the fact that Jewish settlements in Gaza, set up during the Israeli occupation which began in 1967, were sited on some of the most fertile areas containing the best water resources. 'I can see a day coming soon,' a Palestinian economic planner in Gaza said, 'when we no longer have room for agriculture.'

This wedge of fertile land, fringed by desert to the south and east, and by broader sweeps of agricultural development to the north, is in all senses a link between two worlds. For many reasons, historical and political – as well as geographical – Gaza does not fit comfortably with either of its giant neighbours, Egypt to the south or Israel to the north. It has been occupied by the one and administered by the other; and while the links with Egypt remain close (with the Arabic spoken in Gaza tinged by the accent and woven with the colloquial expressions of Egyptian Arabic), Gazans see themselves inextricably linked with Palestine (the ancient territory of Philistia). The recent history of Gaza has been characterized by a struggle on the part of its people to reassert that link.

What follows in the pages ahead is the story of the Gaza crossroads from earliest history to the present day. For centuries different armies fought for control of the land on which, eventually, Syria, Lebanon, Jordan, Palestine (incorporating Gaza) and Israel were created in the aftermath of the 1914-18 World War. In recent times, this region has been the battleground for the Middle East wars of 1948, 1956, 1967, 1973, 1982, 2006 and 2008-09. The Middle East crisis and the various parties involved in it have received international attention at these moments of open warfare; guerrilla campaigns have also attracted the eyes of the world, as has the search for peace in the more recent years. Gaza has been in the thick of this intense activity, wedged between bigger powers, buffeted this way and that by the creation of the state of Israel, by the Suez crisis in 1956, by the Middle East war of June 1967 and by the *intifadas* and their aftermath. This small and insignificant speck on the bottom right-hand corner of a modern map of the eastern Mediterranean has had an important and colourful role to play in the history of this part of the world. Up until very recent times, Gaza has been a crossroads for armies and traders alike, a strategic corridor controlling access between Egypt to the south and the lands of Palestine, Syria and Turkey to the north.

Gaza has never been the subject of biography like some of its illustrious neighbours in the region such as Jerusalem and Cairo. Yet scores of references to Gaza can be found in ancient texts – from reports of conquests of the pharaohs carved in stone to references in cuneiform script on clay tablets – as well as in more recent records. Gaza has also been mentioned in numerous memoirs and biographies written by soldiers and politicians who came into contact with this part of the world. Archaeologists have dug beneath the surface of Gaza and discovered physical evidence of its past, recording their experiences in learned journals. By piecing together these disparate references – sometimes a mere mention in a list of place names – it becomes clear that Gaza has its own story.

Of the two areas where the Palestinians have lived under Israeli occupation the Gaza Strip has tended to be overshadowed by the West Bank which is rich with religious associations for Muslims, Jews and Christians. It is also less crowded, scenically more attractive and considerably the more prosperous of the two physically unconnected (since 1948) regions of Palestine. In the second half of the 20th century Gazans had good reason to feel themselves unwanted. While the clamour for control of the West Bank was considerable among many nationalist and right-wing Israelis, as much as among all Palestinians, neither Israel nor Egypt (which administered the territory from 1949 to 1967) showed enthusiasm for continuing to administer or possess Gaza. There is little in Gaza, for example, to attract fervent followers of Islam, Judaism or Christianity; Gaza cannot boast about its Jerusalem, Hebron or Nazareth.

The Palestinians of Gaza, as much as the place itself, have had to survive in recent years accepting the indifference of the world at large. Gaza has been living in the shadow of neighbouring states which have attracted international attention. It is not surprising, therefore, that Gaza's past has been largely forgotten by the outside world.

Gaza today is part of the Arab world and has been inhabited mostly by Muslims of the mainstream Sunni branch of Islam (with a small community of Christians) since the birth of the religion in the 7th century. But even earlier than this, traders from the Arabian peninsula, modern-day Saudi Arabia, had settled there. Gaza had been a crossroads for many centuries before the arrival of either Islam or Christianity. And like any junction of trading routes or region of strategic military importance, its people were prepared to absorb foreign influences as much as they were determined to resist and repel foreign domination. Like other eastern Mediterranean coastal cities, the people of Gaza in the earliest years of history were fused with the races of the lands nearby. The history of Gaza cannot be seen in isolation: it is linked with the sagas of Egypt, Babylonia, Assyria, Persia, Greece and Rome. All the great dynasties of the Middle East fought to possess Gaza – a 'land with a long experience of war'.

Notes
[1] The Reverend Father Waggett. Quoted in Foreign Office Documents held at the Public Records Office (PRO) in Kew. (FO 371 3413) The records give no information on his identity – but his sensitive observations make interesting reading and are quoted in Chapters 10 and 15.
[2] Interviewed by the author, 1994.
[3] PRO 371 3413.

CHAPTER 2

A City on the Border

Driving south from Gaza City there is a point where the main road dips down briefly. It is not immediately clear that you are crossing a wide river bed. But if you look up to the right you see a narrow bridge which spans the dry river and once carried the old railway line running up from Egypt. Up the river bed to the left you can see vegetation and greenery – evidence of the rainwater that feeds the soil of the river banks in winter. This is the Wadi Ghazzah (*wadi*, meaning valley, and *Ghazzah*, the Arabic word for Gaza). Since the earliest times it has been the city's front line of defence to the south.

Where the wadi reaches the sea it opens out into a broad estuary. In the winter, when rainwater flows down from the Naqab (Negev) desert, it carries soil and sand with it into the sea, colouring the water of the shoreline a muddy brown. Just on the other side of the estuary is a small, rounded sandy hill – no higher than a circus marquee. This is Tell Jemmeh (*tell*, the Arab word for hill), the closest to modern Gaza City of a series of *tells* that line the Wadi Ghazzah. It is from beneath these *tells* that archaeologists have discovered much of the evidence which has enabled them to build up a picture of Gaza and the surrounding land in the earliest years of recorded history.

These *tells* have yielded clues to the earliest occupants of the area, the buried signs of the people who occupied the Gaza area from the time when small groups of Chalcolithic hunters and farmers established communities in the late 4th millennium BC. Successive excavations over the past 80 years have scraped away the layers of Tell Jemmeh, Tell al-Ajul and Tell al-Farah to reveal evidence of the peoples who came and went for nearly two thousand years. Archaeologists have pieced together a story of a land constantly under threat, a land seized and occupied by a succession of invaders from neighbouring superstates.

From its beginnings, Gaza was part of 'a land, whether we call it Canaan or Israel or Palestine, doomed... to be the land bridge and meeting place and battlefield of great Empires – Egypt, Assyria, Babylonia, the Hellenistic kingdoms and Rome. Their peoples and armies moved up and down the Way of the Sea, one of the oldest roads in the world, which spanned the country from North to South, traversing the coastal plains and the plain of Jezreel, the site of many armed clashes.'[1] Biblical descriptions and the writings of ancient Egypt add weight to the idea that Gaza itself, in the two millennia before the Christian era, was witness to many of those armed clashes. It was a city of strategic importance. For armies approaching from Egypt, Gaza was the first city on the coastal plain to be encountered on the route towards the richer territories of Syria and Phoenicia. The Egyptians knew that control of Palestine was important for access to the timber reserves of Phoenicia and also imperative if the Valley of the Nile itself was to be protected.

Study shows that small groups of hunters and farmers established communities on the *tells* as early as 3300 BC. The territory should, therefore, be an archaelogical treasure chest. Gaza has a private museum which opened in 2008 and displays

A City on the Border

a fine range of pottery and other items, based on the 3,000-piece collection of Jawdat Khourdary, accumulated over a 20-year period. This is a rich and important resource for preserving Gaza's history. But inevitably, as is the case with any strategic territory repeatedly fought over, Gaza has lost much of its archaeological treasure to foreign plunderers. The Israel Museum in Jerusalem, for example, has a fine collection of excavated material from this very early period. It includes the largest and oldest metal horde ever discovered, consisting of copper mace heads and ceremonial maces.

In subsequent centuries the Canaanites – a Semitic people – began to move into the region. Archaeological evidence suggests that the earliest Canaanites established settlements in the Gaza area around 3000 BC, although the Biblical land of Canaan did not come into existence until much later. Material remains from the earliest period suggest that the economy was based on agriculture and crafts, as well as organised trade. The Canaanites imported copper from Sinai and luxury items made of alabaster from Egypt, in exchange for the export of olive oil.

Between 1800 and 1500 BC (the Middle Bronze Age) Canaan truly came into existence. A reference in the first book of the Bible places Gaza firmly in Canaan. But even this first mention shows clearly Gaza's function as a border town with all the strategic importance that implies. Gaza has never lost that importance. 'And the border of the Canaanites was from Sidon as thou camest to Gerar, unto Gaza as thou goest.' (Genesis X v 19)

Excavation of the *tells* along the Wadi Ghazzah has revealed much pottery evidence of this period of settlement. For example, the Israel Museum has among its collection a broad-based painted chalice taken from Tell al-Ajjul. It stands about 30 centimetres high and is decorated with dark terracotta-coloured stripes. From Tell Nagila, 35 kilometres east of Gaza, is further evidence of the period. In an excavated tomb 150 pottery vessels were found, as well as objects made out of alabaster, bronze, bone and ostrich shell. Some of these had clearly been imported from Egypt and Cyprus, showing how even in these early years Gaza was becoming a trading centre and a place of settlement for travellers. At that time large numbers of immigrants had moved through Canaan to seize control of lower Egypt. These were the Hyksos pharaohs, the 'rulers of the desert uplands', as one historian described them, and they controlled the city states in Canaan. Two fortresses, one at Tell al-Ajjul (also called Betheglaim and close to modern Gaza) and the other at Joppa (modern day Jaffa) enabled them to control the coastline. Gaza was already beginning to experience the disadvantages as well as the advantages of its strategic location: Canaan, including Gaza its capital, had become an Egyptian province. Gaza was a pawn, its fate resting in the hands of powerful neighbours.

But the people of Gaza continually asserted their independence – as they were to do for centuries thereafter. Although Egyptian rule over Canaan, first by the Hyksos pharaohs and subsequently by other dynasties, lasted for 400 years, Egypt's control of the coastal area of the eastern Mediterranean was often weak. Successive pharaohs were obliged to march north at the head of their armies to reassert authority there. The governors of Gaza swore loyalty to Egypt only under pressure.

The end of the Hyksos era came in 1580 BC when they were driven out of Egypt by Ahmose, the founder of the XVIIIth Dynasty; but by this time Egyptian control over the lands of the eastern Mediterranean had diminished, and powerful leaders in Syria threatened the Nile valley itself. Ahmose's descendant Tuthmosis III, a century or so later, gained full control of the eastern Mediterranean coastal plain. He began the process of re-establishng Egyptian supremacy in the area by the conquest of Gaza.

The man who led the Egyptians back into Gaza was a

A City on the Border

formidable warrior. As one historian, P H Newby, has written, 'if ancient Egypt can be said to have had its Napoleon it was Tuthmosis III.'[2] He had been hampered in his kingship by a powerful stepmother and aunt, Hatshepsut, who had acted as co-regent with him since he had come to the throne while still a child. During her lifetime Egyptian power in Syria and Palestine had waned and the local warlords had seized the opportunity to exploit their own strength. On the death of Hatshepsut, the Syrian princes, anxious to take advantage of instability in Egypt to further their ambitions to control it, united and became a powerful threat. Thus Tuthmosis III rode out at the head of a vast army from his frontier fortress at Tjel (near modern Kantara on the Suez Canal) to 'overthrow that vile enemy and to extend the boundaries of Egypt in accordance with the command of his father.'[3]

Travelling at about 15 miles a day, Tuthmosis III and his troops would have reached Gaza, the first major settlement on the road, about 10 days later. The firmer soil of the coastal plains around Gaza would have made the going speedier for the chariots after the sand of desert. Archaeologists believe that Gaza had defensive mud-brick fortifications at this time. A sentry posted on the walls could have spied a formidable army approaching, the dust from thousands of hooves signalling its approach. Newby has created a vivid picture of how the scene might have been: 'A desert patriarch encamped with his family in the hills of Sinai could have looked west one morning during that spring of 1468 BC and seen the pharaoh's army as a cloud of dust moving north with the blue Mediterranean behind it. As the day progressed and the angle of light changed he would see the glint of the chariots and spears. It was an army that intended to live off the land, one not so fat as Egypt no doubt but, in its pockets, rich. Nevertheless, hundred of trotting donkeys carried basic rations of bread, fruit, and oil to see them through to Gaza. A certain amount of water was carried in jars, though the army depended for its main supply on the wells that had been sunk along this already ancient road for just this purpose. Tents, furniture, battering rams, spare poles, axles and wheels for the chariots, were packed either into the chariots themselves or tied on to the backs of the donkeys. Tuthmosis drove his own chariot. Attempts had been made over generations to make the desert road practicable for chariot traffic and a special effort had been made following Tuthmosis's own sortie against Gaza on an earlier, minor campaign during Hatshepsut's lifetime.'[4]

Tuthmosis's troops are said to have numbered 20,000, charioteers, infantry, bowmen and all manner of supply troops. In those days, before stirrups made horse-back warfare effective, the charioteers were the elite, enjoying all the prestige of later cavalries. From his small chariot platform the Egyptian warrior could hurl a javelin, swing a short sword and shoot arrows.

Land which more recently has heard the thunder of tanks and artillery and the scream of jets overhead would have echoed then to the rumble of wooden chariot wheels, the clash of spears and the pounding of hooves as the first battles for this much fought over territory took place.

It seems that Gaza fell quickly to the Egyptian ruler. The army took provisions and pushed on to the north. The capture of Gaza had occurred simply because it was there, the first city on the Way of Horus (as the Egyptians called the ancient Way of the Sea), not a great prize in itself, but of strategic importance and the first chance of the great army to test its might. It was an event set to repeat itself.

So, in 1468 BC, Canaan was again firmly under Egyptian control. Its governors were answerable to the pharaohs. Evidence of this period has come from an extraordinary source. In 1887 AD the villagers of Tell al-Amarna in Egypt found a hoard of 382 clay tablets covered with cuneiform text. These writings (some of which can be seen in the British Museum in London) turned out to be extant samples of diplomatic

A City on the Border

correspondence between the pharaohs and the great powers of the day, as well as the local vassal states of Syria and Canaan. During this period the Egyptians maintained several centres for administrative purpose in Canaan; Gaza was one of the centres where they posted a commissioner.

Canaanite society appears to have functioned in a way similar to that of Europe in the Middle Ages. Each small city state usually consisted of a major town with subordinate neighbouring towns around it. All the villages were subject to the overlordship of the local 'king' and his nobles. The land appears to have been cultivated by tenant farmers working for the nobles; they also served as infantry. Every city state was subject to tribute payments and its fighting men were liable to call-up whenever the Egyptian king required them to march in his army. In one of the texts, Yahtiri, governor of Gaza and Joppa (Jaffa), writes to the pharaoh for permission to come to Egypt to serve in his army. 'To the king my lord, my pantheon and my Sun-god, seven and seven times I fell. Moreover, I am a faithful servant of the king my lord. I looked here and I looked there, but there was no light; I look to the king my lord and there is light. And even though one brick might move from beneath its neighbour, I will not move from beneath the feet of the king my lord. And let the king my lord ask Yanhamu, his deputy! When I was young he brought me to Egypt, and I served the king my lord and I stood in the gate with the king my lord. And let the king my lord ask his deputy whether I guard the gate of Azzati and the gate of Yapu. And I, with the troops of the king my lord, will go wherever they go. And now indeed have I set the front of the king's yoke upon my neck and I will bear it.'[5]

The Amarna letters show clearly how different the relations were between the pharaohs and the powerful states on the one hand, and between Egypt and the lesser vassals in Syria and Canaan on the other. In communications with Egypt, the leaders of the powerful states like Babylon and Assyria address the pharaohs as 'brother'; whereas the Canaanite leaders were more likely to affect humility, like Yahtiri, and refer to themselves as the 'dust under the feet' of the pharaohs. They positively grovelled in their communications with Egypt, indicating the low status of Gaza at this time within the land under pharaonic control.

The clay tablets describe in great detail the gifts – given more often than not to buy loyalty – that were constantly being exchanged between the powerful foreign 'kings and their "brother" the pharaoh. Horses, chariots, inlaid furniture, lapis lazuli, and ivory *objets d'art* were the most common objects exchanged, but the most valuable and sought after commodity was gold.'[6]

The pharaoh's 'brothers' in the neighbouring superstates had gold on their minds, whereas the leaders of the weaker states were more concerned with their personal safety and with the safety of their villages. Gaza and the other cities of Canaan were vulnerable, weak militarily, subject to Egypt and fearful of attack from the increasingly powerful Hittites to the north. 'The city weeps and her tears are running, and there is not help for us,' reads one of the Amarna tablets from a town in Syria. 'We have been sending to the King... of Egypt for twenty years; but not one word has come to us from our Lord.'[7]

The letters also shed light on another group causing concern for the towns and cities of Canaan. This was the Habiri (also spelled Apiru), so-called outlaws and outcasts, who were only too willing to ally themselves with the disloyal Egyptian subjects. The Habiri were 'runaways who for various reasons had to flee from their own city states. They tended to band together in isolated hill areas... whenever they appear in the Amarna letters they are portrayed as engaged in violent or subversive activity.'[8] The Amarna letters speak frequently of their actions. Several of the letters are pleas to the pharaohs for support against these marauding bandits. 'The Habiri plunder

A City on the Border

all the lands of the king. If the archers are here this year, then the lands of the king, my lord, will remain; but if archers are not here, then the lands of the king, my lord, are lost' (Amarna letter 287). The inhabitants of Gaza and the other cities in Canaan were under threat from more than one enemy.

There exists much excavated material to throw light on this period between 1450 and 1200 BC. Remnants of a large building of that time, possibly a palace, have been revealed and excavations have shown that the *tells* on the Wadi Ghazzah were fortified from this period – no doubt in response to the waves of attacks from the Habiri. According to a study published in *Archaeology* magazine, a short stretch of mud-brick wall of the Tell Jemmeh fortification still survives, along with one of the gateways. Large quantities of pottery from this period, much of it imported from Greece and Cyprus, can be seen in the Gaza Museum and the Israel Museum in Jerusalem.

Also in the Israel Museum from this period are the spectacular finds from Deir al-Balah, a town just south of Gaza City, which illustrate a high level of sophistication in society at that time – the 1200s BC. The core of the collection is made up of several large pottery sarcophagi – resembling in shape Egyptian mummy coffins. Human faces and tiny arms are depicted on the lids. The headdresses and ornaments also echo the Egyptian style. Stored inside the sarcophagi along with the bodies was a fine collection of pottery and delicate jewellery, including a bone scarab inscribed with the name Tuthmosis III set in a bronze ring. Another scarab, this time faience set in gold, is also inscribed with his name. The identity of the occupants of these extraordinary sarcophagi remains unclear. The speculation must be that they were either Canaanites influenced by the Egyptian belief in the after-life; or perhaps that they were Egyptian officials stationed in Canaan by the pharaohs. Either way the quality and individuality of the workmanship indicate that the people of the Gaza area at that time were used to handling finely crafted and beautiful objects – either locally made or imported from Egypt.

Tuthmosis's success in re-establishing Egyptian control over Canaan was short-lived. Subsequent pharaohs found the subjugation of the territories to the north increasingly difficult to maintain. The people of the Gaza area, true to form, did not relish foreign control. Egypt's prestige in those lands fell in the century following Tuthmosis's campaigns. Around 1300 BC, about 150 years after Tuthmosis had marched north, another pharaoh, Sethos I, set out in the first year of his reign to restore influence in Canaan and Syria. His aim was to restore the glory of Egypt and define again the outlying frontiers of the pharaoh's suzerainty. He referred to his reign as a period of renaissance.

Like Tuthmosis, Sethos was a warrior and set about his task with great energy. In his mission he was no longer guided by the god of his predecessors, Aton, who 'filled every land with beauty'. In keeping with his aggressive aims he marched northward protected by the god Amon whose 'heart is satisfied at the sight of blood... (who) cuts off the heads of the perverse of heart... (who) loves an instant of trampling more than a day of jubilation.'[9]

Sethos's campaign trail, like that of Tuthmosis III before him, began at the fortress of Tjel (close to modern Kantara and a place well known to soldiers more recently in the two world wars of the 20th century and the subsequent Middle Eastern wars). By now Egyptian communications were less secure. Sethos's army had to fight even in Sinai where he found many of the 'migdol' fortresses, built to protect the wells along the military route, under siege from bedouin tribesmen. According to one historian 'the Egyptian army had to begin fighting as close to home as the southern Sinai where the Shasu Bedouin were disrupting the smooth flow of travellers and material along the approximately 120-mile roadway known as the Way of Horus that led from Egypt to Gaza.'[10]

A City on the Border

Pictorial evidence of Sethos's march north at the head of his army comes from wall reliefs in the great Hypostyle Hall at Karnak in Upper Egypt. The illustrations show clearly Sethos's aggressive and warlike character. One scene depicts him walking with a Syrian prisoner under each arm. The climax of the relief shows Sethos returning in triumph to be greeted by the god Amon. Behind Sethos come long lines of captives who are to become slaves in the workshops of the temple at Karnak – in all probability some of the defenders of Gaza were among the prisoners.

But much of the relief at Karnak concentrates on the campaign march itself in the form of a pictorial map which depicts Gaza and confirms its status as a significant strategic city needing to be captured along the way.

The lowest line of pictures on the eastern side of the wall at Karnak shows the various landmarks along the route, including the besieged water sources. Access to these was essential to this and all later campaigns against Gaza from the south. The map indicates 'the military road along which Sethos's army had to pass before he could reach his main objectives in northern Syria. The way led across the waterless desert of the Sinai peninsula beyond a small canal now replaced by that of Suez. The reliefs display in correct order the many small fortified stations built to protect the indispensable wells, and these together with a town of lost name which is evidently Raphia (Rafah), 110 miles from Tjel, constitute the earliest equivalent of a map that the ancient world has to show. Twenty miles further on, described as the "town of Canaan" is Gaza.'[11]

Tuthmosis's easy victory over Gaza was not to be repeated. Sethos found a city more strongly fortified than in the past. By this time Gazans had experience of defending their city and would not give up without a fight. For Sethos it was an all-important battle; this was the first year of his reign and Gaza was the first city standing in the way of his declared renaissance of Egyptian supremacy. Sethos took Gaza by storm; the details of the battle are obscure, but it is fair to surmise, given the reports of Sethos's bloodthirsty nature, that Gazans took a considerable bruising. But, having secured the city, the conqueror moved on to the north, leaving the inhabitants of Gaza to carry on as before.

By the end of the Bronze Age (around 1200 BC) Gaza was important enough a place to be marked firmly on a map; it was the site of a thriving Canaanite settlement; and it had its own governor and ruling hierarchy, even though it was subject once more to the pharaohs.

In its first 2,000 years of recorded history the pattern of Gaza's relationship with its powerful neighbours was established. On several occasions armies from the south had succeeded in crossing the Wadi Ghazzah and taking the city. But Gaza was never the goal of the campaigns; no invader stayed to enjoy it as a prize. As a result the city, between invasions, could develop a certain autonomy. The inhabitants of Gaza seemed able to pay lip-service to foreign masters while maintaining the city's independent spirit.

Around 1300 BC Gaza and the rest of Canaan had become a wedge between the two big powers of the day, Egypt to the south and the Hittites of Syria to the north. The great pharaoh Rameses II spent at least a decade in efforts to recapture Egypt's Syrian possessions. Inevitably in these northern campaigns, Gaza, on the Way of the Sea, had a role to play. In particular, in Rameses's second campaign he used Gaza (the most important Egyptian provincial city controlling the southern coastal area) as a garrison where he divided his force into two units to confront the Hittites on two flanks.

During the rule of Rameses II and his successor Merneptah, Egyptian scribes continued and refined the tradition of recording and collating information collected during forays into Canaan. One document contains a gazetteer of the 12

A City on the Border

principal forts along the coastal route from the Egyptian border to Gaza. These forts were built specifically to protect wells, the sweet water which was vital for the success of military campaigns.

While Merneptah was in power a postal register was established, recording the movement of the pharaoh's messengers to and from Gaza and cities further to the north. Another interesting record from this time is an inscribed basalt stela. It contains a hymn of triumph to the pharaoh for his victory over Canaan, and mentions the towns in the province. The stela also talks about victory over a new people called Israel settled in the foothills to the east of the coastal plain. This is the earliest mention of Israel in ancient texts. Although never settling in Gaza, these newcomers were to play a major part in the history of the city. However, another set of new arrivals who came from much further away did settle, changing the character of the city for ever.

These travellers did not arrive via the Wadi Ghazzah as the Egyptians had done, but by sea from the west and by land from the north.

Notes
[1] Michael Grant, *History of Ancient Israel*, London, 1984, p. 7.
[2] P H Newbym *Warrior Pharaohs – The Rise and Fall of the Egyptian Empire*, London, 1980, p. 46.
[3] Sir Alan Gardiner, *Egypt of the Pharaohs*, Oxford, 1961, p. 109.
[4] Newby, *op. cit.*, p. 58.
[5] *The Times Concise Atlas of the Bible*, London, 1991, p. 25.
[6] *Biblical Archaeologist*, March 1989.
[7] Al-Amarna letter number 59, quoted in *Biblical Archaeologist*, March 1989.
[8] *The Times Concise Atlas of the Bible*, p. 2.
[9] *Biblical Archaeologist*, March 1989, p. 2.

[10] *Ibid.*, p.2.
[11] Gardiner, *op. cit.*, p. 253.

CHAPTER 3

The Roots of Palestine

From the centre of Gaza City you get no sense that you are close to the sea – yet the Mediterranean shore is only about five kilometres away. Life in the city has traditionally focused on the land routes through Gaza rather than its sea approaches. In past centuries the port was a separate city beyond a barrier of sand dunes and shrubbery, influenced by its proximity to Gaza but with a character of its own. Today the city has sprawled westward to the sea shore. The hope is that a time will come when the modern port can function normally, thus breaking the links with Israel and re-establishing Gaza as a coastal trading city in its own right, echoing its status as a major trading terminus 2,000 years ago.

In the 1200s BC, when Gaza remained a province of pharaonic Egypt, the sea began to play a more important part in the city's history. It was from the sea that waves of new settlers started to arrive in about 1175 BC – immigrants who created strong, prosperous city states along the coast and left an indelible cultural imprint. The largest group amongst them, the

39

Philistines, gave their name to the land – Philistia, a name which survives today in the word Palestine.

These immigrants were called the Sea People and in their thousands they represented the 'greatest threat to the stability of the countries of the southeastern Mediterranean since the movement of the Hyksos three centuries earlier.'[1] In fact the Sea People came by land as well as by sea. By land they travelled from Anatolia southwards into Syria, bringing their families and goods by ox-drawn waggons. They were heading for Egypt, a land of legendary wealth in gold and abundance in food.

By sea the new arrivals came mainly from Crete and Cyprus, bringing with them the cultural traditions of the Mycenean world. Much of our evidence of the arrival and settlement of the Sea Peoples comes from the Old Testament of the Bible. Their displacement of the people of Gaza is mentioned in the book of Deuteronomy (II v 23): 'As for the Avim, who had lived in settlements in the vicinity of Gaza, the Caphtorim, who came from Caphtor [Crete], destroyed them and settled in their place.'

The appearance of such large numbers of new inhabitants, many of them fighting men, posed a threat to Egyptian supremacy as much as it unsettled the local Canaanite population.

Some 150 years after the pharaoh Sethos had restored Egyptian rule in Canaan, one of his successors, Rameses III, had to commit a huge land and naval force to counter the new threat. His warriors fought the Sea People on two fronts and their victories were recorded on impressive stone reliefs.

One scene of battle where the invaders were defeated by the Egyptian army was the coastal plain north of Gaza. The newcomers from the north battled, in the manner of the Hittites whom they had clearly encountered on their march from southern Anatolia, from chariots, each with two armed men and a driver. Formidable fighters, the Philistines were depicted on

The Roots of Palestine

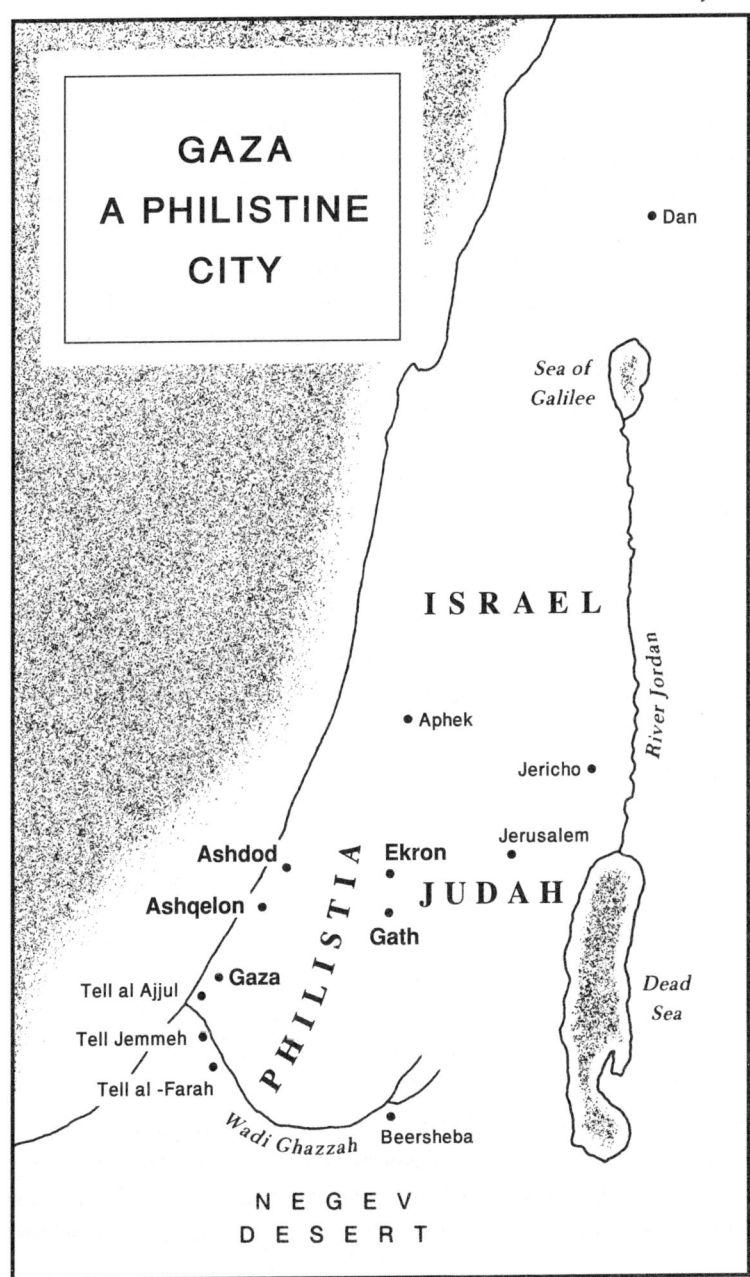

Rameses's victory frieze as tall warriors wearing tasselled kilts and distinctive ribbed helmets.

Off the eastern shores of the Nile Delta, meanwhile, Rameses's forces engaged the Sea People in a great maritime battle. The superior Egyptian navy with its powerful ships manoeuvred by skilled oarsmen trapped the sailors from across the Mediterranean, whose vessels were powered by sail only, near the shores where bowmen were waiting to pick them off. One historian recounts that for 'those who came forward together on the sea, the full flame was in front of them at the river mouth while a stockade of lances surrounded them on the shore. They were dragged in, enclosed and prostrated on the beach, killed, made into heaps from tail to head. Their ships and their goods were as if fallen into the water.'[2] While the newcomers were defeated on both fronts, the cost to the Egyptians was such that they could not drive them away permanently.

Egypt was victorious but drained of resources. From this period, exhausted of both revenue and resolve, Egypt fell into decline that lasted for centuries, removing the threat to Gaza from the south.

But Gaza had to come to terms with the increasing number of new settlers on the land, because Rameses, the victor in the battles against the Sea People, had no option but to allow them to remain in the land of Canaan. The southern part of the coastal plain, a fertile strip some 70 kilometres long and up to 35 kilometres wide, became Philistia. Power was concentrated in a pentapolis consisting of the cities of Gaza, Ashqelon, Ashdod, Ekron and Gath, each of which was ruled by a local lord. Gaza, with its former status of a capital, became the most powerful of the Philistine city states. Three of the cities, Ashqelon, Ashdod and Gaza, were beside the coastal road. Ashqelon had long possessed a harbour and enjoyed prosperous trade. The same was true of Gaza. In addition to the five recorded city states,

The Roots of Palestine

there were other Philistine settlements as well. Two of the most notable were a busy fertile town called Yavneh (Jamnia) which in ancient times included a port, and another harbour town at Tell al-Qasili near the northern extremity of Philistine occupation on the bank of the River Yarmuk.

Despite the fact that Egypt was in decline, the Philistine leaders, while responsible for the defence of their own cities, still nominally answered to the pharaohs and were obligated to raise tributes for them. But gradually their role as vassals or mercenaries of the Egyptians diminished as the influence of the pharaohs faded. A striking illustration of the change in relationship between the peoples of the coastal province and Egypt comes in the reports of one of the pharaonic envoys, Wen Amun, who was dispatched to Byblos in Phoenicia around 1100 BC to procure cedar wood. The prince of Byblos apparently would not even receive Wen Amun and forced him to camp on the beach for almost a month, all the while sending him messages to 'get out of my harbour'. Such behaviour by a Canaanite leader towards a high ranking Egyptian official during the reign of Tuthmosis III or Rameses II would have been unthinkable.

For all practical purposes, then, the city states of the Philistines became independent. Their people put down roots and became settled, flourishing as merchants, traders and warriors. Excavations and the reports of Wen Amun show how the Philistines established maritime trading with Phoenicia in the north, and actively competed with them for control of the lucrative eastern Mediterranean sea trade. Trading was also conducted by land in caravans moving into the deserts of the interior.

Archaeological evidence in the form of imported pottery shows that the Philistines maintained trade links with their former homelands, Crete and Cyprus. Pottery manufactured by the Philistines during this period can be seen in the Israel

Museum in Jerusalem. The shapes of the pottery and some of the decorative features clearly reflect styles from the Aegean which the Sea People presumably brought with them. The display shows bowls with horizontal loop handles, stirrup jars and other vessels, all decorated with distinct Philistine patterns. Red and black are the dominant colourings and most have a wide band of colour in which spirals, triangles and other patterns are painted. Another common decorative feature is a leaf-shaped bird, its wing spread and its head turned backwards.

Philistine deposits have been uncovered all over Tell Jemmeh, on the Wadi Ghazzah, which appears to have been a 'daughter town' of Gaza, a neighbouring town under Gaza's control. The most important find of this period on the *tell* is an enormous 12th century technologically advanced ceramic kiln.

But while maintaining links with their homelands, 'over the years in which they were settling down in their new homes the Philistines gradually became assimilated to the civilisation of the Canaanites and presumably intermarried with them as well; even their language [non-Semitic] was eventually replaced by a local Canaanite dialect. Excavations at Ashdod have shown how many Canaanite elements became blended with their originally non-Semitic way of life. Thus the gods of Aegean origin whom they brought to the country were given the names of Canaanite deities. These included Dagon,[3] to whom a large temple was devoted in Gaza and which figures in the Biblical story of Samson.

The five strong Philistine cities, which were ruled by military elites, soon came into conflict with another group of immigrants, the tribes of the Israelites (Hebrews) who, according to the Book of Exodus and Jewish tradition, had been led by Moses out of Egypt where they had been in slavery. The frequent references to Gaza and the Philistines in various books of the Old Testament appear in the context of the developing conflict between the Philistines and the tribes of Israel. The accounts inevitably view the friction from the perspective of the Israelites.

In the earliest reference to the Philistines, the area of their supremacy is defined when the Lord reminds Joshua of the land waiting to be claimed by the Israelites. 'This is the land that still remains: all the regions of the Philistines, all those of the Geshurites from the Shihor, which is east of Egypt, northward to the boundary of Ekron, it is reckoned as Canaanite: there are five rulers of the Philistines, those of Gaza, Ashdod, Ashqelon, Gath and Ekron' (Joshua XIII vv 2-3). Later in Joshua (XV v 47) the inheritance of the tribe of the children of Judah is listed according to their families: 'Ashdod with her towns and her villages, Gaza with her towns and her villages into the river of Egypt.' Gaza was seen as rightfully belonging to the nascent Israelite state, God-given, to be gained and held. It did not yield easily.

As the Philistine city states grew they became established as independent military powers, and even though they had no central government were still able to present a united military front when necessary. Conflict with the Israelite tribes occurred when the Philistines attempted to extend their influence inland into the hill country. There were constant skirmishes between the Israelites and the Philistines. Israelite patrols targeted Philistine trading caravans travelling to the coast from the desert, and threatened constantly to make incursions into the plain. The Philistines, for their part, set up frontier posts to the east of their cities which encouraged the Israelite tribes to believe that the rulers of the coastal plain were about to invade their hill settlements.

In the several mentions of Gaza in the book of Joshua, it is always referred to as the furthest point of Philistine territory in the sights of the Israelites. For example, in the chronicles of his great battles (Joshua X v 41): 'And Joshua defeated them [the enemies of the Israelites] from Kadesh-barnea to Gaza and all the country of Goshen as far as Gibeon.'

There is no complete chronicle of the encounters between the Philistines and the Israelites, but the Bible paints a picture of an era marked by battles interspersed with periods of calm. The Israelites held the high ground, but were faced with a formidable enemy on the plain – a string of city states built on military might which united when necessary against a common enemy. But they also had one other enormous advantage over the tribes of Israel: they 'enjoyed a local monopoly on the manufacture of iron, the secret of which they had presumably learned from the Hittites who had had a similar monopoly.'[4]

The Philistines were skilled smelters of ore, particularly of iron. Thus they could manufacture chariots from which to fight, while the armies of Israel consisted of foot-soldiers. As one historian has written, 'the ill-trained, ill-equipped Israelite tribal levies could stand little chance against such a foe in open battle.'[5] Frequent references in Joshua and Judges bemoan the military superiority enjoyed by the Philistines because of their technological skills. In Joshua XVIII v 16 one reads: 'The tribe of Joseph said, "The hill country is not enough for us; yet all the Canaanites who live in the plain have chariots of iron."' And again in Judges I v 19: 'The Lord was with Judah, and he took possession of the hill country, but could not drive out the inhabitants of the plain because they had iron.'

The Bible also records the Philistines' unwillingness to share their knowledge with the Israelites. 'Now there was no smith found throughout all the land of Israel: for the Philistines said, "Lest the Hebrews make them swords or spears."' (I Samuel XIII v 19)

There are many Biblical stories, in which the threads of myth and history are tangled, about the conflicts between the Philistines and the Israelites. Gaza is the setting for one of the most dramatic of these. It is the story of Samson, who is portrayed as a superhuman figure from the Israelite tribe of Dan.

The tribe had been forced by the Philistines to leave the foothills and settle to the north. Scripture sees him as a *nazirite* – a person consecrated to God – born to deliver the tribe from their misfortune. As Judges (XIII v 5) puts it: 'It is he who shall begin to deliver Israel from the hand of the Philistines.'

Samson had a soft spot for Philistine women and his exploits in Gaza began when he went to visit a prostitute within the city. The Gazans saw an opportunity to ambush this Israelite giant as he left the city at dawn, and lay in wait for him. But Samson departed at midnight, and seeing his way out barred 'took hold of the doors of the city gate and the two posts, pulled them up, bar and all, put them on his shoulders, and carried them to the top of the hill that is in front of Hebron.' (Judges XVI v 3)

Samson then fell in love with a Philistine woman, Delilah, who was persuaded by the Philistine lords to coax out of him the secret of his extraordinary strength. Finally he told her 'a razor has never come upon my head: for I have been a nazirite to God from my mother's womb. If my head were shaved, then my strength would leave me: I would become weak and be like anyone else.' (Judges XVI v 17)

Delilah was paid by the lords to cut Samson's hair as he slept. And then, while he was weakened, the Philistines seized him and gouged out his eyes. 'They brought him down to Gaza and bound him with bronze shackles; and he ground at the mill in the prison.' (Judges XVI v 21) While there, the story goes, Samson's strength began to return as his hair grew again.

The Philistines offered a great sacrifice to their god Dagon in thanks for the capture of Samson. And when their hearts were merry, they said, "Call Samson, and let him entertain us." So they called Samson out of the prison and he performed for them.' He asked to stand between two pillars of the temple where he could feel the columns under his hands. Three thousand men and women were watching him when he said, '"Let me die with the Philistines." He strained with all his might and the house fell on the lords and all the people who were in it.' (Judges XVI vv 25-30)

The descriptions of Samson's superhuman strength are clearly mythical. But the setting of a city of considerable stature, well fortified, with a prison and with a temple big enough to accommodate at least 3,000 people, is probably accurate. In which case Gaza under the Philistines was a solidly established city with a justice system and a flourishing practice of pagan worship. This temple may have been built over the one of Amon which Rameses erected.

As for Samson's exploits, they are clearly folk tales. However, according to one historian, 'he was probably an historical individual all the same: not perhaps one of the judges as the Bible regards him, but a tough resistance leader who made a name for himself.'[6]

The tribes of Israel eventually managed to unite for a time to face their common enemy, the Philistines. In 1050 BC a large Philistine army gathered at Aphek, a frontier post close to the Israelites. They faced an army consisting of members of practically all the tribes of Israel. On this occasion the Israelites suffered total defeat and the Ark, the shrine housing the Ark of the Covenant, the throne of the invisible Yahweh [God] and the focal point of the Israelite tribes, was captured by the Philistines. It was taken to Ashdod and placed in the temple of Dagon there. The only account of these events is Biblical and is inevitably coloured by the Israelite version of history. The Bible relates how the presence of the Ark brought plague and calamity to the Philistines wherever it was taken. After seven months it was sent back to the Israelites. From this point on, in the face of the increasing integration of the Israelites and their growing strength, the Philistines no longer enjoyed automatic supremacy either in military or commercial affairs, and victory was not always a foregone conclusion.

The Roots of Palestine

The Israelites, acting more and more in unison, looked for a leader 'because a unified military command was needed to drive the Philistines out of Israel's hills.'[7] Saul became the first king of Israel, spending the whole of his reign at war, much of it facing the major challenge from the Philistines 'whose efficient united forces still held down the greater part of the country.'[8] Saul defeated them in at least three major battles, compelling them to withdraw their forces from the inland regions and redeploy them on the coastal plain. The Philistines were becoming less of a military threat, with their monopoly of iron taken from them. But Saul could not deal the major blow needed to subdue them definitively.

Saul's end came in a disastrous battle against the Philistines in which his three sons, including his heir Jonathan, were killed. Saul, wounded in the fighting, died by falling on his own sword. The Philistines displayed his severed head in one of their temples, and nailed his body, together with that of his sons, on to the city wall at Beth-shan. And they reoccupied the greater part of the country.

Around 1000 BC, David, who as a boy soldier during the reign of Saul had earned fame when he killed the great Philistine soldier Goliath, became king. He won decisive battles against the Philistines and fought unprecedented wars of conquest, vastly enlarging the Israelite dominion.

David's victories over the Philistines ushered in a new era of Israelite supremacy, with Jerusalem for the first time the centre of power. The Bible portrays David as carrying out the word of God in defeating the Philistines. Once again the Philistines made a raid in the valley. When David again inquired of God, God said to him, 'You shall not go up after them; go around and come on them opposite the balsam trees. When you hear the sound of marching in the tops of the balsam trees, then go out to battle; for God has gone out before you to strike down the army of the Philistines.' (I Chronicles XIV vv 13-15) Thus, it is said, David drove the Philistine armies from Gibeah to Gezer. It is not clear whether he annexed Gaza and the other Philistine city states. However, 'they had been completely deprived of their power: pinned into a narrow strip of territory, they lost both their maritime and land traffic to David and their trading town of Tell el-Qasili became a commercial centre of the Israelites instead. A new sort of Israelite pottery, derived from Philistine models, began to appear, with a hand-burnished slip coloured dark-red with haematite (natural ferric oxide).'[9]

Gaza and the other Philistine city states were helpless, no longer militarily powerful and obliged to recognise Israelite supremacy. In the first book of Kings (IV v 21) Philistine subjection to Israelite rule in the reign of king Solomon, David's successor, is spelled out. 'Solomon was sovereign over all the kingdoms from the Euphrates to the land of the Philistines even to the border of Egypt; they brought tribute and served Solomon all the days of his life.'

The reference to 'the borders of Egypt' seems to indicate that Gaza and the other Philistine city states may have been tributaries to David and Solomon.

However, it appears that the Philistines began to escape Israel's domination towards the end of Solomon's reign and to look to Egypt for aid against the Hebrew kings.

Five years after Rehoboam (Solomon's son and successor — around 928-911 BC) came to power Egypt reasserted itself, and once again a pharaoh sent a force to the north. This time it was the pharaoh Shishak who led the march. At this point the land of the Israelites had become divided into Israel and Judah — the latter occupying the hill country to the east of Philistia and encompassing Jerusalem.

The route of Shishak's march is unclear, but the best evidence suggests that he passed through Judah into Israel; and Gaza once again featured in the campaign. 'According to the places listed on the Temple of Amon at Karnak the starting point

The Roots of Palestine

of Shishak's campaign in Asia was apparently Gaza. From there one force advanced to the north, and another to the Negev. On his way home Shishak must have passed Gaza again; in the last row of the record is the name of Raphia [Rafah]. Since no other Philistine town is mentioned, apparently an understanding existed between Egypt and the Philistines and in particular between Egypt and Gaza.' Shishak died shortly after the campaign and before he could restore Egypt's grip on Asia. However, the tribes of Israel were never again a threat to the stability of Gaza.[10]

Documentary evidence of Shishak's campaigns in Palestine is slight and questionable. Over the next century fleeting historical references to Gaza depict a city subject to changing fortunes and to shifting alliances aimed at protecting its increasingly important status as a terminus for the valuable trade in spices and incense from the Arabian peninsula.

As the power of Israel declined, so the lands of the eastern Mediterranean became vulnerable again to powerful neighbours.

The period of Philistine rule was one of the most significant in Gaza's history. There is a clear echo today of the Philistine heritage in the name Palestine — in Arabic, Filastin. At same time, though, the word Philistine has been used rather unfairly in Western culture over recent centuries in a completely different context. It has acquired a pejorative sense, the origins of which are not easy to understand. One English language dictionary defines a Philistine as 'a person of material outlook, indifferent to culture.' The Philistines, it is true, were aggressive fighters; and their treatment of Samson, as reported in the Bible, showed awful brutality. Whether or not they were indifferent to culture is not clear. But in any case it seems unreasonable that history, witness to the rise and fall of numerous barbaric groups, should have decided to single out the Philistines for particular abuse.

Notes
[1] *Biblical Archaeologist,* March 1989.
[2] *Ibid.*
[3] Grant, *op. cit.,* p. 69.
[4] John Bright, *A History of Israel,* Philadelphia, 1981, p. 169.
[5] *Ibid.,* p. 180.
[6] Grant, *op. cit.,* p. 69.
[7] *Ibid.,* p. 72.
[8] *Ibid.,* p. 73.
[9] *Ibid.,* p. 80.
[10] *Anchor Bible Dictionary,* volume 2, New York, 1992. p. 913.

CHAPTER 4

Assyrians, Babylonians and Persians

At the northern edge of the Gaza strip Israeli-registered trucks can be seen entering a huge compound encircled by a high wire fence. The compound is filled with factories and warehouses. It is an industrial zone established by Israel on Gazan soil at Erez, next to the main crossing point into the territory. Gazans would prefer it if compounds like this one were in their own hands and that trading and business affairs in the territory were under their control, with direct access with the outside world, as was the case for many centuries. The history of trading in Gaza dates back at least to the days of Philistia, and its strength in commerce made it an attractive prize for successive foreign invaders.

Although confined to the coastal plain it appears that Gaza and the other Philistine cities continued to function as effective ports and trading centres during the period of Hebrew domination. In the 8th century BC another neighbouring power, Assyria (a region to the north-east, centred on the river Tigris), laid claim to the towns and cities of the eastern Mediterranean. Gaza, with its unique position on the major international trade routes, its flourishing port and its proximity to the bigger prize of Egypt, was once again a natural target for conquest.

Assyrian rule in Philistia lasted only a century, from about 730 to 630 BC, and the Gazan role in resisting the invaders is well documented. Much of the evidence comes from letters on clay tablets in cuneiform script.

The Assyrian invasions began in 742 BC with the campaigns of Tiglath-Pileser III whose initial target was control of the trade from the Phoenician ports of Byblos, Arvad, Sidon and Tyre, on the Mediterranean. Once Assyrian rule over those cities was established, Philistia became the next target.

Trade was uppermost in the minds of the Assyrians. The text of a letter found in Calah (a city in Assyria) to Tiglath-Pileser from an official stationed in Tyre sheds light on the background to Assyrian aims in Philistia. The official states that he has sent instructions to the inhabitants of Sidon that they should not trade with the Philistines and the Egyptians. It appears that the Assyrians wanted to monopolise Phoenician trade in timber. The date of this letter is unclear, but it is thought to be about 738-734 BC. If so, the letter would support the argument that the main aim of Tiglath-Pileser's first campaign in Philistia in 734 BC was to secure Mediterranean ports and gain control over their trade.1

A fragmentary inscription to Tiglath-Pileser from Calah gives some detail of the first Assyrian campaign into Philistia and specifically refers to Gaza. According to this fragment of clay tablet the Assyrian army set out from Phoenicia marching south along the coast.

The only Philistine city mentioned is Gaza, which was captured and sacked – something that happened repeatedly throughout history and which accounts for the paucity of ancient remains in Gaza today. The king of Gaza at the time of the Assyrian invasion, Hanun, receives special mention.

It appears that although the royal family was captured he managed to escape the attacking army and flee to Egypt where he unsuccessfully sought the help of the king of Bubastis. Having failed, he returned to Gaza where he was pardoned by Tiglath-Pileser and, surprisingly, reinstated as king. But Gaza became an Assyrian vassal, incorporated into the realm of Tiglath-Pileser's tribute bearing states. Nevertheless, following normal Assyrian practice, the conquerors allowed it to retain autonomy as the largest commercial city on the threshold of Egypt. The Assyrians only annexed territory that bordered directly on Assyrian lands and at that time their southernmost province was Simirra in Phoenicia.2

Having captured Gaza, like conquerors before and after, Tiglath-Pileser moved on, this time south as far as the 'City of the Brook of Egypt (at or near modern al-Arish) where he set up a stela to indicate the southernmost limit of his empire. The erection of this stela symbolized the final military achievement of the Assyrians in 734 BC. 'Now, having conquered all of Syria and Palestine, from the Taurus to the Egyptian border, the Assyrian emperor could justifiably declare himself ruler over all the lands "from the Bitter Sea of Bit Yakin... as far as Egypt, from the horizon to the heights of heaven."'3 The list of vassal leaders who paid tribute that year included almost all the kings of southern Anatolia, Syria and Palestine – among them Hanun of Gaza.

The effects of Tiglath-Pileser's ventures into Philistia were felt for some years afterwards, and news of his death in 727 BC caused unrest across the country. It was this event that prompted Isaiah to prophesy against Philistia: 'Do not rejoice, all you Philistines, that the rod that struck you is broken, for from the root of the snake will come forth an adder and its fruit will be a flying fiery serpent. ' (Isaiah XIV v 29)

The Philistines' resentment against foreign domination was not strong enough at this time, however, to tempt them to join Samaria in its last war against Assyria. Samaria was defeated and fell to Shalmaneser V, Tiglath-Pileser's son andsuccessor.

But when Sargon II ascended the throne at the end of 722 BC, Hanun of Gaza joined a coalition of cities, led by Yaubi'idi, king of Hamath (a city in northern Syria), opposed to Assyrian domination. This Syro-Palestinian revolt, which was supported by Egypt and encompassed cities across Syria and Palestine including Simirra and Damascus, failed. In 720 BC Sargon suppressed the rebellion in the west, then defeated the coalition in central Syria before turning south towards Gaza crushing all of Philistia on the way.

Once again Hanun called for help from Egypt and although an Egyptian force set out it was intercepted at Raphiah (Rafah), just south of Gaza. Raphiah was taken and, without the aid of the Egyptian forces, Gaza was doomed. The city offered no resistance, and Hanun was captured and led to Assyria in chains, leaving Gaza once again a vassal city. After this abortive blow for freedom, despite the unrest and resentment that simmered away in Palestine during the reigns of Sargon and his successors, Gaza remained loyal to Assyria.

In an economic sense the relationship between Gaza and its Assyrian overlords appears to have been mutually advantageous because, as has been seen, the motives for Assyrian control over southern Philistia and the borders of Egypt seem to have been largely commercial. Gaza, by then, was a city of considerable economic importance. Control of the city enabled Assyria to extend her rule further into Arabia while Gaza would continue to reap profit from the Arabian trade – spices, incense, perfume and other luxury goods being in particular demand.

Following a further campaign to consolidate his strength in the Egyptian border region Sargon appears to have established a military garrison in the vicinity of the destroyed town of Raphiah. This was a settlement of exiles forming a buffer region which, while not being annexed to Assyria, remained loyal to it. The pharaoh of the time, Osorkon IV, also appears to have had commercial interests at heart and was not interested in fighting Assyria. Both sides seem to have wanted peace and normal trading. Economic endeavour rather then territorial acquisition and the subjection of foreign populations was the achievement of Sargon's military victories in Philistia.

In return for relative autonomy the cities of Philistia continued to pay tributes to Assyria. One letter from this period (some time after 716 BC) informed the king that foreign chieftains from Egypt, Gaza, Judah, Moab and Ammon (western Jordan) had arrived at the capital with tributes. Gaza's tribute of 24 horses is singled out for a special mention. Another interesting example of rich tribute levied on Philistia is found in a letter sent to Sargon, most probably by Sennacherib, then crown prince. It is a detailed account of the tributes of two Philistine cities. Parts of the letter are broken making identification of the cities difficult, but it is believed that one of them was probably Gaza. The tax consisted mainly of silver, linen suits, robes, tent cloth, dried fish and sheaves of papyrus for the chief scribe.

Sargon's death on the battlefield in Anatolia in 705 BC sparked off rebellions throughout the Assyrian vassaldoms. Babylon rebelled first and the majority of the territories in the west soon followed. In 701 BC, after settling affairs in Babylon, his successor Sennacherib set about quelling the rebellions in Philistia, consolidating them once again as a semi-neutral buffer area between Assyria and Egypt; but again neither annexing them nor exiling their inhabitants.

However, Sargon's son, Esarhaddon, favoured a much more aggressive military policy and it is from the period of his rule that the excavations at Tell Jemmeh revealed remarkable evidence of the military control of Philistia by the Assyrians at that time.

In 679 BC, approximately a year after his accession, he undertook his first expedition into Philistia and plundered the town of Arsa, a hitherto unknown place on the border of Egypt (Arsa is the town associated with the excavations at Jemmeh some 20 miles from Gaza City), and carried its king Asuhili back to the Assyrian capital of Nineveh (near Mosul in modern Iraq). This campaign against what must have been an insignificant town was probably intended as a show of force against the new Nubian king Tirhaka who was having some success in extending Egypt's sphere of influence into Philistia. Archaeological evidence suggests that Esarhaddon built a new military base at Arsa (Jemmeh), to guard the border of his empire and to serve as a base for his campaigns against Egypt in 674, 671, and 669 BC.

One of the finds at Tell Jemmeh was evidence of a large building with a mudbrick barrel vaulting, unique in the region and dating back to the period of the Assyrian occupation. Archaeologists believe that it may have served as the residence of the military governor or general commanding the Assyrian base. The plan of the mud-brick construction corresponds to a well known Assyrian building type. A report on the find in *Archaeology* described the construction of the palace in detail: 'The building's walls were constructed with rectangular mudbricks laid header-stretcher in alternating courses in what is today known as "english bond". The bricks were laid with sand mortar kept in place by a thick layer of mud plaster, large areas of which survive inside the rooms. All rooms are floored with mudbrick, and against the end wall of each small room is a ledge that was probably designed to hold several lamps for these lightless rooms.'

The pottery found inside the structure has led to interesting theories about its original occupants. 'A number of locally made storage jars were found on the floors of the basement rooms; one had apparently been suspended from the vault by ropes. In one room, where a thick ash layer rested on top of the fallen portion of vaulting and continued under the intact vault, archaeologists found many fragments and one unbroken bowl of a type of pottery known as Assyrian Palace Ware. It seems certain that the building's pantry or kitchen was directly above this room, and that this fine dinner service had been stored there. If this magnificent vaulted building did indeed serve as the residence of an Assyrian military governor or general it is quite possible that the imported Assyrian Palace Ware was his personal dinner service. In one corner of the room where the floor bricks were missing was a debris-filled cavity with a cache of about 150 carnelian and faience beads. A few iron spearpoints and arrowheads were also found in these rooms.'4

The vaulted building survived Esarhaddon's death in 669 BC and probably continued as the major residence during the reign of Ashurbanipal who carried the conquest of Egypt as far as Thebes in 663 BC. But there it seems Assyria overreached itself and Egypt soon broke free, forcing Assyrian troops back into Philistia. No reference to the Philistine cities has survived from the latter part of Ashurbanipal's reign, and Assyria's supremacy rapidly declined after his death.

Nineveh (Mosul in modern-day Iraq) fell in 612 BC and with its fall came a resurgence of nationalism among the nations previously under Assyria's power. Egypt was enjoying one of its periodic moments of self-confidence, looking once again beyond its own borders to the north. Indeed, an Egyptian army joined forces with the Assyrians to confront a new power threatening the region, Babylonia. They fought the Babylonians on the banks of the Euphrates river. The Egyptian army must have passed through Gaza on its way northwards and the assumption is that, for this brief period at least, the city was once again a vassal of Egypt. 'There can be no doubt that Gaza was Egypt's vassal in 609 BC when Neco II (610-595 BC) hurried to Harran to help the Assyrians against the attacks of the Babylonians. In that battle

Life at the Crossroads

(605 BC) Nebuchadnezzar, still as crown prince, totally defeated the Egyptian forces.'5 The Bible's account portrays the Babylonian victory as absolute: 'The king of Egypt did not come again out of his land, for the king of Babylon had taken over all that belonged to the king of Egypt from the Wadi of Egypt to the River Euphrates.' (II Kings XXIV v 7)

Despite this emphatic statement by the Judaean chronicler in the Book of Kings, it appears that further battles occurred in Philistia between the Babylonians and the Egyptians. Given the location of Gaza it is safe to assume that the city became a pawn in the hands of the two great powers. The great Babylonian ruler Nebuchadnezzar II, the most powerful of the six kings who ruled Babylonia between 629 and 535 BC, undertook several campaigns in the south between 604 and 586 BC to establish authority. Gaza came under Babylonian control in 601 BC, subdued yet again by an army on the move. It is thought that a great battle between the Babylonians and the Egyptians took place on the Gaza plain in that year. Documents of a later period indicate the likelihood that Gaza became, for the Babylonians, a garrison town at that time – as it has for other foreign armies so often in its history. By the end of those early campaigns Babylonian influence held sway as far as the City of the Brook of Egypt (al-Arish) on the Palestine-Egypt border.

There is little to suggest that life in Gaza changed dramatically with the transfer of overlords. Tribute still had to be paid, only it was now sent to Babylon instead of Nineveh. The last mention of the Philistine leaders in cuneiform documents is a reference to the kings of Gaza and Ashdod, together with the kings of Tyre, Sidon and Arvad. Their names appear at the end of a list of high court officials who performed certain duties on the completion of Nebuchadnezzar's palace.

Babylonian domination of the Near East was

shortlived. The Babylonians had been coming under increasing pressure from the Persians. A new and powerful state had been created in Persia with a fusion of Medes and Persians. Between 559 and 530 BC, King Cyrus created an empire which eventually covered most of the modern Middle East. In 539 BC Cyrus and his army entered Babylon and effectively Gaza had new rulers from afar. In 525 BC Cyrus's successors overran Egypt and 'it could be said that for the Egyptians 2,000 years of foreign rule had begun.'6

Gaza and the cities of the Mediterranean coast during the time of Persian rule cannot have been considered as great prizes. Although dominated by and paying tribute to the Persians, there is no evidence that attempts were made to assimilate their populations into Persia. Their individuality appears to have been respected. For the Persians the significance of the old cities of Philistia lay in their location. Like the Philistines before them, the Persians coveted the wealth of Egypt. Gaza, as usual, was the obvious place to prepare for an attack on Egypt. *Tells* in the vicinity of Gaza, Tell al-Farah, Tell Jemmeh, Tell al-Hesi and Tell al-Shariah are thought by archaeologists to have been military installations. The *tells* were in fire-signalling distance of each other, and their proximity to Gaza and Ashqelon, coupled with their ready access to the Egyptian border, would have made them obvious locations for forward-staging areas as well as combat support stations for the Persian army in its campaigns against Egypt.

Cyrus's successor, Cambyses II, invaded Egypt in 525 BC. Maritime support for the invasion was provided by the Phoenicians, while the Arabs protected the water supplies on the desert route from Gaza to Egypt. 'The Arabs are first mentioned in Assyrian inscriptions of about 850 BC as a nomadic people of the north Arabian desert who paid their tribute to their Assyrian overlords in the form of camels –

which had first been domesticated in the Arabian peninsula some 500 years earlier.'7

Gaza, after Cambyses's invasion of Egypt, became the bridge between Persian Asia and Persian Egypt. In 517 BC Cambyses's successor, Darius I (the Great), visited Egypt. It is more than likely that he stayed in Gaza on his journey. Excavations indicate that Gaza became a strong fortress town for the Persians. At Tell Jemmeh two large buildings and storehouses belonging to the Persian period were uncovered; more than likely they had been constructed for Persian troops garrisoned in Gaza.

The strongholds may have been occupied by Greek mercenaries under the command of Persian officers and it is probable that the sites stored food supplies so that the army could fight in the border regions without having to expend precious time foraging for supplies. Much of this is supposition as very little is known about the period of the Persian occupation of Palestine. However, archaeological evidence that does exist suggests that the *tells* contained storage facilities for grain, and the excavation of large quantities of pottery of the period, originating from Attic and other Greek markets, suggests that the occupants of the sites came from further afield.

It appears that under Persian rule at the beginning of the 4th century BC coins were struck in Palestine which imitated coins of Athens showing Athena and an owl. Two such coins are on display in the British Museum in London. One has the letter 'O' in the cheek of the goddess Athena and the second has two Phoenician letters above the wings of the owl which refer to Gaza.

From this time on the five cities of Philistia ceased to hold any kind of position in international affairs. However, within the immediate region Gaza, for one, remained an important urban centre, well fortified and prosperous. The

Greek historian Herodotus, in 450 BC, reported that the city was almost as large as Sardis (a city in Asia Minor). Under the control of regional administrators called satraps, Persia allowed the different nationalities under its sway to retain their laws and customs, and Gaza presumably continued to function as a trading centre.

In 350 BC, Egypt once again reasserted itself, this time with the help of mercenaries from Sparta – finding themselves in conflict with the Greeks based in Gaza who were fighting alongside the Persians. The Egyptians conquered Gaza in that year and extended their military operations as far as Syria. But this period of Egyptian domination was brief. Another Persian ruler, Artaxerxes III Ochus, began the first of two campaigns to reconquer Egypt, establishing his base in Gaza.

In the light of what was to follow in Gaza's history, it is interesting to see how Greeks were beginning to play a role in the military campaigns for the control of Egypt and the eastern Mediterranean. And just as Gaza had been strategically important for the hirers of Greek mercenaries, the Egyptians and the Persians, so its position on the eastern Mediterranean crossroads ensured that it would regain its prominence when Greek culture became dominant – in the Hellenistic age.

Notes
[1] *Biblical Archaeologist*, vol XXXIX 1963, p. 88.
[2] *Ibid.*, p. 88.
[3] *Ibid.*, p. 89.
[4] *Archaeology*, January-February 1983, pp. 17-18.
[5] *Anchor Bible Dictionary*, p. 914.
[6] Peter Mansfield, *A History of the Middle East*, London, 1991, p. 5.
[7] *Ibid.*, p. 6.

CHAPTER 5

The Rule of Greece and Rome

Gaza in the 20th and 21st centuries has been caught up in the waxing and waning fortunes of successive superpowers; its history, like that of any small city trapped between powerful and ambitious neighbours, has been one of reaction, entrenchment and self defence. In the past two centuries, the ambitions of Turkey, Britain, Egypt and Israel have all had a bearing on Gaza's fate. For much of the time the events in Gaza were played out in the context of the battle of the Cold War, as the United States and the Soviet Union sought to secure zones of influence in the Middle East. More recently, Gaza has been characterised by Israel and many Western states as a dangerous centre of radical Islam, a potential target in the global war on terror.

The burden of keeping foreign populations subdued has always involved the outlay of huge resources – in the ancient world no less than in the modern one. In Palestine, wedged as it

Life at the Crossroads

has always been between superstates, as soon as one power found the weight of empire too heavy to carry, so another was waiting in the wings to take it over.

In the case of the Persians, too, there was a foreign power watching for signs that the empire might be crumbling. The next major player ready to come on stage was Philip II of Macedonia who ruled between 359 and 336 BC. He sought revenge for the Persians' invasion of Macedonia and Greece in the previous century and for their more recent support for his own opponents in Greece. The Persians were the only potential enemy of any size left to threaten Philip's desire for empire, expansion and power.

But long before he had achieved his territorial aims, at the age of only 42, Philip was murdered. His 19-year-old son Alexander III (the Great) took up the mantle with enthusiasm. Alexander's achievements in establishing an empire stretching as far as India and central Asia exceeded by far the ambitions of his father.

Given what Alexander ultimately achieved it is worth recording an anecdote about an incident in his growing years which reveals much about his character – particularly as the story centres on Gaza. 'Once, when the young prince was offering sacrifice, with would-be royal lavishness he scooped up two whole fistfuls of incense to cast on the altar fire. This brought down a stinging rebuke on his head from his tutor. "When you've conquered the spice-bearing regions, you can throw away all the incense you like. Till then, don't waste it." Years later Alexander captured Gaza, the main spice-entrepot for the whole Middle East. As always, he sent presents home for his mother and sister. But this time there was one for Leonidas [his tutor] as well. A consignment of no less than 18 tons of frankincense and myrrh was delivered to the old man (enough to make him rich beyond his wildest dreams on the resell price), "in remembrance of the hope with which that teacher had inspired his boyhood" together with an admonition to cease being parsimonious towards the gods.'[1]

In 334 BC, at the head of 40,000 Macedonian and Greek troops, he crossed the Hellespont (Dardanelles) and began his conquest of the Persian Empire. In 333 BC he defeated the Persian king Darius III Codomannus and then began to make his way down the eastern Mediterranean coast towards Egypt.

Much of Phoenicia came readily over to his side but Tyre refused to allow him access to the temple dedicated to the city's god, Melqart. Alexander thought himself descended from Heracles, and regarded the city god of Tyre as a manifestation of the great fighter. The people of Tyre refused to allow a foreigner – even Alexander – to offer a sacrifice in the city. As a result of this, Alexander prepared to lay siege to the Tyre. His shipborne arsenal was formidable – siege towers on ships equipped with scaling bridges, and powerful torsion catapults capable of firing huge stones. Alexander's army was eventually victorious, the city fell and a gruesome massacre followed with 8,000 of Tyre's defenders killed, 2,000 of them being crucified along the coast as a warning to any of the inhabitants who considered resisting the foreign army.

As reports of the fall of Tyre spread, the coastal cities along the route to Egypt sent notice of their submission to Alexander – with one exception: the walled stronghold of Gaza.

Built as it was on a *tell* a couple of miles inland, Gaza controlled the approaches to Egypt. Its location was also important, standing at the head of the caravan route for the trade in spice and luxury goods from Arabia. This made it a clearing centre for the eastern trade in frankincense and myrrh. Gaza had become an international commercial centre under the Persians, thanks to the political alliance and economic cooperation both with the Persian authorities and with neighbouring Arab tribes.[2] Its inhabitants, a mixture of Philistines and Arabs, were wealthy, making the city something of a prize both economically and strategically.

Gaza's commander, Batis, a eunuch loyal to Persia and one determined to save the city for the Persian crown, apparently decided to stand siege to Alexander. This might seem like an absurdly courageous decision, given that he must have known what had befallen the people of Tyre. Batis laid in weapons, stockpiled provisions and hired Arab mercenaries. He was confident in the knowledge that for the past two centuries, since the assault by the Persian leader Cambyses, the city had not been taken by storm.

Alexander sent one of his generals to Gaza by sea carrying the siege equipment which had been so successful at Tyre. One of the general's important tasks would have been to bring food and water (it was summer and the wadis would have been dry). Battles for Gaza, before and since then, have been lost because of the failure of attacking armies to secure water supplies.

Alexander's army, meanwhile, had an uneventful journey on foot down the coast, welcomed by the inhabitants of the towns on the way. But Gaza stood firm.

The siege of the city lasted two months (August and September 332 BC). Sandy soil around the city walls, which prevented the effective use of siege towers, slowed the progress of the attackers. The defenders fought fiercely; Alexander himself was wounded through the shoulder by a catapult bolt early in the siege. Eventually the city walls were weakened by mines placed in the sandy soil and siege armaments were used in the final assault.

'Three assaults on the ramparts were repelled, but they were gradually stripped of defenders by the artillery barrage and the walls were finally occupied, the hypaspists as usual leading the attack. Alexander was in the forefront and received a second, minor, wound in the leg. His blood was up and his troops were ready for the slaughter, their temper soured by the

The Rule of Greece and Rome

weeks of hardship preparing for the assault (water in particular would have been in very short supply over the months of September and October). The predictable massacre followed, as the fighting men of Gaza were exterminated, resisting until the end. Women and children became the prizes of war.'[3]

Accounts of the capture of Gaza speak also of Batis, the commander of the city, being taken prisoner and, because he refused to honour Alexander by kneeling before him, being executed in horrible fashion. He was bound by his heals to Alexander's chariot and dragged round the city, 'thus sharing a fate similar to that of Hector who was killed by Achilles in the Trojan War.'[4]

Defeat at the hands of Alexander had been total: the city was bereft of all its fighting men, and its women and children were sold into slavery. It seems that Gaza was then repopulated with people brought in from towns and cities round about and established as a military base, as ever, to control the route to Egypt. With Gaza secured, Alexander moved on towards the Nile Delta, having subdued all the cities of coastal Palestine.

The conquest of Gaza was vital in Alexander's ambition to gain control of the source and markets of perfumes and spices. From Gaza he sent to Macedonia a cargo of 10 ships loaded with the booty he had captured there, and these ships had to bring back new recruits to fill the ranks of the army which had suffered heavy losses in Gaza.[5]

Alexander died in 323 BC and his empire did not survive beyond his death. He died without a competent heir and a period of fighting ensued. Gaza became caught up in a power struggle in which his generals fought for shares of his vast empire. After about 40 years of conflict three big states emerged, each of them a hereditary monarchy, with the Antigonids ruling in Macedonia, and the Seleucids in Syria, Babylon and the east. Ptolemy Soter, Alexander's governor in Egypt, seized power there on the emperor's death and his descendants subsequently

69

ruled the province for nearly 3,000 years. Egypt was the largest and richest of the successor states and initially swallowed up the Palestinian cities.

A major archaeological discovery dating from this time supports the notion that Gaza had become a military stronghold, perhaps a garrison town. It appears that Jemmeh, the excavated *tell* closest to modern Gaza, 'became the site of a vast grain storage depot, not unlike the large grain centres in the American midwest, but unique in the ancient Near East. In addition to 10 large granaries that Petrie [Sir Flinders Petrie, the eminent British archaeologist who in the late 19th and early 20th centuries uncovered much evidence about ancient Palestine] excavated, in whole or in part, archaeologists working in 1970-2 excavated one on the west side of the *tell* and, in 1978, partially excavated another on the previously untouched east side. It is virtually certain that the entire site was covered with these structures in the late fourth to third centuries BC. There may have been a few houses scattered among the granaries for officials and keepers, but most of the other buildings from the period appear to be warehouses constructed of two parallel walls and partitions formed by cross walls.'[6]

Careful measuring of one of the largest granaries led to a calculation that its capacity would have been about 156 cubic metres, capable of containing about 132 tons of wheat. That is, apparently, enough to feed 1,000 people, each consuming two pounds per day, for just over four months.

Archaeologists saved every potsherd found in the excavations, and hours of painstaking work have gone into the re-assemblage of many jars and pots. A remarkable amount of Greek sherds, including Attic Black and Red-Figure ware, Black Ware and plain amphorae were found in the granaries.

One of the potsherds found in the granary has a painted Arabic monogram spelling the name 'Abum. This name appears in at least three other inscriptions found along the Arabian

The Rule of Greece and Rome

incense route and indicates that Arabs from southern Arabia (Yemen) had visited Jemmeh probably as caravaners bringing frankincense and myrrh to Gaza. It is highly likely that caravans stopped at Jemmeh to purchase wheat for the long journey – made in 65 stages, according to the historian Pliny – along the western fringe of the 'Empty Quarter', the great desert in Arabia, back to southern Arabia.[7]

As one historian has written, 'in view of the long history of grain management in Egypt, it is not surprising that the Ptolemies established a central grain storage depot in the southernmost cereal growing region of Palestine, an area that earlier had served as the border between Palestine and Egypt. In all probability, grain from all over was brought to this centre from which it could be transported to Egypt, shipped overseas through Gaza, or traded locally.'[8] Because Jemmeh was situated close to the military stronghold of Gaza it would obviously have meant that Egyptian troops on the march would be able to replenish their supplies there.

From 301 to 198 BC Gaza was under Ptolemaic rule and became a thriving commercial centre for trade with Egypt. An Egyptian record known as the Zenon Papyri specifically mentions Gaza's prosperity. Zenon was the chief agent of Apollonius, the Ptolemaic equivalent of a minister of finance, and after his visit to Palestine in 260 BC he cited Gaza as one of the most important Palestinian cities. Commodities being traded in the markets of Gaza were slaves, olive oil, Syrian wheat and other grains, fish, wines and dry fruits. More importantly, Gaza was renowned as the centre of 'the Arab trade' – in spices and perfumes. The Zenon Papyri mentions a Ptolemaic official stationed in Gaza who had the title 'Officer-in-Charge of Frankincense'. Trading activity of the Arab tribes branched out as far as India and the Far East. Goods reaching Gaza from there included Indian tree resin, dyes, aromatic essences, ginger, pepper, balsam, persimmon, fragrant creams, vermilion, specially processed woollen cloth, precious woods, silk, brocade and medical drugs.[9]

During the Ptolemaic period Gaza was deeply involved in the Syrian wars (beginning in 270 BC) in which the Seleucids laid claim to territory of the Ptolemies. In 217 BC, Ptolemy IV defeated Antiochus III (the Great) in the battle of Rafah. But in 200 BC Antiochus was the victor in the battle of Panion (on the Lebanon-Palestine border) against Ptolemy V for control of Palestine. Antiochus annexed Judaea (Judah), the religious state of the Jews, and with it the old Philistine coastal cities down to Gaza which he held under siege. Apart from new masters demanding taxes there is no indication that life in Gaza was any different as vassals of the Seleucids from life under the Ptolemies.

Seleucid control of Palestine provided the setting for a wider extension of Greek culture. Greek became the official language of the whole Near East; and under the Seleucids a union of Hellenistic (meaning, after the time of Alexander the Great, Greek) and oriental civilization developed. 'In both the Ptolemaic and Seleucid empires the senior civil servants, and the leading businessmen, scholars, and intellectuals were Greek. Both empires encouraged immigration from Greece, but the Greeks remained a minority. In their armies the Greeks formed the core or phalanx bearing pikes, but the archers and slingers were Arabs, Kurds and Persians.'[10]

The basis of Seleucid power lay in cities, and immigration of Greeks to the cities of Asia Minor and Mesopotamia, where Hellenistic influence was strongest, was encouraged. The Hellenistic cities of Alexandria and Antioch and the new capital, Seleucia, near Babylon supported populations of between 100,000 and 200,000 each.

Partly destroyed and then repeopled by Alexander, Gaza could well have been one of the first cities of the Greek type in Palestine and as such must have shared in the transmission of

Greek ideas, so much a feature of the city culture of the age. It was an era of academic achievement, especially in science. Huge libraries were established at Alexandria and Pergamon, and Ptolemy I also founded the Museum, an institute for advanced study. Traditions were established that were strong enough to endure through the Christian era, though much of its content has been irretrievably lost.

There are few records to show the nature of Gaza as a Hellenistic city. It is said there was a great library there, although little is known of it. But it is reasonable to assume that Gaza's proximity to the great seat of learning in Alexandria, with its astronomers, scientists and mathematicians, must have led to some transmission along the coast of the scholarship of the day.

Hellenistic civilization was undoubtedly richer than its predecessors. It was a period of prosperity – Alexander's conquests had generated great wealth and made available enormous booty. The ruins of many Hellenistic cities show vast expenditure on the amenities of Greek urban life. One finds the ruins of theatres and gymnasia in many places. It is certain that beneath the crowded streets and buildings of modern Gaza lie the remains of structures built to house the entertainments for the citizens of the city in the 1st century BC. Through the culture of the cities Gaza and the east generally were Hellenized in a way which lasted until the coming of Islam.

After his victory at Panion, Antiochus directed his attention westwards to Rome. Rome had just finished crushing Carthage and the Carthaginian general Hannibal had taken refuge in the Seleucid court. With Hannibal's encouragement Antiochus marched into Greece. Rome quickly declared war and drove Antiochus out of Europe. The Romans followed him into Asia and in 190 BC defeated him at Magnesia near Smyrna. In suing for peace Antiochus had to give up all Asia Minor except Cilicia and pay an enormous indemnity. It was the beginning of the decline of the Seleucid empire.

Life at the Crossroads

The decline of the Seleucids led to a brief period in which the Jews of Palestine gained ascendancy. The Hasmonaean dynasty (beginning in 142 BC) extended the boundaries of Judah to the borders of Egypt. Gaza, which in late Seleucid times had enjoyed a large measure of independence, resisted Jewish control. As a result of its hostility the Hasmonaeans attacked the city and burned to the ground the areas approaching it. Under siege, Gaza successfully sued for peace; however, the Hasmonaeans took some of the city's archons as hostages and carried them off to Jerusalem. Thus Gaza's aim of achieving full independence failed.[11]

The early Hasmonaean control of Gaza was clearly not total. In 103-102 BC, it appears that Gaza was used as a military base by the Ptolemaic governor of Cyprus who wanted to invade Egypt and depose his mother, Queen Cleopatra III. When he failed, Alexander Jannaeus, the Hasmonaean king, jumped at the chance to reconquer Gaza. Reports of this battle for Gaza (in 100-99 BC), unlike all the Biblical reports, are sympathetic to the Gazan position, rather than that of the Jews. They come, ironically, from a Jewish historian, Flavius Josephus, who sided with the Romans. They portray Jannaeus as a bloodthirsty tyrant and the Gazans as victims who were tricked into surrender. 'Jannaeus isolated Gaza from its hinterland by capturing Anthedon in the north and Raphia as well as Rhinocorura (El-Arish) in the south. When the city had been cut off from its own port to the west, the Gazans desperately appealed to Aretas II (the Nabataean king) for aid, but without success. Apollodotus, the city commander, mounted a night raid on the Jewish besiegers, but at daybreak the Jews gained the upper hand. The fate of the city itself, however, had not yet been determined. Only after a fight had broken out between Apollodotus and his brother Lysimachus in which the former met his death did Jannaeus succeed in breaching the walls of Gaza. Fierce fighting broke out in the city streets, and when the Gazans realised that

The Rule of Greece and Rome

they had no chance of victory they set their property on fire and many preferred suicide rather than capture by the Jews.'[12] The campaign, which had lasted a year, had been the longest battle for Gaza thus far in its history.

Gaza remained under the Hasmonaeans for another 36 years. In 63 BC history was set to repeat itself with the arrival of a new power from Europe –whose empire would build on the foundations of that of Alexander. Rome was now the important power in the Mediterranean region. In the 2nd century BC Rome was at war on every front. To the west as a result of the wars with Carthage, it gained the provinces of Hispania (Spain) in 197 BC; and Africa in 146 BC. In the east Roman legions defeated the Seleucids in 190 BC, and Macedonia and Asia were annexed in 148 and 133 BC. In the following century, motivated by the threat posed by pirates from Cilicia (modern day southern Turkey) to corn shipments from Egypt, the great Roman general Pompey set off on a campaign to capture the principalities of Asia Minor, taking Crete and Cyprus on the way, and eventually arriving in Syria in 64 BC.[13]

At the same time Pompey reduced the recently expanded Hasmonaean kingdom to Judaea, Galilee and Peraea. Gaza was freed from Hasmonaean rule the following year and the 20 or so Greek cities which Janneus had captured regained their independence. Local rulers became 'client-kings' and were diplomatically termed 'friends' (amici) or 'allies' (socii) of Rome.[14] As a mark of gratitude to Pompey, Gaza and some other cities adopted the Pompeian calendar, dating the years from 61 BC when the reconstruction of the city began. The full programme of rebuilding Gaza (along with Anthedon, the nearby port, and Rafah to the south) after decades of warfare began a few years later under the eye of Gabinius, governor of Syria.[15]

But even after the Romans were in control of Gaza city, Hasmonaean power in the area was not totally broken. In 40 BC

Gaza was formally assigned by the Romans to the kingdom of Herod whose territory included the whole of Palestine; but Herod took control of Gaza only when he had defeated on the battlefield the last Hasmonaean king.

At this point, Gaza's fate became entangled with the power struggle that ensued in the Roman dominion as the Republic entered its last days. In Rome itself the Republican structure was under severe strain as Pompey and Julius Caesar contested for power. Pompey's victories in the east had been matched by Caesar's conquests in Gaul which became a province in 49 BC. In the following year Pompey was killed in Egypt by Ptolemy XIII. Julius Caesar, who had pursued Pompey to Alexandria, avenged his rival's death. He also stayed on 'long enough to dabble in the Egyptian civil war and became, almost incidentally, the lover of the legendary Cleopatra' – Ptolemy's sister.[16] Back in Rome Julius Caesar was assassinated in 44 BC by Republican sympathizers. They, in turn, were defeated by Mark Antony and Caesar's nephew, Octavian, the man who was to become the first Roman Emperor.

Octavian and Mark Antony fell out, and the latter withdrew to Egypt where he married Cleopatra, the last of the Ptolemies. In 36 BC, when Antony assumed control over Egypt and the lands of the eastern Mediterranean, Herod, the ruler of Judaea, was forced to hand over several city-territories to the new Roman leader. Gaza was one of these cities – which Mark Antony, in turn, gave to Cleopatra.

But this period of renewed Egyptian control of Gaza was brief. In 31 BC Octavian defeated the forces of Antony and Cleopatra. Herod, declared king of Judaea by the Senate in Rome in 37 BC, had backed the winning side. He had supported Octavian against Antony and Cleopatra and his loyalty was rewarded by the successful Roman leader. He was accorded the status of 'client-king', thus producing the new Jewish state that existed under the early Roman Empire. In 30 BC Octavian handed back to Herod Gaza and the cities which had been ceded to Cleopatra. Octavian, who in 27 BC took the title Augustus Emperor of Rome, saw in Herod's rule a chance to secure the region, with its strategic and profitable trade routes, against Nabataean and bedouin elements. The kingdom was divided into city-territories and toparchies, regions without any settlement which had free city status. Some cities remained independent of Herod's direct control. Gaza was one such place with 'free city' status.

Herod initiated many extravagant building projects – palaces, fortresses, temples (including the Temple in Jerusalem, 'twice the scale of Solomon'[17]) and theatres were constructed throughout his kingdom, although Gaza, presumably because of its location far from Jerusalem, was not awarded any such symbol of Herodian power. Also 'it seems that Herod was suspicious of Gaza because of its close relations with the Nabataeans, his enemies. It is possible, therefore, that he rebuilt the port of Anthedon (then called Agrippias after Marcus Agrippa, Augustus' commander-in-chief) in order to compete with Gaza and to diminish its economic power.'[18] Evidence of the workings of the port are expected to come to light when planned archaeological excavations of the area begin.

In general, in this early period of Roman influence in the eastern Mediterranean, Gaza continued to maintain a large degree of independence, enjoying the prosperity accruing from its traditional role as a trading city, while nominally coming under the control of the Roman governor of Syria. In short, the Roman empire was one 'which imposed stability and so made possible freedom of trade and communications throughout a vast area, yet did not seek to regiment ideas or inhibit their exchange and propagation.'[19]

With the Roman empire came a further spread of Hellenization, and cosmopolitanism was encouraged by the Roman administration. 'Rome sought not to impose a uniform pattern of life but only to collect taxes, keep taxes, keep the peace and regulate the quarrels of man by a common law.'[20] Rome's greatest triumph rested on the bringing of peace, helping to create a second great Hellenistic age in which men could travel from one end of the Mediterranean to the other without hindrance.

Rome continued the Hellenistic process of mixing the cultures of east and west, and the Romans themselves made much of their inheritance from the Greeks. Education changed little, Roman literary forms derived from Greek and all educated Romans spoke both Latin and Greek.

Great Roman achievements were in the practical spheres of law and engineering, particularly in building – bridges, roads, basilicas and great places of public entertainment still exist at many locations in the eastern Mediterranean as a legacy of the skill of Rome's engineers, architects and builders. In Gaza, though, because of the numerous occasions in which the city was attacked and destroyed in the centuries which followed, none of these great structures have survived to anything like the extent they have in other cities.

Nor is there evidence to prove that Jesus Christ and his parents, Mary and Joseph, passed through Gaza during this period. But if the Gospel of St Matthew is to be believed, and Mary and Joseph fled with their son to Egypt to escape the wrath of Herod, then they certainly would have done so (the flight to Egypt is not mentioned in the other three Gospels.) St Matthew's Gospel says, 'the angel of the Lord appeared to Joseph in a dream, saying, Arise and take the young child and his mother into Egypt.' (3 v 13) According to a Christian lawyer in Gaza, Faraj al-Sarraf, the tiny Christian community there today believes that 'when the Holy Family returned from Egypt, they passed through Gaza. They rested under a sycamore tree which was later called the "Salha Sycamore" (the Good Sycamore). The Salha Sycamore remained a holy site until the end of the

The Rule of Greece and Rome

Ottoman Empire. Although the actual Salha Sycamore is no more there, the place with its sycamores is still visited by the people of Gaza.'[21]

The period of Roman control was not entirely calm in Gaza. In 66 AD Gaza and Anthedon were attacked by rebel Jewish zealots during the First Jewish Revolt against Roman rule. Josephus, the historian who wrote with an unsympathetic view of the Jews, stated that Gaza and Anthedon were totally destroyed; but subsequent research, based on the discovery of coins from this period, indicate that his reports were exaggerated.[22]

Whatever the true extent of the damage inflicted on Gaza, disruption to the thriving commercial activity in the city appears to have been minimal. Sixty years later, under the rule of the emperor Hadrian (117-138 AD), economic life in Gaza is reported to have enjoyed particular prosperity. The emperor visited the city in 130 AD – an event celebrated by the minting of special coins.

Gaza, one can assume, enjoyed the security of being part of such a large and well organised empire. 'The empire was a huge area and required the solution of problems of government which had not been faced by the Greeks or solved by the Persians. A complex bureaucracy appeared with remarkable scope. To cite one small example, the records of all officers of centurion rank and above were centralized in Rome. The corps of provincial civil servants was the administrative armature, sustained by a practical reliance for many places upon the army, which did much more than merely fight. Bureaucracy was controlled by the adoption of fairly limited aims. These were above all fiscal; if the taxes came in, then Roman rule did not want to interfere in other ways with the operation of local custom. Rome was tolerant. It would provide the setting within which the example of its civilization would wean barbarians from their native ways.'[23] Gaza, therefore, paid taxes to Rome

Life at the Crossroads

and enjoyed all the benefits that membership of such a powerful empire brought it. But, as so often in its history, the city retained much of its traditional character.

The Roman empire was not, however, totally benign. Its prosperity was based partly on brutality – not least on the purchase and sale of slaves, a thriving traffic at the heart of Roman society. Gaza traded in slaves as much as it did in commodities. Trading in slaves was particularly profitable in 135 AD after another Jewish uprising, the Bar Kokhba revolt, against Roman rule had finally been suppressed. The revolt collapsed when the rebels' two-year hold on Jerusalem was broken and their leaders were killed. The slave markets of Gaza and other cities in Palestine are said to have been filled at that time with Jewish prisoners. Many were sold to Egypt, packed off there on ships, or sent over land. Some remained in Egypt, while others were resold and found themselves being transported to cities to the west. In the view of one historian, 'taking into account the long enmity between Gaza and the Jews, it seems that the defeat of Bar Kokhba and the Jewish national disaster were probably cheered by the people of Gaza. It is possible that the city served as an important staging base for Roman troops sent to crush Jewish resistance in the southern parts of Judaea (and in Idumaea [southern Judaea] in particular). Gaza undoubtedly played an important logistical role as a station between Egypt and Judaea, supplying water, equipment, and services to the auxiliary forces coming from the south.'[24]

The material world of the Roman empire was a model of sound organisation, served by a well-ordered bureaucracy and an efficient military. The spiritual life in Roman times is less easy to characterise. While the Jews of the Roman empire had their monotheistic faith, non-Jews practised an eclectic kind of paganism with all manner of beliefs. 'For the most part, the peasants everywhere pursued the timeless superstitions of their local nature cults, townsmen took up new crazes from time to

The Rule of Greece and Rome

time, and the educated professed some acceptance of the classical pantheon of Greek gods and led the people in the official observances. Each clan and household, finally, sacrificed to its own god with appropriate special rituals at the great moments of human life: childbirth, marriage, sickness and death. Each household had its shrine, each street corner its idol.'[25]

As the Roman empire expanded, so the individual and his close world felt increasingly insignificant and powerless. State religion came to be dominated by ritual; and emperors acquired something of the status of gods. The time was right, therefore, for a religion which had appeal on an individual level and offered even the lowliest citizen ultimate salvation. Christianity, with its roots in the lands of the Roman empire, was set to fill the void.

Notes
[1] Peter Green, *Alexander of Macedon 356-323 BC – An Historical Biography*, California, 1974, p. 42.
[2] *Anchor Bible Dictionary*, p. 915.
[3] A A Bosworth, *Conquest and Empire – The Reign of Alexander The Great*, Cambridge, 1988, p. 68.
[4] *Anchor Bible Dictionary*, p. 915.
[5] *Ibid.*, p. 915.
[6] *Archaeology*, January-February 1983, p. 18.
[7] *Ibid.*
[8] *Ibid.*, p. 19
[9] *Anchor Bible Dictionary*, p. 916.
[10] Mansfield, *op. cit.*, p. 8.
[11] *Anchor Bible Dictionary*, p. 916.
[12] *Ibid.*, p. 916.
[13] *The Times Concise Atlas of the Bible*, p. 102.
[14] *Ibid.*, p. 102.
[15] *Anchor Bible Dictionary*, p. 916.
[16] J M Roberts, *The Penguin History of the World*, London,

Life at the Crossroads

1990, p. 239.
[17] Paul Johnson, *A History of Christianity*, London, 1976, p. 11.
[18] *Anchor Bible Dictionary*, p. 916.
[19] Johnson, *op. cit.*, p. 6.
[20] Roberts, *op. cit.*, p. 238.
[21] Faraj al-Sarraf, "Christianity in Gaza", *Christianity in the Holy Land*, London, 1994.
[22] *Anchor Bible Dictionary*, p. 916.
[23] Roberts, *op. cit.*, p. 246.
[24] *Anchor Bible Dictionary*, p. 916.
[25] Roberts, *op. cit.*, p. 250

CHAPTER 6

Under the Byzantine Cross

Gaza was a flourishing centre of paganism up to and beyond the 3rd century AD when Christianity took hold of the region. Proof of this is seen in some of the archaeological finds of the period. Many of the cities under Roman rule produced their own coinage. One coin unearthed in Gaza, and now on display in the British Museum in London, reflects the paganism of the time. It dates from the reign of the Emperor Caracalla (198-217 AD) and portrays the temple of the city goddess along with the inscription 'Gaza'. It is the size of an old English penny, but thicker and made of bronze.

The appearance of Christianity in Gaza has to be seen in the wider context of the gradual establishment of the new faith as a religion separate from Judaism – where its roots lay. It took a considerable time for Christianity even to make an impact on Gaza – even though the city lay only 80 kilometres from Jerusalem where Christians believe the Crucifixion and Resurrection of Christ occurred. But there is New Testament evidence that the Apostle Philip went to Gaza, presumably a short time after the Crucifixion of Christ. According to the Acts of the Apostles (8 v 26), 'the angel of the Lord spake unto Philip, saying, Arise, and go toward the south unto the way that goeth down from Jerusalem unto Gaza, which is desert.' On the way, Philip baptised a eunuch from Ethiopia. But we learn nothing about the apostle's mission to Gaza.

The early 'Jewish' Christians built up a following, more among the Gentiles than the Jews, around the central belief that Jesus was the prophesied Messiah who had been put to death and had come to life again. The emphasis on this belief, combined with the practice of baptism and the celebration of the Last Supper, turned what had been a sect of Judaism into a religion in its own right.

Gaza was not a city to embrace Christianity with enthusiasm. The new faith had more appeal to the poor and disadvantaged, to whom it offered a hope of personal salvation, than to the people of a metropolis like Gaza which was prosperous and commercially-minded.

In the 1st century AD St Mark is credited with having taken the Christian message to Egypt where it spread among the masses. St Peter and St Paul, meanwhile, were heading towards Europe. In the lands of the eastern Mediterranean Christianity was making a limited impact. But by the beginning of the 3rd century there were Christians in all classes and Christianity was enough of a threat to Roman authority to be subject to persecution. The Emperor Diocletian (284-305), against the background of the declining Roman empire, made one last effort to stamp out Christianity and restore the unique, almost godlike, status of the emperor. In 303 he ordered the final Roman persecution of Christians, targeting officials of the church, and the buildings and written works of the new religion. In Egypt and Palestine the persecution was harshest and lasted longer than elsewhere in the empire. Failure to sacrifice at pagan temples incurred the death penalty.

Under the Byzantine Cross

Diocletian's policy failed. Persecuting believers in a religion which drew its spiritual force from a victim of persecution and held up acceptance of suffering as a way of salvation inevitably had the opposite of the desired effect. Within 30 years, Diocletian's successor, Constantine (306-337), through genuine belief or political expediency, had reunited the Roman empire under Christianity, being baptised on his deathbed. Seven years earlier, on the ancient site of Byzantium, he had founded the new eastern and Christian capital of the Roman empire which became known as Constantinople (Istanbul). The emperor in the east 'was a theological as well as a juridical figure; the identity of Empire and Christendom and the emperor's standing as the expression of divine intention were unambiguous.'[1] In time Constantinople overtook Rome in splendour. The city became the centre of the Christian Hellenic-oriental Byzantine world which encompassed Gaza.

It is not known exactly when Christianity reached Gaza, but it is recorded that a bishop Sylvanus, 'the bishop of the churches around Gaza',[2] was put to death under Diocletian. The first half of the 4th century was marked by the activities of Hilarion, a leading figure in the history of Christianity in Gaza. He was born a few miles south of Gaza and studied in Alexandria. Hilarion returned to Palestine and led an ascetic life in the desert, gradually gathering followers around him at Maioumas (sometimes called Meyoma or Majoma), the name of Gaza's port in those days, close to today's al-Shati (beach) refugee camp. Other chronicles speak of him building a church and monastery in what is today Deir al-Balah (*deir* being the Arabic word for monastery); traces of the floor of the church have been found by archaeologists. Hilarion is considered to be the founder of monastic life in Palestine. During the reign of the Emperor Julian (361-363), who tried to restore pagan cults – for which he earned himself the title of 'Apostate' – there were anti-Christian riots in Gaza and Hilarion's monastery was destroyed.

But Hilarion himself had already fled, and he spent his last years in exile. He died in Cyprus in 371, and the Crusaders later named one of their castles on the island after him.[3] His body was later brought back to Palestine and buried there.

Christianity was formally adopted in Gaza at the end of the 4th century, but the process of establishing roots in the staunchly pagan city had not been easy. By comparison, in the adjacent port town of Maioumas there had been a mass conversion of the local population to the new religion, to the anger of the people of Gaza City who made strenuous efforts to keep the port, the outlet to the Mediterranean which was vital for commerce, under their control. The Gazans tried to convince the Byzantine authorities that Maioumas was an extension of the inland city and should, therefore, submit to its will. But Maioumas kept its own bishop and church administration until the 6th century, long after Gaza had become a Christian city.

For the prosperous inhabitants of Gaza, keeping control of Maioumas was more vital than anything else which explains why they showed faint enthusiasm for embracing Christianity. In the words of one historian, the pagans of Gaza 'energetically resisted the expansion of Christianity.'[4] Early converts to Christianity paid a high price for their belief, as another historical account makes clear. 'At Heliopolis in Syria, the great pagan city of Baalbek, and Ashqelon and Gaza in Palestine (the latter the citadel of the great god Marnas, whose hold over the population was only loosed with great difficulty by an energetic bishop around 400 AD) groups of priests and nuns were put to death with horrible savagery, by filling their dismembered bodies with barley and feeding them to the pigs. Unless the sources wrongly attach the same incident to the three cities, the repetition of such bizarre methods would indicate that the pagan rabble of one got the idea from that of another.' Throughout Palestine there appears to have been action on the part of pagans against encroaching Christianity. In one place near modern-day Beirut a pagan fanatic burned down the church and was ordered to rebuild it at his own expense. In other cities, Gaza for one, there was mass pagan rioting. These incidents 'reveal a great bitterness of feeling on the part of pagans in at least some part of the largely Christian provinces of the east Mediterranean, surrounded as they were with flourishing and triumphant Christianity, with its outward and visible signs of multiplying churches, ostentatious processions and the like.'[5]

The 'energetic bishop' referred to above was Porphyry, who had been appointed in 394 and became the leading figure in the establishment of Christianity in Gaza. His secretary, Marcus Diaconus, wrote an account of the life of the bishop and his efforts to suppress paganism. Porphyry's initial efforts to wean people away from their long established habits of pagan worship failed, and in 398 he turned for help to the Roman Emperor Arcadius. An imperial decree ordered the closure of the eight temples in Gaza – but exempted the Marneion, the temple of the Cretan god Marnas, worshipped locally as a rain god.

The continued existence of this major temple stood in the way of the bishop's missionary efforts, so in 400 he travelled to Constantinople to seek the support of the wife of Arcadius, the Empress Eudoxia. She prevailed upon her husband to drop the exemption enjoyed by the Marneion, and a decree to this effect was issued. In the summer of 402, the destruction of all the temples was carried out. The operation was supervised by an imperial official, civil and military governors, and a large body of troops. According to reports from the time, the local Christian community joined in the work with enthusiasm. According to one historian, 'many of the pagans, including most of the richest citizens of Gaza, fled from the city, abandoning their homes.' The temple of Marnas was destroyed, and a large church was built on the site.[6] The church was subsequently called the Eudoxiana as a mark of gratitude to the empress who provided funds for the project. She is said to have assigned to the construction of the church, 200 pounds of gold (14,400 gold pieces) from the revenues of Palestine.[7]

A church built on the site of the Marneion in 402-407 is still in use today, but there is no sign of the 30 or more green marble pillars which were also said to have been donated by the Empress Eudoxia. The current Greek Orthodox church, with enormously thick walls, houses the tomb of Bishop Porphyry who died in 420. The tomb lies next to the iconostasis under the high vaulted ceiling. Porphyry's portrait hangs above it.

St Porphyry's Church, as it is now called, stands in the Daraj district of the old city of Gaza, amid the bustle of money changers, gold sellers, shoe repairers and many other small traders in the covered *souq*. It has the look and feel of a market area in any busy Arab city. The church is situated close to one of the main landmarks of Gaza City the Mosque of Umar ibn al-Khattab (the Gramd al-Umari Mosque), itself a site of Christian worship in the past.

Near St Porphyry's church is one of the oldest streets in the centre of Gaza, called today Hammam al-Samarra (where a Turkish bath was once located). It is crammed with mud-brick and sandstone buildings and runs straight north-south, coming out at what would once have been the west door of the Eudoxiana church. The street clearly formed part of the original grid pattern on which Gaza was built, and shows how the church was once the focus of life in the city.

The first pictorial impression of Gaza during the Byzantine period appears on a 6th century mosaic map discovered in a church in Madaba, Jordan in 1896 and known as the Madaba Map. 'The vignette of the city, only approximately half of which survives, depicts a walled city built on a Roman street plan, with colonnaded main streets running north-south and east-west, leading to gates in the city walls and meeting in a large forum in the centre. A small domed structure in the middle

Under the Byzantine Cross

of the forum may be the elaborate clock described by Procopius of Gaza [a leading figure in the city's Rhetorical School who died around 526]. A semi-circular structure at the south-east corner may possibly represent a theatre, but is more probably simply a colonnaded courtyard. The south-western quarter is filled by one large building, presumably a church, which cannot, however, be positively identified with any of the churches known through literary sources [although some historians believe the building is the Eudoxiana church].'[8]

The houses of Gaza at this time were made mostly from mud-brick and had flat roofs. Also – as is evident from streets like Hammam al-Samarra today – they were packed closely together.

The Byzantine period generally for Gaza was one of great economic prosperity and great cultural achievement – with Aramaic being the common language, and Greek spoken by the upper levels of society. The city was at the peak of its achievements during the reign of Emperor Justinian the Great (527-565). Many new buildings were erected and the city walls were repaired. While Gaza came under attack from time to time from bedouin tribesmen from Arabia and Egypt, the fortifications were such that the assaults had little impact on life in the city. The Byzantine period was one of tranquillity for Gaza (especially when matched against the turbulence affecting the city before and since that time) and it appears to have developed into a flourishing and self-confident metropolis. As a colony of Rome, Gaza was subject to the rules of law and administrative organisation of the empire. A city council ran day-to-day affairs under the supervision of magistrates. In the later years of the Byzantine period bishops assumed an increasingly important role in public as well as church affairs.

The picture of Gaza that emerges from the writings of an Italian pilgrim in 570 – known as the Piacenza pilgrim – is of a thriving and hospitable city. He admired Gaza for its civilisation.

89

'We went to the city of Maioumas of Gaza, the resting place of the martyr Saint Victor. Gaza is a lovely and renowned city, with noble people distinguished by every kind of liberal accomplishment. They are welcoming to strangers. Two miles from Gaza is the resting place of our holy father Hilarion.'[9]

The Piacenza pilgrim is only one of many Christians who began to visit the Holy Land after the 4th century – often including Gaza in their itinerary. The Eudoxiana church was built with a hostel specifically intended to accommodate visiting pilgrims. Gaza and other cities in Palestine and Syria benefited economically from the movement of pilgrims and from the sale of religious artefacts. It was also the habit of Christians to take back home with them cakes of dried earth from the sites of the Holy Places. Special clay stamps were sold to make an impress on the blocks of soil. The Israel Museum has on display a round clay stamp – dated somewhere between the 4th and 7th centuries – showing Mary with the child Jesus. The stamp was found east of Gaza. The inscription reads: 'Blessing of our Lady. Mother of God, Mary'. Such stamps were also used to make impresses on loaves of bread.

Gaza and Maioumas had a tradition of extending a welcome to strangers, partly through the experience of greeting Christian pilgrims but more significantly through dealings with foreign traders. The prosperity of the two cities, as ever, rested on trade. Reports from this period speak of sizeable knots of foreign merchants in the two cities.

While trade was central to the economy of Gaza, the nature of commerce had changed over the centuries. There was still a movement of goods between Gaza and the Arabian peninsula, but the spice trade – on which the city's former prosperity had been built – was coming to an end. Instead, Gaza's economic success stemmed from the export of another commodity, wine. The first mention of wine being sent abroad from Gaza – to Egypt and Syria – comes as early as the middle of the 4th century. Later the scope of the wine producing industry and the range of export destinations expanded considerably. According to one account, 'the economy rested largely on the export of high quality wine, particularly to western Europe. Agriculture in southern Palestine was flourishing as a result of the sophisticated water conservation and irrigation techniques developed by the Nabataeans, and excavations in a number of Negev towns have revealed elaborate wine presses, evidence of wine production on an industrial scale.' By the end of the 4th century, according to Marcus Diaconus [the biographer of Bishop Porphyry] 'a colony of Egyptian wine merchants was resident in Maioumas. From the 5th to the 7th century a number of Latin writers refer to the strength and quality of Gaza's wine. Pottery identified as amphorae from Gaza has been found on several sites throughout Europe and the Near East.[10]

Aside from handling shipments of wine, Gaza continued to be the distribution centre – as it is today – for agricultural produce from nearby villages. Produce which was surplus to the demands of the city was exported through Maioumas.

Local industries serviced the commerce of the city by manufacturing the amphorae for the wine and the pots for carrying agricultural produce and other commodities. Excavations at Maioumas have revealed the existence of a dyeworks. It is clear that some of the inorganic dyes were imported from Italy and Greece.[11]

Another archaeological find at Maioumas points to the existence of a Jewish community in the port city at the beginning of the 6th century. In 1965 archaeologists uncovered the mosaic floor of a synagogue. It had been part of a building next to the sea divided by four rows of columns into a central nave with two narrower aisles on either side. One part of the colourful mosaic, removed by the Israelis after they occupied the Gaza Strip in 1967 to the Israel Museum in Jerusalem, shows King David sitting on a throne portrayed as Orpheus playing his lyre to a group of animals.

Artistic skills during the Byzantine period were matched by achievements of scholarship. Shortly after the emergence of Alexandria as the major centre of learning in the region several centuries earlier, a tradition of scholarship had developed in Gaza. Late in the 5th and early in the 6th centuries the city boasted a school of rhetoric which gained a wide reputation, attracting students from cities far away, including Athens. Its scholars produced a wide range of literary works, some secular, others strongly influenced by Christianity. One of the leading members of the school was Procopius who produced a number of Biblical commentaries which have survived to the present day, along with some speeches and a big collection of letters.[12]

Oratory, originating, no doubt, from the school of rhetoric, provided 'the most elevated form of entertainment in Byzantine Gaza, and was part of the frequent and elaborate festivals which took place there, some under the patronage of the Church, others, such as the "Day of Roses", evidently survivals from the Pagan tradition. Others, perhaps more popular, amusements included mimes, performed in the city's theatres, instrumental and choral concerts, chariot racing, wrestling and athletics.'[13]

But there is little in contemporary Gaza to enable one to picture how the thriving commercial city looked during the Byzantine age and imagine the celebration of culture and learning during this rare period of stability, prosperity and tranquillity. 'What we can see of late ancient Gaza,' an historian in the 21st century has written, 'stands in striking if not pathetic contrast to the stature of the city's literary culture, unique in Justinianic Palestine, and exceptional even in the east.'[14]

This golden era in Gaza under Roman rule lasted for three centuries. For most of this time the eastern Roman empire faced a threat from the 'aggressive and expansionist

Sassanian Persians to the east. However, for at least two hundred years the Byzantines were able to secure peace with the Persians through diplomacy.'[15] The change in the balance of power between the two empires came when the Emperor Justinian the Great turned his attention to the west. He decided to try reconquering provinces in the western half of the Roman empire with a view to re-establishing unity. The Persians saw an opportunity to extend their control. From the early years of Emperor Justinian's rule (in the 530s) until 629, the Persians kept up their attacks on the Roman controlled provinces of Syria and frequently had to be repelled. In 615, under Chosroes II, the last great Sassanid leader, they made even bigger inroads into Roman-held territory, sacking Jerusalem and ravaging other cities in their path. Three years later they took control of the whole of Palestine, capturing Gaza in the process. Their brief sojourn in the city appears to have been peaceful and uneventful; and when in 629 Heraclius, the former imperial viceroy of Carthage and one of the greatest soldier emperors, retook Palestine, life in Gaza soon returned to the way it had previously been under Byzantine rule.

But the calm did not last long. Both Byzantium and Persia, 'the superpowers of the ancient world' were overstretched and weakened.[16] Just as a popular hunger for spiritual fulfilment had helped the rapid spread of Christianity in the opening centuries of the millennium, so the declining political and military power of the Byzantine and Persian empires contributed to the successes enjoyed by the next wave of invaders to take control of the lands of the eastern Mediterranean in the 7th century.

The invaders came from the Arabian peninsula, conquering the land in the name of a third monotheistic religion. This had been born in the Arabian peninsula at the very moments when Heraclius and his army were struggling to evict the Persians from Palestine and Syria. The religion was Islam and its imprint can still be seen on the life of Gaza and its people today.

Notes
[1] Bright, *op. cit.*, p. 280.
[2] *Anchor Bible Dictionary*, p. 917.
[3] *Ibid.*, p. 918.
[4] John Wilkinson, *Jerusalem Pilgrims before the Crusades*, London, 1977.
[5] Diana Bowder, *The Age of Constantine and Julian*, London, 1978, p. 130 ff.
[6] *Anchor Bible Dictionary*, p. 918.
[7] Wilkinson, *op. cit.*
[8] *Anchor Bible Dictionary*, p. 920.
[9] Quoted by Wilkinson, *op. cit.*
[10] *Anchor Bible Dictionary*, p. 920.
[11] *Ibid.*, p. 919.
[12] *Ibid.*, p. 920.
[13] *Ibid.*, p. 920.
[14] Hagith Sivan, *Palestine in Late Antiquity*, Oxford, 2008. p. 344.
[15] Mansfield, *op. cit.* p. 12.
[16] *Ibid.* p. 12.

CHAPTER 7

The Arrival of Islam

Shafiq, when I met him, was a man in his late seventies living in the densely packed Shuja'iya neighbourhood of Gaza city in a house built in the Turkish style with high, domed ceilings and a central courtyard. 'My family came originally from the Arabian peninsula during the Ottoman period,' he said. 'His name was Khalil and he was a merchant in camels, goats and sheep. He travelled between Jeddah, Gaza and Turkey. He sold mainly to the Turkish army. He decided to settle in Gaza. He married five times and had 15 sons.'[1]

The Shafiq family history, like that of many others, is interesting because it contains echoes of the connection between Gaza and the family of the Prophet Muhammad in Mecca in the Arabian peninsula in the 6th century. By this time Gaza was well established as a trading centre. Not only were commercial links with the Arabian peninsula firm, but an Arab community had settled in Gaza and in other cities further north. A key figure in this trading pattern was Hashim ibn Abd al-Manaf, the great-grandfather of the Prophet Muhammad who saw that 'the

Life at the Crossroads

struggle of the two great powers [the Byzantines and the Persians] to dominate the trade routes and centres in Arabia was coming to a standstill... The real change in Makka's [Mecca's] fortune occurred with the change of its trade from local to international. This is now proved to have been the achievement of Hashim, great-grandfather of Muhammad, who lived around the middle of the sixth century. It is a remarkable tribute to the astuteness of Makkan merchants that they were quick to perceive the vacuum created in the international commerce of their time.'[2]

Gaza was already experienced in international trade, so it is not surprising that the merchants of Mecca saw the city as an important outlet to the world across the Mediterranean. Hashim, therefore, had become well known in Gaza as he passed through the city en route to Egypt or to Syria. On one such journey he died while staying in Gaza and was buried in the city. His body is said to lie in a tomb in a small domed building with decorated, curved iron bar windows, in an eastern corner of the courtyard of the Sayyid Hashim mosque. Gazans say that the tomb was discovered in a cave early in the 7th century, before the birth of Islam. After the spread of Islam to Gaza the cave is said to have became the focus of attention for travellers through the city and is mentioned by Arab travellers in later centuries. Not until 1855 was a mosque built in Hashim's name. It is significant, the citizens of Gaza say, that, being a trader, he stayed and died in the mercantile centre of Gaza City where the mosque in his name is located. Because of the connection with the family of the Prophet, Gaza is known among Arabs and Muslims as Ghazzata Hashim – Hashim's Gaza.

The Prophet Muhammad was born into a world dominated by commerce ('It is impossible to think of Makka [Mecca] in terms other than trade; its only *raison d'etre* was trade. It was first established as a local trading centre around a religious shrine.'[3]) and there are suggestions that the Prophet

The Arrival of Islam

had experience in the business himself. He certainly understood the workings of Mecca well enough to realise that the corruption practised by a handful of rich manipulators and the growing appeal of idolatry were endangering the prosperity of the city. The Prophet Muhammad had the Call of God as he was approaching the age of 40. When he began denouncing the religions of Mecca and preaching about the unity of God and the prospect of divine judgement, he won support from the poorer people; but at the same time he encountered fierce opposition from the powerful figures in business who saw their prosperous livelihoods being threatened.

In 622, in the face of increasingly hostile opposition to his preaching, Muhammad moved from Mecca to Medina – known in Arabic as the *Hijra* (flight), a key event in the development of Islam. (The Islamic calendar takes this year as its starting point.) No longer was Muhammad a private citizen advocating reform in the name of God; now he was a religious, political and military leader.

This broad range of leadership responsibilities was passed on by the Prophet to his successors – known as caliphs from the Arabic word *khalifa* – and reflects the way in which Islam is a religion that directs all aspects of a believer's life as well as that of the community in which he lives. The universality of Islam, with none of the metaphysical mysteries of Christianity, combined with the emphasis on the life of the community, gave the religion immediate popular appeal. This was the case particularly after the death of the Prophet Muhammad in 632, when Islam burst out of the Arabian peninsula. The Arab armies were able to make progress precisely because of what the Prophet had achieved in his lifetime. In the view of one historian, 'to the pagan peoples of western Arabia he had brought a new religion which, with its monotheism and its ethical doctrines, stood on an incomparably higher level than the paganism it replaced. He had provided that religion with a revealed book [the Quran] which was to become in the centuries to follow the guide to thought and conduct to countless millions of Believers. But he had done more than that; he had established a community and a state well organised and armed, the power and prestige of which made it a dominant factor in Arabia.'[4]

The dominance of the Arab Islamic armies coming out of the Arabian peninsula soon spread far across the region. 'If the achievements of the Islamic faith in the lifetime of Muhammad were remarkable, those during the brief rule of his three successors... were even more astonishing. The small forces of the faithful went on to challenge the two great empires of Byzantium and Persia.'[5] But both empires were exhausted, and resistance to the invaders was remarkably weak. The march of the invading army followed the well-known caravan route, leading from Mecca and Medina northwards to Damascus, along what in later decades and centuries became the route taken in a southerly direction by Muslim pilgrims to the sacred cities of the
Hejaz. The first territories that came under the control of the Islamic armies were those east of the River Jordan and the Dead Sea. Only when Damascus and territory in the north had been taken did Galilee, the lowlands of Jordan, and Palestine, fall to the Muslims.

The Arabs began attacking Palestine in 634. The army of the Byzantine Emperor Heraclius was defeated at the battle of Yarmuk in 637 and his forces pulled out of Syria. The Arab conquest of the rest of Syria was achieved without great difficulty. Gaza' s reputation both as a trading centre and a strategic crossroads was well known, and there are indications that the commander of the army of 'Amr ibn al-'As decided that the city should be one of his first objectives. Some of the earliest battles against the Persians (who had occupied Gaza in 618) were fought in this area. A troop of Persian soldiers defended

The Arrival of Islam

Gaza but were overcome; they were later put to death by the conquering army for refusing to convert to Islam. But aside from the resistance put up by the Persians, the Arab conquest of Gaza was swift and peaceful; it was completed in June or July 637. According to one account by a contemporary writer, 'the inhabitants of Gaza welcomed the Muslims, and many were converted to Islam. It is recounted that Amr ibn al-As was warned by a Ghassanid Christian [a member of a tribe that came originally from southern Arabia] about a plot to kill him. The warning saved his life.' As a result, Amr ibn al-As divided 'the two churches that existed at that time between the Christians and Muslims.' The Christians kept St Porphyry's, while the Muslims took over the one that was to become the Grand Mosque of Umar, named after one of the earliest caliphs.[6] The Arabs set up an administrative centre in the city and it was from here that the surrounding region continued to be governed.

Two aspects of the Islamic conquest of Gaza and other cities in the region are remarkable. One is the lack of resistance, either military or popular, to the spread of Islam. The Gazan people responded with alacrity to the call to convert to the new religion (in contrast to their response to the arrival of Christianity), and they readily accepted, according to local historians, that the great church in the centre of the city be converted into a mosque. It was named after one of the earliest caliphs, Umar. According to two Arab writers of the late 10th century, Umar had a personal connection with Gaza: 'Here in Gaza, too, was once the man who later became the Caliph Umar Ibn al-Khattab. In the days of ignorance [before Islam] he grew rich here; for this place was a great market for the people of the Hejaz.'[7]

Another interesting aspect of the Arab conquests is the degree to which the new arrivals left the administrative structures which they found in place. The attitude of the Arab conquerors to the countries they now invaded 'was one of caution. They themselves had little understanding of the economic system of the region where they had obtained control, and with remarkable restraint decided as far as possible to preserve the existing order. Thus they avoided disrupting the commerce of the area, which was far in advance of what they had known in the cities of the Arabian desert. They permitted Christians and Jews to remain in their own religions on condition that they paid poll tax, and they carried out the occupation of their newly conquered lands not by monopolising the existing cities but by building camps, usually on sites not hitherto occupied. Thus it was that Ramla eventually came into existence as the capital of Palestine. In contrast with the Persian invasion, the Muslim conquest seems to have caused little material damage.'[8] The fact that Gaza already had strong trading links with Arabia as well as an Arab community of its own within the city must have contributed to the ease with which the newcomers took it over. It is quite conceivable, too, that the invaders may have encountered friends or family when they entered Gaza.

It seems generally in Gaza and elsewhere that the local population welcomed the change of rulers, finding 'the new yoke much lighter than the old, both in taxation and other matters. Even the Christian populations of Syria and Egypt preferred the rule of Islam to that of the orthodox Byzantines.'[9]

In the early years of Arab rule in the eastern Mediterranean, during the Umayyad dynasty (661-750) when Damascus was the capital, Syria was divided into four military districts, each of which was called a *jund* – meaning literally an army – so called because a special body of troops was assigned to each. The military districts corresponded exactly to the earlier Byzantine provinces. Gaza was part of the Palestine district.

While Arabic was the language of the new power in the region as it was the language of the Quran, Greek and Aramaic continued to be spoken for some time after the Arab conquests of

The Arrival of Islam

Syria. Indeed, matters involving writing and translation, as well as the control of fiscal matters, were frequently left in the hands of Christians and Jews who tended to be fluent in Greek, the *lingua franca* of the time.

Not until the fall of the Umayyad caliphate in 750 and the rise of the Abbasids, who moved the capital from Damascus to Baghdad, did the Arabs break their ties with Byzantine traditions. Even in styles of pottery in the early Islamic years, the Arabs copied the Byzantines. The Israel Museum in Jerusalem has examples of 'slipper-type' clay oil lamps from this period which mirror the Byzantine style. But the move to Baghdad signified a major change in outlook. Arabic became the dominant language of a vast empire in the same way that Islam had already become the dominant religion. Once the empire was established, by the 9th century, Islam had developed a character and style that were easily recognisable. These, in themselves, helped to unify the empire. But it was a time of great movement within the boundaries of empire. The spread of Islamic influence was achieved in part by the movement of armies and people. But trade also flourished. Textiles, metalwork, soap and perfumes were carried vast distances over land, and across the Indian Ocean and the Mediterranean Sea. Artists and craftsmen were lured to move from one city to another by the promise of patronage. Goods bearing the distinctive Islamic style formed the body of long-distance trade.

Gaza, although situated a long way from the heart of empire, was at the crossroads of the movement described above. In this period Gaza adopted the strong Arab and Islamic character which it retains today.

Even in the early days of the Islamic empire, Gaza gained a reputation as a centre for Islamic study. It was also the birthplace of Imam al-Shafi'i (767-82), the founder of the Shafi'i school of Islamic law. But still as late as the 10th century, the Arab geographer and historian, al-Muqaddasi (born in Jerusalem in

Life at the Crossroads

946) noted how Christians were continuing to play an important role in formulating Islamic law. 'It is seldom recorded that any jurisprudist of Syria propounds new doctrines, or that any Muslim here is the writer of aught; except only at Tiberias, where the scribes have ever been in repute. And verily the scribes here in Syria, even as is the case in Egypt, are all Christians, for the Muslims abandon to them entirely this business, and, unlike the men of other nations, do not hold letters a profitable subject of study.'

But by the time al-Muqaddasi was writing, Arab scholarship was starting to come into its own. For the first two centuries after the death of the Prophet Muhammad the study of history and geography was slow to develop, and so the written records of what Gaza and other cities were like during the early periods of Islam are scanty. The earliest extant Arab books on geography and history date from the 9th century. From this period onwards, though, one finds some interesting and detailed portraits of aspects of life in Gaza, seen through Arab eyes.

A glimpse of economic life in Gaza in the 9th century is provided by the great Arab historian of the 14th century, Ibn Khaldun. He found records on this subject dating back to around 780. They show both the degree of organisation and the considerable contribution of Gaza and the surrounding area to the coffers of the Arab empire. Palestine, the documents say, provided 310,000 dinars (gold coins), and 300,000 *ratls* [variable measurement of weight from this region] of olive oil to the central revenue of Syria in Damascus. During the reign of Harun al-Rashid in 800 a similar record also shows Palestine paying 310,000 dinars. In addition, all the Syrian *junds* provided 300,000 pounds of raisins. In 903, the Palestinian contribution had risen to 500,000 dinars.

In the 9th century the Arab geographer, Ya'qubi, noted that the ancient capital of the military district of Palestine was

The Arrival of Islam

Ludd (Lydda), on the coastal plain north of Gaza. 'The Caliph Sulaiman ibn Abd al-Malik subsequently founded the city of Ramla which he made the capital, and Ludd fell into decay... The population of Palestine consists of Arabs of the tribes of Lakhm, Judham, Amilah, Kindah, Kais and Kinanah.' Ya'qubi described Gaza as 'a city of Palestine on the sea-coast. It stands on the limit of the Third Climate. There is here the grave of Hashim ibn Abd Manaf.' He also identified Gaza as 'the last town in Syria on the road from Ramlah to Egypt.'

Not surprisingly, many of the writers comment on Gaza's continuing role both as a centre for agriculture and a flourishing trading city. Al-Mas'udi, who wrote in 943, gave the following account of the arrival of oranges, today one of the most common fruits in the lands of the eastern Mediterranean, in Palestine. 'The orange trees were brought from India beginning in the year 912 and were first planted in Oman. Thence they were carried by caravans from Al-Basra to Iraq and Syria... The trees have now become very numerous in all the Syrian coast towns, with those of Palestine and Egypt, where, but a short time ago, they were unknown.' Bait Lahya, near Gaza, close to the northern edge of the Gaza Strip today, was described by another traveller in 1300 as 'a village with many fruit trees,' as it still is.

Al-Muqaddasi wrote the following about commerce in Palestine in the 10th century: 'The trade of Syria is considerable. From Palestine comes olives, dried figs, raisins, the carob-fruit, stuffs of mixed silk and cotton, soap and kerchiefs.' Al-Mas'udi travelled extensively through the Islamic world of the day, and was also much impressed by Palestine. 'The lower province of Syria is even more excellent than the north, and pleasanter, by reason of the lusciousness of its fruits and in the great number of its palm trees... Unequalled is this land of Syria for its dried figs, its common olive oil, its white bread and the Ramlah veils. Also for the quinces, the pine-nuts called "Kuraish-bite" [*snowbar* or pine nut]", the Ainuni and Duri raisins, the Theriack antidote [drug against dangerous bites], the herb of mint, and the rasaires of Jerusalem. And further know that within the province of Palestine may be found gathered together six-and-thirty products that are not found thus united in any other land. Of these, the first seven are found in Palestine alone: pine-nuts called Kuraish-bite, the quince, the Ainuni and Duri raisins, the Kafuri plum, the fig called al-Saba'i and the fig of Damascus. The next seven are the water lily, the sycamore, the carob or St John's bread (locust tree), the lotus-fruit, the artichoke, the sugar-cane and the Syrian apple.'

Gaza, al-Muqaddasi said, was 'a large town lying on the high-road into Egypt, on the border of the desert. The city stands not far from the sea. There is here a beautiful mosque; also to be seen is the monument of the Caliph Umar.' Exports of agricultural produce and other commodities passed through Maioumas port (the outlet to the sea adjacent to Gaza). Al-Muqaddisi described it as 'a small fortified town which lies on the sea and belongs to Gaza.'

Istakhri and Ibn Haukal (who wrote in the latter half of the 10th century) were merchants by trade; but in a double book, they produced a systematic Arab geography defining the territory and mentioning the limits of Philistia. Gaza in this latest period, too, was clearly an important strategic city. 'The frontiers of Syria are the following: on the west, the Bahr Rum (the Greek or Mediterranean Sea)... The furthest point south of Syria towards Egypt is Rafah.' They described Palestine as 'the westernmost of the provinces of Syria. In its greatest length from Rafah to the boundary of Al-Lajjun (Legio), it would take a rider two days to travel over; and the like time to cross the province in its breadth from Jaffa to Jericho... Filastin [Palestine] is watered by the rains and the dew. Its trees and its ploughed lands do not need artificial irrigation... In the province of Filastin, despite its small extent, there are about twenty mosques with pulpits for

The Arrival of Islam

Friday prayer.'

Another Arab geographer, al-Muhallabi, commented on the landscape around Gaza. He wrote (in 990) that about three miles from Rafah in the direction of Gaza are 'many sycamore trees that border both sides of the road, to the right and left. There are near a thousand trees here, their branches touching each the next, and they extend for close on a couple of miles. South of Rafah the lands of the Jifar District begin, and the traveller strikes into the desert.'

Gaza's relations with other coastal cities in Palestine in the 10th century are described in a colourful passage in the works of al-Muqaddasi. 'All along the coast of Filastin (Palestine) are the watch-stations, called Ribat, where the levies assemble. The war-ships and the galleys of the Greeks also come into these ports, bringing aboard of them the captives taken from the Muslims; these they offer for ransom – three for the hundred Dinars. And in each of these ports there are men who know the Greek tongue, for they have missions to the Greeks and trade with them in divers wares. At the Stations, whenever a Greek vessel appears, they sound the horns; also, if it be day, they make a great smoke. From every Watch-station on the coast up to the capital Al-Ramla there are built, at intervals, high towers, in each of which is stationed a company of men. On the occasion of the arrival of the Greek ships the men, perceiving these, kindle the beacon on the tower nearest to the coast station, and then on that lying next above it, and onwards, one after another, so that hardly is an hour elapsed before the trumpets are sounding in the capital, and drums are beating in the towers, calling the people down to the Watch-station by the sea. And they hurry out in force, with their arms, and the young men of the village gather together. Then the ransoming begins. Some will be able to ransom a prisoner, while others (less rich) will throw down silver Dirhams, or signet-rings, or contribute some other valuable, until at length all the prisoners who were in the Greek

105

ships have been ransomed. Now the Watch-stations of this province of Filastin, where this ransoming of captives take place, are these: Ghazzah (Gaza), Maioumas (Gaza port), Askalan (Ashqelon) Mahuz-Azdud (the port of Ashdod), Yubna, Yafah (Jaffa) and Arsuf.'

As for the administrative arrangements in Palestine, changes had been made since the days of the early caliphs. al-Muqaddisi, in 985, described Syria as divided into six districts which differed in some minor points from the original military districts (*junds*). But Gaza still came under the district of Palestine. By this time the need for the cantonment of troops had passed. The system of military districts came to an end in the 12th century with the arrival of the Crusaders. Thereafter, Syria and Palestine nominally belonged to the rulers of Egypt, but in point of fact the territory was divided up among a number of minor sultans.

For several centuries, as an integral part of the Muslim empire, Gaza enjoyed a relatively peaceful and uneventful period. But, as usual, the territory was to become a pawn in the struggle of larger powers for control of the lands of the eastern Mediterranean. The threat to Syria from the Byzantine empire re-emerged in the 10th century with a string of military attacks into the region having to be repulsed. From the south the Fatimids of Egypt also posed a threat to the stability of the eastern Mediterranean. But in the 11th century the three competing powers of the region, the Byzantines, the Fatimids and the Abbasids, were all on the decline. This left the way open for a new military force made up of nomads from central Asia, known as the Seljuq Turks. In 1050 they captured Baghdad, 'reducing the Abbasid caliph to the status of a vassal. In 1071, they took Syria and Palestine and drove the Fatimids back to Egypt. By the end of the century the Seljuq Empire included Persia, Mesopotamia, Syria and Palestine.'[10]

Gaza, then, was once again under foreign domination –

The Arrival of Islam

albeit Islamic, the Seljuqs being Sunni Muslims. One major change brought about by the Seljuqs was in the ownership of land, developing what amounted to a feudal economy. The historian, Imad al-Din, writing in the Seljuq period, pointed out that the only way to give the turbulent Turkish tribesmen and soldiery an interest in the prosperity of agriculture was to give land to officers, assigning to them both the yield and the revenue. The change of system brought about social upheavals. Former landlords were hard hit by the rise of a new class of non-resident feudal lords. 'Trade withered and declined. Perhaps the clearest indication of the decline of trade is to be found in the coin hoards of Scandinavia. During the 9th and 10th centuries Arabic and Persian coins are very numerous and indeed predominate in these hoards. During the 11th century they decrease greatly in numbers; thereafter they disappear.'[11] Gaza's role, therefore, as a major trading city was, for the first time in its history, in decline.

What the people of Gaza and other cities did not know, as they adjusted to the new conditions, was that the arrival of the Seljuq Turks in the eastern Mediterranean, and particularly in the land of the Christian holy sites, was a source of profound concern in territory far to the west. Adding to the concern felt there was the fact that the Byzantine empire appeared to be in danger of collapse. Western Christendom had come to count on Byzantium acting as a shield against Islamic expansion westwards. Unknown to the people of Palestine, in France an army was being assembled to travel to the Holy Land with the aim of wresting the Christian holy sites from the hands of the infidels.

Notes
[1] Interviewed by the author, 1994.

[2] M A Shaban, *Islamic History AD 600-750 (AH 132-448) A New Interpretation,* Cambridge, 1971, p. 6.
[3] *Ibid.* p. 3.
[4] Bernard Lewis, *The Arabs in History,* London, 1968, p. 47
[5] Mansfield, *op. cit.* p. 14.
[6] Al-Sarraf, *op. cit.* p. 59.
[7] Istakhri and Ibn Haukal. Quoted by Guy Le Strange, *Palestine under the Moslems. A Description of Syria and the Holy Land from AD630 to 1500,* London, 1980. This remarkable work is the source, unless indicated otherwise, of the quotations from early Arab geographer and historians that follow in this chapter.
[8] Wilkinson, *op. cit.*
[9] Lewis, *op. cit.* p. 58.
[10] Mansfield, *op. cit.* p. 20.
[11] Lewis, *op. cit.* p. 148.

CHAPTER 8

The Crusades: A Bruising Encounter

In the courtyard on the northern side of the Grand al-Umari Mosque in Gaza City there is an object that you would not expect to find in a place of Islamic worship – a Christian font. It stands at the foot of a weathered buttress on an outer wall of what must once have been a cloister. The grey marble font is in the shape of a cross; today, weeds grow in and around it. At one time a pipe would have protruded from the wall above to allow water to be poured directly into the font.

The font is a relic of the period in the 12th century when the Crusaders took over the Mosque of Umar and used it once again as a church – the mosque having been built on the site of a 5th century church. The Crusaders made another change to the building they called the Cathedral of St John the Baptist – they added a bell tower. The circular interior of the tower, complete with hole for the rope, can still be seen in the mosque. When you pass through the outer entrances and go into the main body of the mosque you are greeted by the dimensions and grandeur of a great cathedral, with baptisteries and grand pillars lining the

Life at the Crossroads

nave. Growing out of the southern side of the former church – the shape and windows of which are still clearly discernible – is a separate structure containing the mihrab (focus of prayer in the direction of Mecca) and an area to accommodate worshippers. Al-Umari Mosque dominates the centre of Gaza city today, as it has for many centuries. Here, compact within the walls of this sacred building, more than anywhere in the Gaza Strip, one can experience some of the layers of history on which the territory sits today.

The process which led to the arrival of a Crusader army in Gaza began with an appeal from the Byzantine Emperor Alexius Comnenus to Pope Urban II in 1095. With his own empire in danger of collapse Comnenus asked for military help in repelling the infidel Seljuq invaders from the Holy Land. Unlike the Muslim Arabs, the Seljuqs – less tolerant of Christianity – restricted the access of the many Christian pilgrims to the holy sites. For the pope, the appeal from Constantinople was fortuitous. The emergence of an outside enemy offered him a chance of distracting the warring knights of Europe from internecine strife. After the fall of the Roman Empire Europe was passing through the Dark Ages. 'War was endemic; every petty lord fought every other petty lord in the district, and there was no central authority strong enough to control them, let alone put an end to their eternal and murderous feuds. War was their business, their pleasure, and their sole occupation except for hunting. A warrior class directly descended from the various barbarians who had conquered the empire now dominated its shattered fragments.'[1]

In November 1095 Pope Urban, a charismatic public speaker, launched a campaign to recruit a fighting force to march to Palestine to protect the holiest of places from the Turks. He told his audiences that the Turks were 'maltreating innocent men and women and desecrating their churches.' He said it was time for Christians in the West 'to rise up in righteous wrath and

The Crusades: A Bruising Encounter

march to the rescue,' setting aside their own petty squabbles. The pope promised 'absolution and remission of all their sins' for those who died in battle.[2]

Within weeks, a huge force was on the march towards the east. They reached Jerusalem in 1099 and laid siege to the city, eventually taking it on 15 July. Their bloody massacre of virtually all the inhabitants of the walled city of Jerusalem has never been forgotten. In the words of an Arab chronicler of the day, 'the population of the holy city was put to the sword, and the Franj [as the Crusaders were referred to by the Arabs] spent a week massacring Muslims.'[3] The Jewish population were herded into their synagogue and burnt alive; and even the Arab Christians, whose oriental rites were despised as alien, did not escape persecution. Arab Christians 'regarded the foreign Crusaders as enemies, and they participated in all battles against them from the start. When the Crusaders occupied Jerusalem, the Orthodox patriarch took refuge in Gaza.'[4]

Reports of the massacre in Jerusalem spread throughout Palestine. In Gaza and other cities civilians feared for their lives as they watched and waited to see what these barbaric invaders would do next. It seems that many people fled from their cities, because the first historical reference to Gaza at around this time speaks of a city with few inhabitants. The prosperity of Gaza, which had been in decline since the arrival of the Seljuqs and the introduction of a feudal-style economy, sank further during the Crusader period. The city, which had once been a thriving commercial centre and a focus for scholars, became nothing more than a garrison town for the competing forces.

On Christmas Day in 1100, one of the leaders of the Crusade, Baldwin, was crowned King of Jerusalem. He reigned for 18 years, during which time the lands of the eastern Mediterranean were divided into four Latin kingdoms. The kingdom of Jerusalem, into which Gaza fell, encompassed Palestine and the coastal area of modern-day Lebanon and southern Syria. The other three Crusader territories were centred on Tripoli, Edessa and Antioch.

The Crusaders' hold on the territory within the kingdoms was patchy. Their firmest grip was on the ridge of hills running north and south of Jerusalem and in the Galilee area. Many villages in these districts, including Bethlehem, had always been Christian; while Muslims had fled in the path of the Crusading armies with their reputation for violence, Christians tended to remain.

In the early days of the Crusader occupation Egyptian troops of the Fatimid dynasty were garrisoned in Gaza. Its location on the fringes of the Latin Kingdom of Jerusalem meant that the Crusaders did not control the city until some years later.

For the civilian population of Palestine the whole period of the Crusades was uncertain and dangerous. For a start, they could never be certain who controlled a particular area at any given time. Aside from the constant struggle of the Muslims to unseat the Crusaders, there was also continual strife among the leaders of the armies from the West, and friction between the Egyptians and the Turks. For example, 'in the south the Negev was dominated by the Frankish [Crusader] garrison at Hebron. But the Castle of St Abraham [the Mosque of Abraham at Hebron], as it was called by the Franks, was little more than an island in a Muslim ocean. The Franks had no control over the tracks that led from Arabia, round the southern end of the Dead Sea, along the course of the old spice road of the Byzantines; by which the Bedouin could infiltrate into the Negev and link up with the Egyptian garrisons at Gaza and Ashqelon on the coast. Jerusalem itself had access to the sea down a corridor running through Ramla and Lydda to Jaffa; but the road was unsafe except for military convoys. Raiding parties from the Egyptian cities, Muslim refugees from the uplands and Bedouins from the desert wandered over the country and lay wait for unwary travellers.'[5]

The Crusades: A Bruising Encounter

Of the four Latin Kingdoms, Jerusalem was the poorest. Its principal source of revenue was the payment of tolls. Because the kingdom controlled the coast it also had the ports within its grasp. Produce from the fertile regions inland was taxed as it left the harbours in the kingdom. However, for the first time in history, Gaza appears to have lost its status as a trading city. In short, 'Palestine was a poor country. Its prosperity in Roman times had not outlasted the Persian invasions; and constant wars since the coming of the Turks had interrupted its partial recovery under the Caliphs.'[6]

Armies continued to pass through Gaza as they have done in every period in history. In the opening years of the 12th century the Egyptian Fatimid leader al-Afdal led his army northwards along the ancient Way of the Sea in a series of unsuccessful attempts to defeat the Crusaders and destroy the Latin Kingdom of Jerusalem. The Egyptians did manage to hold on to the old Philistine city of Ascalon (Ashqelon) which, unlike many other cities of Palestine, refused to surrender or sue for peace.

Towards the middle of the 12th century, resistance to the Crusaders (whose presence later boosted by the Second Crusade of 1147) was gaining in strength. A Seljuq leader, Zengi, captured Mosul in 1127 and set up a new state in northern Mesopotamia and Syria. Seventeen years later he captured Edessa. Zengi was the first leader in the region to see the possibility of Muslims putting aside their differences to face Islam's common enemy. His son, Nur al-Din, carried on leading the resistance to the Western occupation in the north.

The king of Jerusalem at the time, Baldwin III, realised that his army was no match for that of Nur al-Din in the north. But wishing to be seen by his subjects as doing something he turned his attention to the south where Fatimid military power was in decline. In particular Baldwin set his sights on the port city of Ashqelon which had remained in Egyptian hands. In

113

order to block the coastal road and prevent supplies and reinforcements reaching Ashqelon from Egypt, the Crusaders needed to take control of the strategic city of Gaza. Baldwin decided that Gaza would become the base of operations for the attack on Ashqelon and gave control of the city to the Knights Templar.

The Templars were so named because they were based on the Temple Mount in Jerusalem (the site of al-Aqsa mosque and the spot where the Jewish Temple of Solomon once stood). Their primary task was to protect pilgrims from attack by Muslims or common bandits as they journeyed to Jerusalem and the other holy sites. As a knightly order they became a military elite whose courage was said to have been unsurpassed.

When the Templars entered Gaza they immediately began strengthening the city's defences. Fortifications were built. The indications are that Templars were occupying a city that had been abandoned. A Crusader chronicler at the time described the construction of the city's new defences. 'The first fort of 1149 was very small. It was located on a slightly raised hill [where Palestine Square and the Grand al-Umari Mosque are located today], and enclosed a rather large space within its walls. Our people, seeing that their energies would not suffice for the present to rebuild the entire area, occupied part of the hill only; and after they had laid the foundations to a suitable depth they built the structure with a wall and towers.'[7] After a few years a small city grew there. 'As the castle could not occupy the whole hill on which the city was founded, but people who gathered there to settle the place, so that they should stay in more security, tried to fortify the rest of the hill with gates and a wall, though weaker and more modest.'[8] Similar forts began to dot the landscape of the kingdom – one was built at Darum, on the main route to Egypt, just to the south of Gaza [close to Deir al-Balah and the former Israeli settlement of Darom]. The 13th century Arab geographer, Yaqut, mentioned Darum, describing it as 'a castle that you pass after leaving Gaza on the road towards Egypt. It stands about a league from the sea, which you can see from thence. It was dismantled by Salah al-Din when he took possession of the place with the remainder of the coast towns in 1188.'[9]

Once Gaza was secure, Baldwin started assembling a huge army outside Ashqelon. The pick of the Templar Knights from Gaza and the Knights Hospitaller from Jerusalem were with him, as well as the patriarch, archbishop and bishops who carried the relic of the True Cross. Ashqelon was a tremendous fortress and the siege took some months to succeed. Because the Crusaders had control of the land route, at Gaza and elsewhere, the Egyptians had no choice but to send a force by sea to try to help the defenders of Ashqelon. They managed to get supplies into the city, but then sailed away. Eventually, after continued attacks on the city in which many Templars were killed, the Egyptian defenders of the city surrendered on condition that the citizens of Ashqelon be allowed to leave in safety. Thus the Crusaders took over the citadel and port, and the lordship of Ashqelon was given to King Baldwin's brother, Amalric.

The capture of Ashqelon represented a triumph for the Kingdom of Jerusalem; but it was to be its last major success. From this moment on, the Crusader hold on the land came under increasingly united Muslim pressure.

The man credited with mustering the Muslim resistance to the Crusaders and eventually breaking their hold on the land is a Kurdish general, Salah al-Din al-Ayyubi (known in the West as Saladin, perhaps the only Muslim leader to be accorded respect and admiration in traditional European accounts of the Crusades). He was the nephew of one of Nur al-Din's generals. Nur al-Din had captured Damascus in 1154 and had turned Syria into a single Muslim state. The Crusaders were faced for the first time by a strong and coordinated adversary.

Salah al-Din was sent as Nur al-Din's *wazir* (minister) to

the Fatimid court in Cairo in 1169. The Fatimids were in an advanced state of collapse, giving Salah al-Din the opportunity to seize power. This spelt the end of the Fatimid dynasty, to be replaced by the Ayyubids, the brief dynasty of Salah al-Din and his successors. With Salah al-Din in control of Egypt and Nur al-Din in Syria, the balance of power had shifted firmly against the Crusaders. After Nur al-Din's death, Salah al-Din assumed control of Syria as well as Egypt.

In June 1170 fighting between the Crusaders and the Muslims was interrupted by an earthquake. But by the end of the year, Salah al-Din was deploying his forces against the southern frontiers of the Kingdom of Jerusalem. Once again, Gaza found itself one of the first cities under attack. In December 1170 Salah al-Din's army attacked Darum and was successful in breaching the city walls. He then moved on to Gaza, still in the hands of Templar knights. Salah al-Din took the lower part of the city, outside the walls, and massacred the civilian inhabitants. However, the citadel was by this time so strong that Salah al-Din did not attack it. Instead, he took his army back to Egypt.

In August 1177, with the Crusaders in increasing disarray, Salah al-Din assembled a large Egyptian army ready to attack both Gaza and Ashqelon. In November that year Salah al-Din's army crossed the frontier from Egypt 'having decided on a sudden counter-attack up the coast into Palestine. The Templars summoned all the available knights of the Order to defend Gaza; but the Egyptian army marched straight on to Ascalon.' In the end, Salah al-Din decided to march on towards Jerusalem. But the mood of the Muslims appears to have been over-confident, and they were scattered by a surprise attack led by King Baldwin IV.[10]

But such setbacks were rare, and by 1187 Salah al-Din was taking the fight to the Crusaders in a major way. In July of that year he defeated them at the crucial battle of the Horns of Hattin near the Sea of Galilee. It was a catastrophic defeat for the

Crusader army and spelt the end of Latin domination of the Holy Land, even though some Crusader strongholds remained and new waves of Crusaders continued to arrive.

After the victory at the Horns of Hattin, Salah al-Din headed westward to the Mediterranean coast and began to capture with ease most of the cities there. Only Antioch, Tripoli and Tyre stood out against him. In September 1187, the Crusader defenders of Ashqelon surrendered, in return for the liberty of King Guy, who had been captured by Salah al-Din's army. The release of another prominent captive, the Templar Grand Master Gerard, was promised if the Templars defending the fortress in Gaza should surrender. The Templar garrison 'was obliged by the law of the Order to obey the Grand Master, Gerard's command,' so his order that it should surrender 'was carried out at once.'[11] This was a rare occasion when a potential military struggle for control of Gaza was avoided.

With the coastal cities under his control, Salah al-Din focused on the main prize: Jerusalem. He finally captured the city after a two-week siege, in October 1187.

Despite the defeats suffered by the Western forces, this was not the last appearance of the Crusaders either in Jerusalem or in the southern region of Palestine. The Third Crusade (1191) saw the arrival of Philip Augustus of France and Richard Coeur de Lion of England in the Holy Land. The following year Richard recaptured Darum and then moved northwards to Ashqelon. The assumption must be that he took control of Gaza as well.

Although Salah al-Din had retaken Jerusalem in 1187, one of his successors, ruling from Cairo, Sultan al-Kamel, in 1229 negotiated a peace treaty with the Holy Roman Emperor Frederick II under which the city would return to Crusader control, with an agreement for refrain from hostilities for 10 years. Thus 'without striking a blow, the excommunicate Emperor won back the Holy Places for Christendom. But seldom has a treaty met with such immediate and universal disapproval.'[12] In the summer of 1244 a force of several thousand Turkish cavalry attacked Jerusalem and sacked it. Shortly after this, the Turks, joined by a force of Egyptians, drove the last Christian forces out of Gaza.

But before this happened, Gaza was the scene of further battles. In November 1239 an expedition force led by Tibald of Champagne left Acre for the Egyptian frontier. An Egyptian army, commanded by a Mamluk Emir, Rukn al-Din, had been sent from the Nile Delta to Gaza. News reached the Christians that the Egyptian force consisted only of around 1,000 men. There were squabbles among King Tibald's forces, and one group defied the king's orders and planned a dawn raid on Gaza. The group was led by Henry of Bar who was 'so confident of success that when he drew near to Gaza about dawn, he halted his men in a hollow in the dunes of the seashore and told them to rest for a while. But the Egyptian army was far larger than he knew, and its spies were all around. The emir Rukn al-Din could scarcely believe that his foes could be so foolish. He sent bowmen to creep round sandhills till the Franks were almost encircled. Walter of Jaffa was the first to realize what was happening. He advised a swift retreat, for the horse could not be manoeuvred in the deep sand.' Others followed him northwards, but Henry of Bar 'would not leave the infantry whom he had led into the trap; and his closest friends stayed with him. The battle was soon over. With their horses and their heavy infantry floundering in the dunes, the Franks were slain.' More than 1,000 were killed and a further 600 captured and carried off to Egypt.[13]

The recapture of Jerusalem by the Muslims in 1244 brought to prominence in the lands of the eastern Mediterranean the next great wave of invaders, the Mongols. One of the dynasties taken over by the Mongols, led by Genghis Khan, during their initial sweep through central Asia into Persia was

The Crusades: A Bruising Encounter

the Khwarazmian Turks. Their army had fled westward into Syria; and it was the Khwarazmians who put an end finally to the Western occupation of Jerusalem. But the Christians escaped with their lives, thanks to dissent within the ranks of the attacking forces. Having liberated Jerusalem the Khwarazmians joined up with the Egyptian army in Gaza.

In the meantime, the Mongol threat returned. The Mongols had paused in their destructive march westward when Genghis Khan died in Persia in 1227. But in the middle of the century they set off again. In 1258 they conquered Baghdad, killing the last Abbasid caliph and destroying the city. In 1260 they took Syria and Palestine. Gaza, once more found itself in the role of garrison city – this time for the Mongols.

The Mongols were, no doubt, regrouping for an assault on Egypt. But their long period of success was suddenly reversed by the Egyptian army of the newly installed Mamluk dynasty – which had superseded that of the Ayyubids founded by Salah al-Din. The Mamluks were descended from Turkish slaves brought into Egypt as mercenaries and Turkish was the dominant language among them. They gradually became powerful enough to seize control of Egypt. The Mamluk army attacked the Mongol garrison at Gaza, catching the defenders off guard. The Mongols barely had time to organise resistance before they were routed.

In a matter of only a few decades, then, control of Gaza had passed from the hands of the Crusaders, to the army of Salah al-Din and his successors, back to the Crusaders, then to Turks, followed by the Mongols and finally to the Egyptian Mamluks. There can be few more graphic examples of how Gaza's location on one of the major strategic crossroads of the region meant that it was destined to be trampled over by succeeding armies.

The whole two-century period of the Crusader presence in the region was one in which Gaza's importance as a commercial and cultural centre in its own right continued to decline. It became nothing more than a fortified garrison. The experience of contact for the first time with armies and peoples from Western Europe brought little that can be counted as positive to Gaza and the rest of the east Mediterranean region. The Franj (as the Muslims called the Crusaders) were seen as barbaric, uncultured and ignorant in practical sciences like medicine. One Arab chronicler of the time said: 'All those who were well informed about the Franj saw them as beasts superior in courage and fighting ardour but in nothing else, just as animals are superior in strength and aggression.'[14]

One 20th century Western historian makes the following assessment of the Crusaders' influence: 'Apart from a few magnificent castles and some of their blood through intermarriage, the Crusaders left little which endured. Their greatest achievement was drastically to weaken the superior civilization they encountered and to undermine its moral standards. However, in one vitally important respect the Crusaders showed that they had an advantage over their Muslim enemies: this was their ability to create sound and workable political institutions.'[15]

Because of Gaza's position as a strategically important town, many more invaders were to enter it after the Crusaders, eliminating any legacy of Templar rule; and in Gaza there is not even the ruin of a magnificent Crusader castle to admire – the citadel which kept Salah al-Din's forces at bay was destroyed long ago. The last remnants of it disappeared more than a century ago. One Arab traveller of the 13th century, al-Fida, described Gaza as 'a city of medium size, possessing gardens by the sea-shore. There are here a few palm trees, also many fruitful vines. Between it and the sea are sand dunes, which lie beside the gardens. There is a small castle over Gaza.'

The era of the Crusades, which represented the first bruising encounter between the Arabs and the West, still resonates in the consciousness of the Arab people. Many Arabs liken Israel to the Crusader kingdom, an unnatural implant that one day will be removed. Western military action in the Middle East is invariably described as a new Crusade. Yet some Arab commentators point out that the Crusades offered the Arabs a chance to expand their horizons. Throughout the Crusades, wrote Lebanese author Amin Maalouf, 'the Arabs refused to open their own society to ideas from the West. And this, in all likelihood, was the most disastrous effect of the aggression of which they were the victims... Although the epoch of the Crusades ignited a genuine economic and cultural revolution in Western Europe, in the Orient these holy wars led to long centuries of decadence of obscurantism. Assaulted from all quarters, the Muslim world turned in on itself.'[16]

Gaza, too, despite its strategic location, could not escape the mood of torpor that settled over the region. The West, meanwhile, feeding on the heritage of Greek civilization that had been passed into Europe by the Arabs, started to develop skills that would make possible further and longer-lasting forays into the Middle East several centuries later.

Notes
[1] Anthony Bridge, *The Crusades*, London, 1980, p. 18.
[2] *Ibid.*, p. 44.
[3] Ibn al-Athir. Quoted by Amin Maalouf, *The Crusades Through Arab Eyes*, London, 1984, p.50.
[4] Al-Sarraf, cit. op., p. 59.
[5] S Steven Runciman, *A History of the Crusades Volume II*, Cambridge, 1952, p. 5.
[6] *Ibid.*, p. 5.
[7] Quoted by Joshua Prawer, *The Latin Kingdom of Jerusalem*, London, 1972, p. 298.
[8] *Ibid.*, p. 298.
[9] Guy Le Strange, *op. cit.*, p. 39.

[10] Runciman, *op. cit.*, pp. 416-417.
[11] *Ibid.*, p. 462.
[12] Steven Runciman, *A History of the Crusades Volume III*, Cambridge, 1954, p. 187.
[13] Ibid. pp. 214-215
[14] Quoted by Maalouf, *op. cit.*, p. 39.
[15] Mansfield, *op. cit.*, p. 21.
[16] Maalouf, *op. cit.*, p. 264.

Photos

Gaza City in the 1930s.

The Rooftops of Gaza City in the 1930s.

Life at the Crossroads

Fishermen with their boats on the Gaza shore in the 50s - one of the traditional livelihood for Gazans throughout history.

Umar al-Mukhtar Street, Gaza City, in the 1950s.

Photos

Gaza holiday beach in the mid-20th century.

Gaza railway station. The line, built by the British in World War I, has long since disappeared.

Life at the Crossroads

The Grand al-Umari Mosque in Gaza City in the mid-20th century.

The Grand al-Umari Mosque in Gaza City in the 19th century.

Photos

Gaza's southern border with Egypt at Rafah - in the 1920s. (Library of Congress)

Imperial Airways - Gaza (Library of Congress)

Statue of the Unknown Soldier in Gaza City, with the Government Administration Building - mid 20th century

Life at the Crossroads

A remembrance service at the British and Commonwealth War Cemetery in Gaza - in the 1920s or 30s. (Library of Congress)

British and Commonwealth War Cemetery in Gaza after World Word I. "The Crosses Mark the graves of the thousands killed in the Battle for Gaza in 1917. (Library of Congress)

CHAPTER 9

Ottoman Domination

In the centre of modern day Khan Younis, a bustling town south of Gaza city, stands a solid arched stone gateway with a tower at one end. Among the ornamentation in the stonework one can see a lion – symbol of the great Mamluk Sultan Baibars, who ruled from 1260 to 1277. The gateway is part of a khan – inn – built by the Mamluks as a staging post, giving the town its name. The khan was one of several linked by well kept roads for Mamluk postal relays which ran between Cairo and Damascus.

The great achievement of Baibars was to stop the Mongols in their tracks as they threatened Egypt and force them into retreat. He defeated them at the battle of Ain Jalout in Palestine in 1260, a momentous encounter that decisively influenced the fate of the region. In the words of historian: 'In that it saved the heartlands of the Muslim world from being overwhelmed this was one of the decisive battles in the history of the world.'[1] Having done this Baibars was able to unite Syria (including Palestine) and Egypt in a single state. He established a nominal caliphate in Cairo; but power rested in the hands of the Turkish Mamluks themselves.

His other great achievement was to eliminate most of the remaining pockets of the old Crusader kingdoms. Because the Crusaders still had supremacy on the sea, Baibars decided that the best way to keep them at bay would be to prevent them from landing. To achieve this, he destroyed the settlements and fortifications right on the coast, encouraging shepherds to use the cleared ground for grazing. Mamluk viceroys were appointed to major cities, including Gaza. The Arab geographer, al-Dimashqi, writing in 1300, spoke of Syria being divided into nine principalities. One of these was Gaza, with the city as the capital. 'It is a city so rich in trees,' al-Dimashqi wrote, 'as to be like a cloth of brocade spread out on the sand. In the Gaza area at times were counted Ascalon (Ashqelon), which belonged to the Franks, and which the Muslims took and destroyed; Jaffa, Caesarea, Arsuf, Al-Darun and El-Arish. Of towns lying between the coast and the mountains belonging at times to Gaza are: Tell Himar, Tell al-Safiyah, Karatayya, Bait Jibrail, Hebron, and Jerusalem. Each of these has a separate governor.'[2]

The likelihood is that the viceroy of Gaza would have lived in what today is one of the finest of the old buildings still standing and in daily use in the city. It is a solid, imposing structure of stone and marble which has the appearance of a citadel, which is how Gazans today, incorrectly, refer to it. The building, again with the lion of Baibars set in relief in the stonework in several places, would once have dominated the city within the walls. Today it houses al-Zahra' secondary school for girls.

The Mamluks adapted the feudal fiscal system introduced, to the detriment of the landowners and merchants of Gaza, by the Seljuq Turks. Mamluk officers, with units of troops assigned to them, were apportioned areas of land rather than given fixed salaries. As a rule the officers did not live in the areas under their control. They were 'interested in revenue rather than possession. The system therefore developed no châteaux or manors or strong local authorities of the Western type.'[3] With this feudal system in place there was no opportunity for the people of Gaza to revive their traditional role as entrepreneurs. In fact, Gaza and the region as a whole was entering a five-century period of introspection, not to say cultural, political and economic stagnation. In the view of one historian: 'Although the epoch of the Crusades ignited a genuine economic and cultural revolution in Western Europe, in the Orient these holy wars led to long centuries of decadence and obscurantism. Assaulted from all quarters, the Muslim world turned in on itself. It became over-sensitive, defensive, intolerant, sterile – attitudes that grew steadily worse as worldwide evolution, a process from which the Muslim world felt excluded, continued.'[4]

A glimpse of Gaza in the 14th century is provided by the great Arab traveller from Morocco, Ibn Battuta. Passing through in 1329 he wrote later that he was impressed by the stylish architecture and fine markets. He said there were several mosques in the city. Gaza's main mosque, he added, was 'elegantly built, containing a pulpit made of marble. The notables of the town are of the Banu Salim tribe, including Shams al-Din, the qadi [religious judge] of Jerusalem.'[5] But Gaza was much changed when he returned 16 years later after his travels around India. Most of the town, he wrote, was 'empty because many people had died of disease. The city's qadi told us that of the 80 notables, only a quarter remained. The number of dead in the city had reached 1,100 a day.'[6]

Aside from coping with illness, during the three centuries of Mamluk rule Gaza could at least enjoy a period of peace. With the Mongol and Christian threats receding there was the opportunity for scholarship and the arts to thrive again in Cairo, Damascus and Aleppo. At this time these three cities became wealthy trading centres with goods flowing to and from the east. If Gaza did benefit from this cultural renaissance – as it surely must have, given its location on the north-south road – little evidence of fine Mamluk architecture has survived. In Cairo, Jerusalem, Damascus and Aleppo, by contrast, the Mamluk architectural heritage is rich.

While there was stability of a kind, below the surface in the world of Mamluk politics things were anything but stable. The Mamluks rejected the idea of hereditary rulers which in practice meant that succession was decided instead by force of arms. The result was that a sultan's period of rule was rarely longer than a few years. The effect of this lack of continuity was to breed political uncertainty, leading ultimately to the weakening of the dynasty.

Another important factor contributing to the decline of the Mamluks was the undermining of their involvement in international trade between the Far East and Europe. The Mamluks depended on revenue from this commerce. The blow to their status as entrepreneurs was dealt by the Portuguese. In May 1498 the great navigator, Vasco da Gama, discovered the sea route, via the Cape of Good Hope, to India. When he returned to Lisbon a year later with a cargo of spices, Europeans quickly realised that this was a route to the East that was both safer and cheaper than the old one over land. There was nothing that the Egyptians or the Venetians (who also lost revenue after the discovery of the Cape route) could do. Diplomatic intervention failed; and the superior ships of the Portuguese dealt easily with the challenge from Egyptian vessels in the Indian Ocean, the Red Sea and elsewhere when the Mamluks tried to block the new trade route.[7]

Gaza, one can surmise, felt the effects of Egypt's decline as a commercial centre as powerfully as any city in Syria. And it is beyond dispute that the Mamluk viceroys and officers in Syria – as much as the sultans and their aides in Cairo – were too distracted by their own economic and political difficulties to

Ottoman Domination

notice the emergence of a new and powerful force to the north. After the Seljuqs had lost power in Syria in the 13th century, the remnants of their army had moved north to Anatolia. There the area had been divided up into a number of different Turkish principalities. One of these emerged powerful, the Osmanli, named after its eponym, Osman, the son of a tribal chieftan, Ertoghul. In Arabic his name was Uthman and the dynasty which bore his name (Uthmani) has been known ever since in the West as Ottoman. In 1453 the Ottoman leader, Muhammad II, captured Constantinople, and put an end to the Byzantine empire. From there the Ottomans expanded even further to the west. Not until the beginning of the 16th century, when the Mamluk dynasty was in crisis, did the Ottomans turn towards the south and east. In 1516, Selim I, known as Selim the Grim, marched the Ottoman army into Syria, defeating the Mamluks near Aleppo. In a matter of months his army had captured Damascus and Beirut, and marched across the Sinai desert to take Gaza, which once again was regarded as the vital crossroads for Egypt. Once Gaza was secure, Selim took the fight to the heart of Egyptian power, capturing Cairo in January 1517.

For Gaza, Ottoman occupation put the seal on what for centuries had been the gradual increase in Turkish influence in Palestine – beginning with the Seljuqs and continuing with the Mamluks. While the Arabs of Gaza continued to be immersed in Arab-Islamic culture (even though 16th century Ottoman records indicate that 20 percent of Gaza's inhabitants were Christians), they were to be ruled for the next four centuries by Turkish administrators.

Gaza found itself in the new Ottoman province of Syria – at that time divided into three pashaliks: Damascus, Aleppo and Tripoli. A fourth, Sidon, was added in 1660. By the 19th century maps of the eastern Mediterranean show a separate pashalik of Gaza which included the towns of Ramla and Jaffa, and extended south to al-Arish.

Gaza was a largely insignificant part of an enormous empire centred on Constantinople where the sultan, who also held the title of Caliph of Islam, was based. The empire encompassed much of North Africa, Egypt, the Red Sea coast of the Arabian peninsula, spreading up north through the countries of the Levant to present day Iraq; and then westwards from Turkey into the Balkans. The pashas of Syria exercised considerable power, and one of their chief responsibilities was levying and collecting taxes from which the empire drew its wealth. Most of the land continued to be organised along feudal lines, and taxes were collected either in money or in kind. A vast, multi-layered bureaucracy came into existence to manage the empire.

In the early days, the citizens of Syria welcomed the sense of order which Ottoman rule brought after the uncertainties of the last days of the Mamluks. But by the end of the 18th century, popular perceptions had changed. The Turkish rulers were seen as decadent and corrupt; and life stagnated.

At the very end of the 18th century an event occurred which set in process a movement that would lead to the reappearance of European powers in the eastern Mediterranean. While Gaza and other cities in the region in the three centuries since the start of Ottoman rule had barely moved out of the middle ages, Europe had undergone startling changes and had progressed into the industrial age. The event, the French occupation of Egypt under Napoleon Bonaparte in 1798, was a pivotal moment in the history of the Middle East. Curiously, Gaza had a role to play in this crucial episode.

In April 1798, Napoleon assembled a large fleet at Toulon with the aim of clearing the English from all their oriental possessions' and destroy all their stations in the Red Sea. He also intended to 'investigate the prospect of a canal linking the Mediterranean and Red Seas. Cherishing ambitions to follow in the conquering footsteps of Alexander the Great, his ultimate

Ottoman Domination

objective was to supplant the rising British Empire in India. After seizing and annexing Malta from the remnants of the Knights of St John, Napoleon and his army landed against little opposition on the beaches of Alexandria. He then marched on Cairo. Thus was Egypt awakened from a long sleep by the first Christian force to penetrate into the heartland of Islam since the time of the Crusades.'[8]

Having secured Cairo in 1799, Napoleon led his army northward out of Egypt. Like other army commanders before him, his first stop was at al-Arish. Napoleon had with him 'an elite body of troops who laid siege to the fortress of El-Arish where some fifteen-hundred soldiers of the Ottoman Empire, mainly seasoned fighters from Morocco and Albania, were entrenched. Short of food and water, the outnumbered enemy surrendered to the French on February 18, after a ten-day siege, and were paroled on condition they went to Baghdad and no longer bore arms against the French.'[9]

From al-Arish the French continued 'in their hard-slogging march up the coast'[10] along the Way of the Sea, as Tuthmosis III, Salah al-Din, and other legendary generals had done. According to one report, at Khan Younis, he had a lucky escape. Napoleon's 'main army, ahead of him, turned off accidentally into the desert; Napoleon took the direct route and, thus missing them, rode into Khan Younis surrounded only by his staff. He was surprised to see a number of Arabs in the market square hastily mounting and galloping away. They thought it was the French army. Had they waited and captured Napoleon the history of the world since then would have been changed at Khan Younis.'[11] On 24 February 1799 Napoleon's army took Gaza without a fight. According to local tradition, Napoleon spent at least one night in the city while his army remained camped, outside. Again, tradition has it that he stayed in the large Mamluk building in the centre of the city which had been the home of the viceroy in the days of Baibars and is now a

135

school. To this day, Gazans refer to it as Napoleon's citadel. In the course of his visit, local historians say, his army destroyed some of the city's mosques and the remaining fortification. Gaza originally had seven city gates – two to the east, one to the south, three to the west and two to the north.

Also following the example of Tuthmosis and other conquerors, Napoleon did not stay in Gaza but moved his army on to the north. While the French are said to have caused, considerable material damage to Gaza, the lot of the citizens was more fortunate than the inhabitants of Napoleon's next target, Jaffa. Here the Ottomans refused to surrender. When the French eventually took the town they slaughtered many of the citizens. Further north, in Acre, Napoleon encountered further resistance. The French besieged the city for two months. But eventually nine small boats bringing extra siege artillery northwards were captured by the British Royal Navy. They were subsequently used against the French. With British support, the Ottomans were able to break the siege and roundly defeat the attacking force.

Napoleon's Syria campaign was ultimately, then, a resounding failure. Many of his men died of plague, and he did not have a force large enough to secure the cities that he had conquered. In May, the ragged band of surviving French troops were transported by sea back to Cairo. Napoleon was coming under increasing threat from Britain, a new power in the eastern Mediterranean which was intent on protecting the route to its imperial lands in India. Admiral Nelson had sunk Napoleon's fleet shortly after the French had first come ashore in Egypt. The French army was weakened and demoralised. Napoleon escaped from Egypt by sea in August 1799, leaving his army behind.

Britain cooperated with the Ottoman authorities in plans to oust the French. As negotiations to secure a peaceful French withdrawal continued, an Ottoman-led army was assembled

Ottoman Domination

ready to march into Egypt. Once again, Gaza was the garrison town chosen for the new force. In January 1800, with the negotiations having failed, the army moved south and overran the nearest French position at al-Arish.

Napoleon's venture into Egypt and Syria was a mere brushstroke on the canvas depicting foreign military intervention in the lands of the eastern Mediterranean. But there was an important secondary dimension to the brief French presence in the region. Napoleon was accompanied not only by an army of 40,000 men, but also by scientists and academics. The French set up an Institut d'Egypte to study antiquities and languages, and began making geological surveys. Put succinctly, the French breached the wall that had been keeping the peoples of the Middle East isolated from the rapid scientific and technological progress of the Europeans.

Another effect of the Napoleon venture was to alert Britain to the threat posed by the French to the routes to India. From this point on the British could not be indifferent to the fate of Egypt and other lands in the region which lay mid-way between Europe and India. The fate of Gaza, a strategic city on the approaches to Egypt, was bound to be of concern to the British.

But before the day came when Britain committed itself on the ground in the Middle East, Gaza experienced another period of direct control from Egypt.

After the French had been forced out of Egypt by an Ottoman army, supported by Britain, the country nominally came back under the umbrella of Constantinople. But developments in Egypt in subsequent months showed that the ability of the sultan to keep the outlying provinces under his control was declining fast. Within the Ottoman army that had gathered in Gaza prior to driving the French out of Egypt in 1801 was a unit of Albanians. Their leader was Muhammad Ali. He remained in Cairo, building up his power base, until a point came when the Ottoman authorities had no choice but to accept him as governor of Egypt. Muhammad Ali realised the value of Western ideas and technology, not least in the creation of a strong army. He sent hundreds of young Egyptians to study in France and set up schools in Cairo. This was the beginning of a process in which Arab nationalism had its origins.

Egypt quickly became the strongest province in the Ottoman Empire, presenting a clear challenge to the authority of Constantinople. Muhammad Ali decided that to consolidate his power he should bring the human and material resources of Syria under his control. In 1832 he dispatched a force of his modernised and reorganised army, with his eldest son Ibrahim in command, to conquer Syria. The Egyptian army headed northward, taking Gaza and most of the coastal cities without a struggle. Only Acre held out, as it had done against Napoleon, before submitting to the Egyptians.

For the people of Gaza, the arrival of the Egyptians was a mixed blessing. At first they welcomed the new rulers who established local councils to run day-to-day affairs and involved the people of Gaza in a way that the Ottomans had not. But the city was subject to a new centralised form of government which required high taxation and which cut across the interests of powerful semi-autonomous sects and clans. There was another unpopular measure introduced by the Egyptians – a ruthless campaign to enlist the people of Palestine into the army. Under Turkish rule the population had not been required to serve in the Ottoman army. Gazans view this period in their history as one of the darker ones. At this time, according to one Palestinian, 'Gaza suffered many disasters. There were pestilence and disease, as well as invasions by the bedouin. Disorder and injustice prevailed. Economically, Gaza was no longer important. The international trading thoroughfares to Gaza were displaced. There was destruction and ruin.'[12]

The British, who were becoming increasingly sensitive to

Ottoman Domination

events in the Middle East, viewed with alarm the emergence of a powerful new state in the region. They decided that the new power cut across their interests and tried to enlist the support of France and other European states to force the hand of Muhammad Ali. In the end, through a combination of military pressure and the instigation of a revolt among the disaffected population of Syria, Britain was able to force the withdrawal of the Egyptian army from Syria.

In 1840, with Muhammad Ali's forces having passed through Gaza on their way back to Egypt, the city fell once again under Ottoman control. A number of tough new economic reforms were introduced to raise central taxes and break the hold of the local landowners. The effect of these measures was to increase the general economic prosperity of Palestine. But Constantinople began to demand, as Cairo had done during the brief period of Egyptian rule, that young men from Syria and Palestine should join the army. Many were recruited in the 1870s to fight in the Ottoman army during the Russian and Balkan wars.[13] The grievance felt by these young Arab conscripts increased when they were sent to Yemen to fight in the Ottoman army against other Arabs.

The population of the eastern Mediterranean were alienated further from Ottoman rule after the revolt of the Young Turks began in 1908. The Young Turks believed that Constantinople could keep the empire together only by stressing its Turkish roots. This caused a reaction among the Arab communities, which resented the imposition of the Turkish language in place of Arabic in schools and public offices as much as they continued to dislike being administered by Turkish officials sent from Constantinople. A comment by the distinguished British archaeologist, Sir Flinders Petrie, suggests that Ottoman officials had little in common with the Arabs under their administration. On a visit to Gaza in 1890, Sir Flinders had commented on the cosmopolitan background of the

Ottoman *Kaimmakam* or District Governor. He found him to be 'much Europeanized in ways and feelings', having spent much of his life in Berlin and Vienna.[14]

This growing sense of dissatisfaction with Ottoman rule was accompanied by an increasing awareness of the changes – political and cultural, as well as technological – that were taking place in Europe. In 1882, the British had invaded and occupied Egypt, taking that country out of Ottoman control in everything but name. At the same time Christian missionaries from Europe and the United States were beginning to establish themselves in Arab countries. The Americans and the French concentrated on Lebanon and Syria, founding, among other things, the American University of Beirut and the College Protestant; while in Egypt and Palestine, British missionaries were active. The Church Missionary Society (CMS) began to offer limited medical services to the Palestinians of Gaza in 1882. In 1891 the CMS rented a house near the centre of Gaza city which it turned into a rudimentary clinic. Sir Flinders Petrie, recording his visit to Gaza in 1890, spoke of being received kindly at the home of a medical missionary: he found it reassuring to learn that the doctor had a fully equipped dispensary 'within human reach' of the archaeological site (Tel Jemmeh) where he was working.[15]

Despite the limited facilities, the two Britons who ran the clinic were soon treating up to 70 people a day. It was the only medical centre of its kind for the whole of southern Palestine and northern Sinai; and reports from the end-of-century years spoke of patients coming to the Gaza clinic from El-Arish, Beersheba and beyond, sometimes travelling by camel or donkey for up to 18 hours to get there. In 1893 a priest from Germany was responsible for building a second floor to what then was being called a 'hospital' to cater for female in-patients. He was followed around the turn of the century by a certain Canon Sterling MD; and the hospital and its facilities continued to expand. The expansion included facilities for a nursing school. In 1908 the Bishop of Jerusalem opened a new hospital building with 46 beds; and records for 1912 show that around 30,000 people were treated as out-patients and 700 were admitted that year. Given that the total population of Gaza at that time was less than 40,000 it is easy to see the extent to which the city had become a regional centre for medical treatment.

Dr Sterling's name became closely associated with the hospital during this period. As a result it became known either as the English Hospital or Dr Sterly's (a corruption of Sterling's). Today the facility, having been rebuilt on the original site by Dr Sterling's son, Robert, after being damaged in the First World War, lies to the south-east of Palestine Square in a quiet compound with trees and gardens. It is known officially as the Ahli Arab Hospital, operated by the Anglican Church in Jerusalem. But staff at the hospital say that elderly patients still sometimes call it the English or Dr Sterly's hospital when they are asking for directions there.

By the time the First World War broke out in 1914, Britain was ensconced as the power behind the throne in Egypt. British officials in Cairo were beginning to consider what might become of the eastern Mediterranean lands once the Ottoman Empire had collapsed. Similar thoughts were going through the mind of the French government. Europe was poised to move into the Middle East in a major way.

But while Ottoman power was crumbling, the Turks still occupied large areas of the eastern Mediterranean and the Red Sea coastal strip of the Arabian peninsula. For Britain, the power in Egypt, to oust the Turks from Palestine and Syria, it would have to do what dozens of military powers before it had done: capture Gaza.

Notes
[1] Mansfield, *op. cit.*, p. 22.

[2] Le Strange, *op. cit.*
[3] Lewis, *op. cit.*, p. 156.
[4] Quoted anonymously by Mansfield, *op. cit.*, p. 21-22.
[5] Ibn Battuta, *Travels*, Beirut, 1992, p. 73.
[6] *Ibid.*, p. 666.
[7] Lewis, *op. cit.*, pp. 157-158.
[8] Lord Kinross, *The Ottoman Centuries: The Rise and Fall of the Turkish Empire*, New York, 1977. pp. 424-425.
[9] Paul Fregosi, *Dreams of Empire*, London, 1989, p. 160.
[10] *Ibid.*, p. 160.
[11] Rennie MacInnes, *Notes for Travellers by Road and Rail in Palestine and Syria*, London, 1933, p. 119.
[12] Al-Sarraf, *op. cit.*, p. 60.
[13] Mansfield, *op. cit.*, p. 119.
[14] Margaret S Drower, *Sir Flinders Petrie – A Life in Archaeology*, London, 1985, p. 159.
[15] *Ibid.*, p. 159.

CHAPTER 10

The First World War
'A Scene of Sad Desolation'

In the closing years of the 19th century, as the Ottomans' grip on their empire weakened, Europe's interest in the eastern Mediterranean region grew. While politicians and diplomats coveted the land and resources of the region, it was becoming fashionable for individuals with sufficient wealth to make pilgrimages to the Holy Land and explore areas close to it. Baedeker's *Palestine and Syria* guide of 1898 includes a section on Gaza. But its author did nothing to encourage a Christian pilgrim to visit Gaza, stating in bald and unequivocal language, that since the defeat of the Crusaders in the mid-13th century 'Gaza has been a place of no importance.'

Nevertheless, the author went on to provide practical information for the visitor to Gaza. Accommodation was available, according to Baedeker, at 'Hotel Gaza (proprietors J. Blaich & Co); also at the Latin Hospice (Mr. Gatt), or at the Greek Monastery (Introduction from Jerusalem desirable). The best place for pitching tents here is near the Serai.'

Life at the Crossroads

The visitor was told that Gaza 'has grown considerably within the last few years, and now contains 325,000 inhabitants, including 700 Greeks (who possess a church), 50 Latins and 100 Jews. The English and the Roman Catholic missions have stations there. Gaza is the seat of a *Kaimmakam* and has a small garrison.'

The Baedeker guide described the city of Gaza in the following way:

> 'The town is of semi-Egyptian character; the veil of the Muslim women, for example, closely resembles the Egyptian. From time immemorial Gaza has formed a connecting link between Egypt and Syria, and to this day, although the caravan traffic is almost extinct, its market is not unimportant for the Beduins, being in particular abundantly stocked with dates, figs, olives, lentils, and other provisions. The bazaar, too, has an Egyptian appearance. Gaza is moreover an important depot for barley; its olive-harvest is considerable; and it contains numerous potteries and a steam mill in German possession. An unusually large proportion of the inhabitants suffer from ophthalmia, a fact which is generally attributed to the want of light and ventilation in the miserable houses, and to the filthiness of the narrow streets which are never flushed. The town-wells are 100-160 ft. deep, but the water is slightly saline, except in a few wells to the N. As the town lies on a hill about 100 ft. high, in the midst of orchards, it is difficult to say exactly where it begins. Owing to the abundance of water contained by the soil the vegetation is very rich. At the present day the town has neither walls nor gates. The ancient town was a good deal larger than the modern one, and to the S. and E. elevations of the ground are visible, marking the course of the town wall. The newer houses are generally built of

The First World War - 'A Scene of Sad Desolation'

ancient materials, and old fragments of marble may frequently be detected in the walls.'

Living conditions for most Gazans at the turn of the century, as the description above makes clear, were basic. Nevertheless, the city of Gaza was continuing its traditional role as a thriving marketing centre for agricultural produce from the fertile land round about. Above all, Gazans were enjoying years of welcome peace. In 1914, Gaza was, according to one chronicle, 'a white walled town in a shallow fertile valley between sand-dunes on the west and irregular hills to the south and east. It is surrounded by small fields and gardens, delineated by high cactus hedges.'[1]

On to this quiet and untroubled landscape landed, in 1917, the horrors of the First World War.

In November 1914, the authorities in Constantinople announced that they were supporting Germany in its war with Britain. In doing so they were taking a step which would ultimately bring an end to centuries of Turkish domination of the lands of the eastern Mediterranean.

Jemal Pasha, one of the leaders of the Young Turk Revolution, was put in control of the Ottoman forces in Syria, declaring that he would not return before he had entered Cairo.[2] In January 1915, assisted by an inspired German chief-of-staff, Kress von Kressenstein, Jemal Pasha launched an attack on what had become the most precious link in Britain's route to India, the Suez Canal. The British, with many of their troops from Egypt deployed in France, were poorly placed to defend the canal. But with the assistance of the French navy the Ottoman-German assault was repulsed. In April 1915, French warships close off the shore of Gaza bombarded the city in an attempt to relieve the military pressure on Egypt. But the attack did not weaken the Turkish hold on Gaza. Over the following year and a half von Kressenstein, with supplies of men and equipment passing southwards through Gaza, continued to tie down the British

145

Life at the Crossroads

army in the Suez Canal zone. By the summer of 1916 the Allies were well prepared for another strong attack on the waterway. Not only did they finally repulse the Turks, but they also drove them out of Sinai. In December 1916 the British army, led by General Sir Archibald Murray, was in El-Arish ready to head northward to Gaza.

While this was happening British officials in Cairo and the French government were musing over what might become of the territories of the eastern Mediterranean if the Turks could be defeated there. Britain had already taken steps to win Arab support in its military campaign. In the Hejaz, the eastern Red Sea coastal strip of the Arabian peninsula, the traditional leader of Mecca, the Sharif, had promised to help the Allies. Sharif Hussain said he was prepared to lead a revolt against the Turkish occupation in return for what he took to be a British promise to grant the Arabs independence in the former Ottoman lands of the Middle East. In June 1916 he declared that the Arab Revolt had begun.

But Britain and France had other ideas. In a series of secret meetings they reached agreement which envisaged the liberated Turkish territories being divided into areas of British and French influence. The secret deal, worked out in London with the agreement of Imperial Russia, came to be known as the Sykes-Picot agreement.

In the early weeks of 1917 only a handful of people knew about the existence of the Sykes-Picot accord. Sir Archibald Murray and his advisers, who almost certainly did not know about it, were working out how they might dislodge the Turks from Gaza and cities to the north. In February, the cavalry of the Egypt Expeditionary Force (made up of British and Dominion forces) set off from al-Arish. On 27 February they entered Khan Younis, midway between Rafah and Deir al-Balah. The Turks had withdrawn their line to Gaza, Tell Shariah and Beersheba, strengthening it along the way.

The First World War - 'A Scene of Sad Desolation'

As the Allies advanced northwards they set down, with the help of Egyptian labourers, a railway track and a pipe to bring water from Egypt. The construction of the railway was an important development both for the Allied war effort and for the future of transport connecting Egypt and Palestine after the war. It was an immense and difficult task. The Right Reverend Rennie MacInnes, the Anglican Bishop of Jerusalem from 1914 to 1931, commented wryly in Notes for Travellers by Road and Rail in Palestine and Syria that 'when our armies, with the magnificent assistance of the Egyptian Labour Corps, began to make this railway, they called it the "Milk and Honey Railway". Later, finding nothing but sand all the way, they called it the "Desert Railway".'[3]

The pipe alongside the track eventually brought water from the River Nile, when the railway was extended, all the way to Gaza. Bishop MacInnes recalled that there was 'an old tradition in South Palestine that the Turks would hold the country "till the waters of the Nile flow into Palestine" – i.e. an almost impossible contingency. But it was eventually effected by General Sir Archibald Murray.'[4]

From Khan Younis the Allies moved on to Deir al-Balah which became the site of an enormous railhead. An aerodrome and camps were established there. According to Bishop MacInnes, Deir al-Balah was 'commonly called by the British troops "Dear Old Bella".'[5]

The Turks, meanwhile, with their German advisers had built an impressive defensive shield in Gaza which consisted not just of infantry, but also artillery – including four heavy batteries and two batteries of desert guns – in addition to machine guns and other lighter weapons. They used the Grand Mosque as a store for their provisions and ammunition. The civilian inhabitants of the city were told to leave for their own safety.

On 26 March 1917, Sir Archibald Murray led an Allied army force of 44,000 men in an attack aimed at surrounding and

Life at the Crossroads

driving the Turks out of Gaza. It was a city described in one contemporary newspaper account as 'this fortress of long standing, situated on the coast road into Palestine. But capturing it would not be easy. Its natural defences from an attack from the south [primarily, the Wadi Ghazzah] were strong. And British movements were constricted by the problem of supplying water (not least for the 9,000 horses) beyond the railhead. To surmount the latter problem, an attack must capture Gaza, where wells could be found in abundance, within 24 hours.'[6]

It is striking how the problems faced by an army commander trying to capture Gaza in the 20th century were so similar to those confronting other commanders many centuries earlier. For a start any advancing general had to fathom how to cross the natural defensive line of the Wadi Ghazzah, while concentrating all the time on securing enough water for his army. The provision of water supplies had been one of the priorities of the Egyptian pharaoh Sethos II, for example, as far back as the 12th century BC when he took the route that was to be followed by General Murray.

Sir Archibald's idea was to approach the city from three directions: Tell Jemmeh and Wadi Ghazzah in the south; from Tell Al-Mantar from the east; and from Beit Hanoun and Jabaliya (two villages in the Gaza Strip today) from the north. The operation against Gaza 'was skilfully planned and well executed. The infantry pressed up from the south with determination. Meanwhile the cavalry outflanked the town on the landward (eastern) side and then swung west to encircle it. Within the allotted time Gaza was cut off, and its capture was imminent.'[7]

But a problem arose. The third force was delayed taking the northern positions. Because of poor communications its fate was unknown. The British army commanders assumed, incorrectly, that the force had run into an ambush. 'With the coming of sunset the point had been reached where it seemed

The First World War - 'A Scene of Sad Desolation'

that the forces must be withdrawn for lack of water. Further, the British command had learned that Turkish reinforcements were approaching from the north.'[8] So, Sir Archibald Murray ordered a withdrawal of the rest of the force that had been moving in on Gaza. During the retreat more losses were suffered, bringing the total number of Allied soldiers killed to 4,000, with Turkish losses only half this number. But Sir Archibald declared the battle a major success.

The lie which he told is exposed in an awesome way at the British War Cemetery close to the highway to the north of Gaza. To pass through the austere granite archway into the cemetery is to step from one world to another – from the bustle and disorder of modern Gaza to a silent and immaculately manicured garden. Here, under trees, and amid flowering jacaranda and oleander, lie ranks of gravestones – many hundreds of them. One only needs to start reading the inscriptions on the headstones to realise that the First Battle of Gaza was a disaster. 'Private W Pearson, Essex Regiment. Died 26th March 1917; Private G Dickens, Aged 26, Died 26 March 1917, Private S P Spurgen, Aged 21. Died 26 March 1917... '

But because of the optimistic assessment of the battle reaching the War Cabinet, Sir Archibald was ordered to make another attempt to capture Gaza a month later. According to T E Lawrence (Lawrence of Arabia), the British commander knew that the task was hopeless, but was 'too weak or too politic to resist... and we went into it, everybody, generals and staff-officers, even soldiers, convinced that we should lose.'[9]

Sir Archibald's second attempt was no more successful than the first. By this time, any element of surprise had gone, and the Turks had had an opportunity to greatly reinforce their positions in Gaza city.

Sir Archibald's plan for the second assault on the city was for bombardment to come from the sea from the south-west, and the land attack would follow from the south and south-east.

A land force, strengthened by a unit from the Indian army, came up the coast as far as Shaikh Ijlin – a coastal village a few miles to the south of the city – today almost an outer suburb. But the Allied force 'lacked the artillery for a direct frontal assault,[10] and could make no further progress under the heavy defensive artillery barrage from the Turks. Once again, the lines of graves in the British cemetery in Gaza (as well as the small cemetery in Deir al-Balah) testify to the military failure. The headstones show that scores of young men were killed on 19 April 1917. Many of the graves carry no name, describing the person buried there simply as 'A Soldier of the Great War – Known unto God'.

After these two military fiascos, Sir Archibald was replaced by General Sir Edmund Allenby. Two defeats in the battle for Gaza had not deterred the British government. Prime Minister Lloyd George 'wanted Jerusalem "as a Christmas present for the British nation".'[11]

Aside from being a more astute military commander than his predecessor, General Allenby had the advantage that the Turkish supply lines were being increasingly stretched. Because of the succession of battles in and around Gaza, for example, the local population had had little opportunity to work the land and harvest crops – or to attend to cattle. This all contributed to a food shortage among the military and the civilian population.

The Ottoman forces were also at a psychological disadvantage in their relationship with the Arab communities among whom they were deployed. By this time, Sharif Hussain's Arab Revolt was under way and Arab forces were helping the Allies harass the Turks in a number of positions. The British had done their best to maximise the propaganda benefit of Sharif Hussain's revolt in trying to win over the Arabs in Turkish-occupied land. The result was that the Ottomans were receiving less than full cooperation from the Arabs of Palestine and Syria who were looking to a day when

The First World War - 'A Scene of Sad Desolation'

Turkish rule would end.

Under the command of General Allenby the attacking force was well organised and larger than that defending the city. Allenby had under his command seven infantry and three cavalry divisions, giving him superiority over the Turks of two-to-one in infantry and eight-to-one in cavalry.

During the long build-up to the third battle for Gaza, Allied troops found time heavy on their hands. A senior British civilian official noted that 'the army had been encamped for five months in this uninteresting stretch of sand country, and it was exceedingly difficult to find any form of recreation beyond riding about in very featureless scenery.' But not all members of the unit were bored. 'The only people who were really happy were a small group of skilled ornithologists who occupied their spare time by increasing considerably the world's knowledge of migratory birds.' Gaza, it turned out, was a crossroads for birds as much as for conquering armies. 'Fate had dumped them down in the very best spot for studying the big annual migration at the right time, and they made the most excellent use of this exceptional opportunity.'[12]

The bird watchers had an ally in their commander-in-chief. 'Lord Allenby,' a correspondent of the Daily Chronicle of London noted, 'stationed a Yorkshire sergeant at a watering place which migratory birds frequented and whenever a new species arrived the commander-in-chief would forget the cares of the campaign and slip off to the pond to see the bird for himself.'[13]

Most of these long days were taken up in getting men and equipment into place for the next stage in the military campaign. The Turks, too, had been using the time to prepare for the expected assault from the Allies, as a correspondent for The Times of London reported. 'In the six months between the second battle and the opening of General Allenby's offensive they [the Turks] had constructed formidable defences on the

Life at the Crossroads

Gaza-Beersheba front. Strategic railways were built, the garrison of southern Palestine was largely reinforced and provided with powerful artillery; the air service was enlarged and rendered very efficient. In all these measures the Turks had the active help of the Germans, who were concerned for the prosecution of their own interests in the Near East.' Gaza city, the correspondent wrote, 'had been made into a strong modern fortress, heavily entrenched and wired, offering every facility for protracted defence.'[14] In the view of the British pilot of a seaplane of the East Indies and Egypt Seaplane Squadron who watched many of the preparation from the air, by far the greatest strength in the Turkish defence line, 'so far as entrenchments and batteries are concerned, was concentrated around Gaza, and the reason for this was the perfectly sound assumption that any attempted advance by the British must keep touch with the sea coast, since the country inland, with its waterless desert, presented almost insuperable difficulties of supply.' As a result, Gaza was fortified with a 'wide scheme of trenches which were regarded as absolutely impregnable. An officer prisoner taken before the advance ridiculed the idea of capture, and there was found afterwards, when the position was captured, that there were many dugouts with head-cover 9 feet thick, and winding stairs leading to shelter a dozen feet underground.'[15]

The correspondent of The Times pointed out, too, that the Turks had the advantage of terrain – their land was fertile and they had good water supplies. The Allies, on the other hand, were mainly occupying desert.

The front line of the Allied force extended some 35 kilometres from the coast south of Gaza, following roughly the line of the Wadi Ghazzah, eastward. At his headquarters at Kilab, just south of Khan Younis, General Allenby worked on his strategy for capturing the city. Writing to General Sir William Robertson, of Eastern Command, three months before the assault on the Turks began, Allenby indicated that he would not

The First World War - 'A Scene of Sad Desolation'

be copying General Murray's tactics in launching a frontal attack from the south. There the Turks were well dug in with lines and lines of trenches. 'I think from what I have so far seen that the Turks expect us to renew our attacks on Gaza. They probably think we shall cling to the coastline. If we make our attack there it will probably be costly... To make the best use of the mounted troops and our mobility it will most likely be preferable to strike further east.'[16]

General Allenby had in mind to attack Beersheba ahead of Gaza; but he was still keen to give the impression to the Turks that he would be going to Gaza first. As he wrote to General Robertson towards the end of July 1917, 'my policy is to encourage the belief that my attack will come against Gaza. Lately we have carried out one or two successful raids on the front of Gaza and others are contemplated.'[17]

In August, Allenby, in another communication to General Robertson, neatly summed up his strategy for defeating the Turks: 'Success depends on surprise and speed, speed depends on transport and water.'[18] Aside from the element of surprise, General Allenby wanted early control of Beersheba because it was an important source of water. His army (both men and horses) was consuming 400,000 gallons of water a day.[19]

On 31 October 1917, the town of Beersheba fell to the Allies. The attack had involved one of the last great cavalry charges in British military history. General Allenby summarised the battle for Beersheba as 'a smart little battle, achieved by careful preparation and good staff work.'[20]

The Allied army then concentrated its attack on Gaza. On the night of 1-2 November, Allenby's army broke through the Turkish line between the coast and the city. The next morning he wrote to his wife, Mabel: 'This morning at 3 o'clock I attacked the south-west part of the Gaza defences. We took them on a flank of some 6,000 yards and a depth of some 1,000-1,500 yards.

We now overlook Gaza and my left is on the sea coast north-east of the town. The navy cooperated with fire from the sea; and shot well. We've taken some 300 prisoners and some machine-guns so far.'[21]

General Allenby mentioned the successful supporting fire from Royal Navy ships offshore, but he omitted to mention the role played by the Port Said-based seaplane squadron. The purpose of the bombardment from the sea was to cut the railway and road north of Gaza to prevent the Ottoman forces using them to retreat. As a seaplane pilot recalled, 'the proximity of the road and railway to the coast made it possible to extend the Gaza cannonade much farther back than would have been practicable by means of land artillery. The bombardment of these lines of retreat was undertaken by battleships which, lying fairly close inshore, could range on them with the greatest ease, though their targets were generally invisible. It was here that the seaplanes came in. They were employed in spotting; that is to say, they circled above the targets, and the observers, noting where the shots fell, corrected the aim of the gunners by wireless signals.'

This same method was used to destroy supply dumps. An airborne observer spotted what looked like a dump beside the railway station at the village of Deir Sineid: 'It was impossible to make out whether the dump consisted of ammunition or of other stores less flammable, but in any case it provided a good target. So a signal was sent and the 6-inch gun was ranged upon it. Half a dozen or so test shots were fired, and then there was a direct hit. The dump made an immediate and gratifying response by proclaiming itself to be ammunition. It exploded and continued to explode for thirty-five minutes, demolishing the railway station and tearing up many yards of line.'[22]

In the days that followed the initial attack, the Allies closed in on Gaza. On 6 November, in another letter to his wife,

The First World War - 'A Scene of Sad Desolation'

General Allenby wrote: 'We've had a successful day. We attacked the left of the Turkish positions, from north of Beersheba and have rolled them as far as Sharia [Tell Shariah]. The Turks fought well but have been badly defeated... Gaza was not attacked; but I should not be surprised if this affected seriously their defenders. I am putting a lot of shell into them and the Navy are still pounding them effectively. There was a sky with mist this morning; which cleared at 8 o'clock. It was in our favour as it veiled our start and the day has been bright and cool. I have no details, yet, of the battle, and don't know what our casualties and captives may be.'[23]

The pounding of Gaza had the desired effect. A correspondent of The Times reported that the evacuation of the city had been completed during the night of 6 November, 'and though a certain amount of movement on the roads north of Gaza was observed by our airmen and fired on by our heavy artillery there was nothing indicating a general retirement. By this prompt retreat General von Kressenstein avoided a battle, for another attack on Gaza was the natural sequel to the Sharia battle, and an attack had been ordered for the night of November 6th-7th.'

On the morning of 7 November, the Allies encountered minimal Turkish resistance around the city. British army patrols cautiously approached the city along the coast and, according to the correspondent of The Times, 'found the enemy gone... and the old capital of the Philistines, before which the British had been held up for nine months, was now won.'

In a letter home, General Allenby summed up the day's achievement: 'Dear Mabel, The Turks have had an awful hammering. We attacked Gaza early this morning; and got it almost without opposition.' This letter ended with the comment, 'No rain here; but the weather is perfect for campaigning and now we have captured all the water supplies we need.'[24]

Although the Allies entered Gaza city almost without

opposition, the whole area had paid a high price for the three assaults of the previous months. Local historians say the bombardments during those battles did more than anything else in recent times to destroy what was left of the historical and architectural heritage of the city. The roof of the Grand al-Umari had been destroyed and its minaret was no more than a jagged stump. The 'English' Hospital, set up by the Church Missionary Society (CMS) in the 1880s and 90s, 'was almost totally destroyed.'[25]

Three eye-witness accounts of Gaza in the immediate aftermath of the battles paint a terrible picture of destruction. A correspondent of The Times of London wrote that houses had been 'ruthlessly plundered [by the Ottoman forces] for the furnishings of dug-outs and the linings of trenches. Our troops found sand-bags made of rich silks. And on evacuating Gaza the Turks did what further damage they could – in particular choking all the wells. When the British entered the town through the orchards, palm trees and cactus which formed a deep fringe of green around it, there was disappointment that such a famous place presented so poor an appearance. But there was evidence of former greatness in the marble used to beautify modern buildings – columns and slabs taken from ancient temples and churches. Relics, too, of the Crusades were found. The west end of the town, an intricate maze of narrow dirty streets, was promptly dubbed "Belgravia" by the soldiers, all of whom seemed to make a point of climbing Al-Muntar ("the watch tower") to which, according to tradition, Samson carried the gates of the city.'

A more emotional response to the destruction of Gaza is found in an article by Reverend Father Waggett which was published by the Church Times in London. He began the article by summarising the importance of Gaza throughout history, first as a centre for pagan worship, then as one of the earliest outposts of Christianity and finally as a city revered for being the burying

The First World War - 'A Scene of Sad Desolation'

place for a forebear of the Prophet Muhammad. 'It is a story,' Father Waggett wrote, 'of worldly splendour and religious heroism, very difficult to stage in imagination in what Gaza now is or has lately been. Before the war it would have been seen as a modest stone-and-mud-built town with Mosques and Churches and market and 40,000 inhabitants... After the battles of this war Gaza was a very lamentable spectacle. The Great Mosque was used by the Turks as a dump for small-arms ammunition, and consequently in the bombardment the whole place was terribly injured by a Turkish explosion... It's a scene of very sad desolation... It was mainly due to the removal by the defenders of the roofs to provide wood for trenches and duck boards and other military works.'[26]

General Allenby visited Gaza on 9 November 1917. He, too, was shocked by the way that the Turks had scavenged for wood. Gaza, he wrote to his wife, 'is badly knocked about; besides the effects of our shells, the Turks took all the wood out of the town. Wide gardens of fig trees, olives and such like, [still] spread all around it; but many fine old olives have been cut down for railway engine fuel. There is an old and a new town, but I had no time to explore either... Tomorrow is likely to be a critical day. If the Turks can't stop us tomorrow, they are done.'[27]

In the tradition over the centuries of army commanders capturing Gaza, General Allenby did not stay in the city, pressed on, arriving triumphantly in Jerusalem a month later. Gaza, as ever, was a crossroad city that needed to be taken, no matter what the cost; but it was not a prize in itself.

But Gaza was henceforth, for the next 30 years, under British occupation. In the early days a certain Major W O Kenny of the Royal Inniskilling Fusiliers was appointed military governor of Gaza and 'the clearing of wells and the sanitation of the town was taken in hand. The extension of the main railway line from Egypt, which then ended at Deir al-Balah, some 10 miles south of Gaza, was begun almost at once; for one of the most urgent problems facing the Expeditionary Force, as the area of operations extended north, was that of transport.

There were also the injured to be attended to, and the dead to be buried in the British Military Cemetery in Gaza. The total there rose to more than 3,000, with around 700 more in Deir al-Balah. Allied servicemen, brought in from field ambulance stations, continued to be buried there until March 1919.

Bishop MacInnes, who was in Palestine during the First World War, reflected on the human cost of the successful military campaign against the Ottoman army by relating it to the concomitant construction of the railway. 'It should never be forgotten that the building of this railway, first by Sir Archibald Murray and then by Lord Allenby, in their campaigns of 1915-1917, was at the cost of more than 10,000 British soldiers' lives – an average of twenty-seven lives every kilometre.'[28]

When Allenby's army had marched on northwards, the people of Gaza started returning to the city and began picking up the pieces of their lives. Father Waggett, observing Gaza several months after the defeat of the Turks, wrote that 'her famous orchards have suffered, but her plentiful, rather brackish, wells will soon be in working order. Some of the streets of stone-walled shops have been put in order and trade goes on busily and grows. But anyone who sees Gaza even now after the very remarkable improvement and the return of about 10,000 people to the city must see how great the need will be for a long time yet of fostering care if Gaza is to recover its former prosperity. And it ought of course go far beyond that in a new and renovated Palestine. But here, as everywhere, the hope is in the security and regular work of the inhabitants, not in favour and gifts.'[29] Nine decades later, the people of Gaza are still looking in vain for security and regular work.

Another person to see Gaza in the aftermath of the Ottoman defeat there was Ronald Storrs, who passed through the city on his way from Cairo to Jerusalem where he was to take

The First World War - 'A Scene of Sad Desolation'

up the position of Military Governor. In his diary he, too, commented on the scale of the destruction of Gaza. But he was able to put those horrors out of his mind when he described the beauty of the winter landscape. 'The country undulating, the sand at this time of year covered with a faint green growth... Riotous hedges and lots of cactus; sand roads, far better at any rate than those through the Euphrates desert and covered for miles with wire netting, giving a surface and appearance of tarring. General effect... European and, with the sea in the background, Flemish dune or low Sussex.'[30]

The process of rebuilding Gaza was slow. Three years after the battles for the city it was still in a devastated condition. 'The town of Gaza suffered probably more from military action during the war than any other town in this theatre of operations,' wrote the British High Commissioner in Palestine at the time, Sir Herbert Samuel, in a despatch to the Foreign Office in London. 'Almost all its buildings have been destroyed and its present appearance is comparable only to that of the devastated areas in France and Belgium.' Sir Herbert asked the Foreign Office if any funds could be made available to help restore the city so that its original inhabitants could return. He emphasised the city's importance before the war. 'It was of considerable commercial importance being the natural emporium of the rich grain districts lying south and east of it [before the war Gaza was a major supplier of barley for the brewing industry in Britain]. The original population has now dwindled to something like one third of its number, and in the present ruinous condition of the town there is little to attract the remainder of its inhabitants to return or fresh population to settle there... I trust that some means may be devised by which His Majesty's Government may be instrumental in helping to restore the prosperity of a town whose past history bears eloquent testimony to its potentialities.'[31]

Sir Herbert also expressed the view that the provision of

Life at the Crossroads

aid from Britain could make the idea of British rule in Palestine more popular. In reality, though, the chances of the British being truly popular in Palestine had evaporated even before their rule began. This was because of a promise made by the government in London to the Jews that it would support the idea of a Jewish homeland being established in Palestine.

Gaza, it is true, was set for a rare period of security from outside attack; but the seeds had also been sown for further bloodshed, leading – before the 20th century had ended – to yet another period of military occupation.

Notes

[1] Taken from the introduction to the official list of names of soldiers buried in the British War Cemetery in Gaza city.
[2] Mansfield, *op. cit.*, p. 149.
[3] MacInnes, *op. cit.*, p. 10.
[4] *Ibid.*, p. 10.
[5] *Ibid.*, p. 11.
[6] Trevor Wilson, *The Myriad Faces of War*, London, 1986, p. 499.
[7] *Ibid.*, p. 499.
[8] *Ibid.*, p. 499.
[9] T E Lawrence, *Seven Pillars of Wisdom*, London, 1935, p. 329.
[10] Wilson, *op. cit.*, p. 500.
[11] *Ibid.*, p. 500.
[12] Major C S Jarvis, *Desert and Delta*, London, 1938, p. 22.
[13] *Daily Chronicle*, 10/9/17.
[14] *The Times, History and Encyclopaedia of the War*, part 187, volume 15, March 19 1918, p.145 ff.
[15] C E Hughes, *Above and Beyond Palestine*, London, 1929, p. 206.
[16] Papers of William Robertson, Liddell Hart Centre for Military Archives, King's College, London, July 1917. Reference: 1/32/62. Quoted with the permission of the Trustees of the Centre.

[17] *Ibid.*, reference: 1/32/64.
[18] *Ibid.*, reference: 1/32/69
[19] Wilson, *op. cit.*, p. 501.
[20] The Letters of General Allenby to his wife Mabel, 1917. The Liddell Hart Centre for Military Archives, King's College, London. Reference: 1/8/16. Quoted with the permission of the Trustees of the Centre.
[21] *Ibid.*, reference: 1/8/17.
[22] Hughes, *op. cit.* pp. 213-14.
[23] Liddell Hart Archive, *op. cit.*, Allenby Letter, reference: 1/8/19.
[24] Liddell Hart Archive, *op. cit.*, Allenby Letter, reference: 1/8/20.
[25] MacInnes, *op. cit.*, p. 12.
[26] PRO 371 3413.
[27] Liddell Hart Archive, *op. cit.*, Allenby Letters. Reference: 1/8/22.
[28] MacInnes, *op. cit.*, p. 11.
[29] PRO 371 3413.
[30] Ronald Storrs, *Orientations*, London, 1939, p. 285.
RO 371 5287.

CHAPTER 11

The British Road to Disaster

Few buildings remaining in Gaza evoke echoes of the days of the period of British rule in Palestine after the First World War. It is appropriate or unfortunate, depending on one's perspective, that the single prominent structure from this period has become an infamous landmark: Gaza military prison. This is a stark and sharply angled child's-drawing of a building lying between the centre of the city and the sea. It is similar in style – having been designed by the same architect – to several others built by the British across Palestine. Such is the enduring structure of the prison that it continued after the end of the mandate period to serve the Egyptians when they administered Gaza. The Israelis, as the next occupying force in the territory, also found plenty of use for the prison; and now the Palestinian authorities are locking their prisoners in the same building. The people of Gaza associate the prison most closely with the years of oppressive Israeli occupation and are both bewildered and angered by the insensitivity of the Palestinian authorities' decision to go on using the building in the same way.

Life at the Crossroads

The end of the First World War saw Britain and France taking control of the former territories of the Ottoman Empire in the eastern Mediterranean. The Arabs might have thought that a promise had been made by Britain to grant them independence in these lands in return for having received their help in defeating the Turks. But Britain did not feel obliged to fulfil its commitment, abiding instead by an amended version of the secret Sykes-Picot agreement of 1916. As the Arab lands were carved up between the two European powers. Since the fall of Gaza in 1917 and General Sir Edmund Allenby's sweep northwards, Palestine had been under British military control, its inhabitants governed by military rule from Jerusalem.

The future of the east Mediterranean region had been one of the subjects of discussion at the Paris Peace Conference in 1919. With Feisal, the son of Sharif Hussain of Mecca, making an impassioned plea for Arab independence, President Woodrow Wilson of the United States gave his backing to the idea of an international commission of inquiry to establish what the citizens of Palestine and Syria wanted. Britain and France, with their own interests in mind, were unenthusiastic. When a two-man American commission visited the region and reported that there was overwhelming opposition to the idea of foreign mandates, the governments in London and Paris ignored the findings. In May 1920, a meeting of the Supreme Council of the League of Nations declared that Syria was being divided into two French mandates, Syria and Lebanon; Palestine and Iraq were being assigned to the British. On 3 November 1920, military rule in Palestine was ended, and the territory became a British mandate under the first High Commissioner, Sir Herbert Samuel (a Jew who had been a member of the British government).

In the earliest years of British rule, the authorities in Palestine made only minor changes to the legal and administrative structures inherited from the Ottomans. But in

The British Road to Disaster

1922 the Palestine Order in Council served as an organic law, providing the basis for executive rule and legislation, with the high commissioner the representative of the British government. The legal system 'perpetuated the coexistence of civil and religious courts. The civil courts followed Ottoman decrees, along with orders published by the mandatory government in Palestine and British common law and equity law, in so far as these filled gaps in Ottoman legal practice and did not conflict with local conditions. The religious courts recognized the judicial privileges awarded to religious denominations in Ottoman times, in matters of personal status; but the mandatory granted parallel authority, in several cases, to the civil courts.'[1]

In the years during which Britain held the mandate for Palestine (until 1948) Gaza became embroiled, along with all other areas, in the three-way tussle between the British authorities, the Palestinians and the Jews. Jewish immigration to Palestine had started in the early part of the century; but by the start of the First World War the total had reached about 85,000, compared with the Arab population of 600,000. The problem for the British authorities was that they had made a commitment to the Jews in November 1917 (while the Sharif of Mecca's Arab Revolt was under way) to establish in Palestine 'a National Home for the Jewish people'. This promise was made by the British Foreign Secretary, Lord Balfour, and has been known ever since as the Balfour Declaration. The root of the problem facing Britain was the fact that the Declaration also promised that nothing would be done 'which may prejudice the civil and religious rights of existing non-Jewish communities in Palestine.' In other words, the British had made two self-contradictory promises. From the first day of British mandatory rule Hebrew was declared to be one of the three official languages along with English and Arabic. The whole period is overshadowed by the unsuccessful attempts by the authorities in Jerusalem to reconcile the two irreconcilable promises made to the Arabs and the Jews. One Arab historian summed up the contradiction in the following way: 'The Jews claimed Palestine, both on grounds of need and because of their traditional connection with it; the Arabs could not abandon it, both because by any ordinary political criterion it was theirs and because its geographical position made it essential for the unity of Arab peoples.'[2] But the Jews in Palestine in the early decades of the 20th century had one major advantage up their sleeve: 'Their influence in the game of imperial politics would prove to be immeasurably greater' than that of the Arabs.'[3]

On the daily practical level Sir Herbert Samuel established a government in Jerusalem which included members of the Muslim, Christian and Jewish communities. He also set up an advisory council made up of members from the three communities, 'which he hoped would lead ultimately to a partly elected legislative council for a joint community. But the Arabs, who fundamentally rejected both the mandate and the Balfour Declaration, boycotted the elections and demanded a national government.'[4]

Palestine as a whole was divided into three districts, each under a District Commissioner: Jerusalem, the north and the south. Gaza, the largest city in Palestine with an exclusively Arab population, was the district capital in the south. Religious matters were in the hands of a Supreme Islamic Council which was established in 1922 under the Mufti al-Hajj Amin al-Hussaini. Al-Hajj Sa'id al-Shawa was the first representative from Gaza. Each town, including Gaza, had its own mayor, while the elected village representative was the *mukhtar*. Shuhadah Qudaih is a former *mukhtar* from Khuza'a, a quiet and orderly village in the south-eastern corner of the Gaza Strip. During the British mandate period he worked with the British administration, as well as being *mukhtar* (1944-48). The chief British administrator, he says, had his office in Gaza city, and passed on instructions and regulations through his representative in Khan Younis. Shuhadah Qudaih recalls that there were no particular problems in day-to-day relations with the British because they generally stayed away from villages and towns. 'There was no police station in this village. We were aware of the British running the administration of Palestine. But their soldiers weren't employed around the Gaza Strip in the way that the Israelis were. Mostly we just were aware of the British presence without directly feeling it.' However, Mr Qudaih, like most other Palestinians in Gaza and elsewhere, accuses the British of failing to stop the Jewish immigrants putting down roots in the land. 'The British were helping the Jews to take the land from Palestinians, to steal the land. And we believe the British were helping Palestinian collaborators to buy land and sell it to the Jews. That's why in the end we were angry and why fighting broke out.'[5]

Internal security during the mandate days was in the hands of the Palestine Police, a mixed Arab and Jewish force with British officers. The headquarters for the British officers and for the civilian administrators was the building close to the Grand Umari Mosque which is today al-Zahra' girls' secondary school. This had also been used as a police garrison by the Ottomans, and was said to have been the building where Napoleon stayed during his brief visit to Gaza in the late 18th century.

The biggest difficulty faced by the people of Gaza was the task of rebuilding their city and their lives after the destruction of the First World War. Only slowly did the population return, and in the absence of major financial investment on the part of the mandate authorities, Gaza's role in the economic life of Palestine was modest. But its position close to the Egyptian border meant that it was still a crossroads which travellers in and out of Palestine had to pass. Gaza was one of the stops on the railway line connecting Kantara in Egypt with Lydda in Palestine. For many Britons and other foreigners, Gaza represented the first glimpse of Palestine. Charis Waddy arrived from Australia in 1919 as a small child; her father had been a chaplain during the First World War and had reached Jerusalem in 1917 with General Allenby's army. After the war her father stayed on as a teacher at St George's School. Two years later his family joined him. 'We came by train from Port Said,' Miss Waddy said, 'and my first impression was waking up in that train when it stopped at Gaza. There was the most extraordinary growling outside the window. It was a camel.'[6] Today taxis and trucks line up alongside the main north-south highway near the centre of Gaza city where the railway station once stood.

Once again, the guide books of the day made less than flattering comments about the city of Gaza. The 1924 edition of *Cook's Traveller's Handbook: Palestine and Syria* described it as 'an unprepossessing town, with an appearance pleasant enough from a distance, but which, on closer study, does injustice to the town's historical importance... Its approximate population is 15,000, which is something like 25,000 less than its pre-war number. It is built on a lofty mound, and possesses a small harbour, screened from the town itself by low sand-dunes; through this harbour moderate quantities of wheat, barley and dari-seed are exported. Its principal industries are weaving and the making of black pottery; the manufacture of lace, a cottage industry for which Gaza was at one time celebrated, is now reviving under the care of the British Administration, and specimens of this work may be purchased in the town.'

The railway, with the trade it brought in passengers and goods, was an important source of income for Gaza. The standard of passenger accommodation on the rail service was impressive, in the view of an American newspaper correspondent who travelled on the route from Egypt, through Gaza, to Jerusalem in 1925. When he boarded the train at Kantara, he wrote, he was pleasantly surprised. 'I was prepared to be uncomfortable on a long night's journey, as I had been in

The British Road to Disaster

Europe where the sleeping cars have a lot to learn from the dear old USA. But here I found the very finest sleeping car, better than anything I had seen in the whole of Europe.'[7]

Gaza during the mandate years was, once again in its history, primarily a frontier town: Its remote location on the edge of the desert, combined with the fact that neither the city nor the area round about contained sites sacred to the Jews, meant that Jewish immigrants were not eager to acquire land there, as they were in many other areas of Palestine. But Gaza was inextricably linked by both blood ties and sentiment to the Palestinian issue; and the anger at what was regarded as Britain's connivance with the Jews in the gradual creation of a Jewish state in Palestine was displayed as clearly on the streets of Gaza as on those of any city under British rule. The people of Gaza, indeed, had a reputation of being (along with the inhabitants of Nablus) among those Palestinians mostly violently opposed both to the policies of the British mandate authorities and to the aims of the Zionist movement. Centuries of foreign occupation had bred in the spirit of the people of Gaza a hatred of occupation. This would be seen most clearly of all during the time of Israeli rule in the territory in the last quarter of the 20th century.

The first anti-British riots broke out after the failure of Sir Herbert Samuel's attempt to set up a legislative council – a move which led to the publication of a White Paper in Britain (the first of several during the mandate period). This stated that a balance would be maintained between the Arab and Jewish communities. 'However, the Arabs were convinced by this that the true intention [of the British] was to wait until the Jews in Palestine had grown sufficiently in numbers and power to become dominant, and they continued to demand an immediate national government, citing the promises made to the Arabs during the war.'[8]

Throughout the 1920s, the Jews continued to acquire property and land. In 1929, Britain allowed the creation of an expanded Jewish Agency, with half the members 'recruited from Zionist sympathizers outside Palestine. The Zionists acquired a new sense of confidence.'[9] The move resulted in widespread riots across Palestine. Members of the Jewish community in Hebron were killed by angry crowds. According to one Palestinian historian, the people of Gaza 'rose up against the Jewish community who were forced to flee the city under the cover of darkness. The Jews had been living in Gaza peacefully and safely before the emergence of the Zionist movement. Some of them had been watchmakers, dentists, millers and fishermen. During the riots, too, a group of youths surged over to the British military airfield to the east of Gaza, and the British forces had difficulty in blocking them... The reaction of the mandate authorities to the troubles in Gaza was to arrest and torture many Arabs. Three were executed. At the same time, Jewish settlers in southern Palestine were given arms.'[10]

An example of how the people of Gaza were becoming radicalised both by events in Palestine and by the rise of Arab nationalism throughout the region can be seen in the choice of a new name for one of the main streets in the city. Since Ottoman times the main thoroughfare heading from the city to the sea had been called Jemal Pasha Street. In the closing weeks of 1931, during the time when Fahmi Bey al-Hussaini was mayor, it was proposed that the street should be given the name of a Libyan nationalist hero, Umar al-Mukhtar, who had been captured and hanged by the Italians in September of that year. The proposal was accepted by the people of Gaza and the name was retained, despite strong protests from the Italian Consul in Jerusalem, passed on to the Gaza municipality by the British authorities. The street is still called after Umar al-Mukhtar.

During the first half of the 1930s Jewish immigration into Palestine increased. There was a realisation, too, among the Arabs that the Zionists were smuggling arms into Palestine with the clear intention of fighting, if necessary, to create a Jewish state. In 1936, political parties banded together to form an Arab Higher Committee led by the Mufti al-Hajj Amin al-Hussaini. On 20 April 1936 the committee called for a general strike by Arabs throughout Palestine. The response was immediate and solid. Tala'at Ibrahim, when he was in his late seventies, recalled being a teenager in Gaza in 1936. Speaking quietly and slowly he recalled the days of the general strike. 'It was a very big event. Everybody here was involved, from all sections of society. The British tried to break the strike. They arrested lots of people – the organisers. But they failed, because the strike went on for six months.'[11] Telephone lines were torn down to impede the communications of the British authorities, and a lengthy curfew was imposed on the city when two British soldiers were shot dead. At other times large number of Gazans were arrested after anti-British and anti¬Zionist demonstrations in the city. The houses of a number of families, from whom alleged ringleaders or perpetrators of violence came, were blown up.

The strike ended, after 176 days, on 13 October 1936; but the violence against the British continued, in Gaza as elsewhere. Army and police patrols were attacked, explosives set off under cars and telephone lines ripped down. The railway line through Gaza was also frequently the target of attacks, and rail services from Egypt to Palestine – a vital lifeline for the British – were frequently interrupted. 'Palestine was in turmoil,' recalled Sir Gawain Bell, who arrived by train from Egypt in 1938 to take up a government posting. 'We crossed into Palestine, and from there on all the way up to Haifa it was slow progress. The telegraph lines were down and the posts were lying on the ground.'[12]

The British did their best to catch those carrying out the attacks, but were not successful. From the minarets of mosques in Gaza city and in the towns and villages round about, warnings were broadcast when British patrols were approaching - a tactic also used to good effect in the violent rebellions in the

Life at the Crossroads

1980s and 90s against Israeli rule. While the effectiveness of mass arrests may have been limited, the numbers of Arabs in detention grew so fast that the need arose for the construction of the military prison.

The Arab rebellion had been given new impetus in 1937 by the publication of a report by Lord Peel which 'concluded that Britain's obligations to Arabs and Jews were irreconcilable and that the mandate was unworkable. It therefore for the first time recommended the partition of Palestine into Jewish and Arab states. The Zionists' response was ambivalent... The Arabs, on the other hand, were unanimously outraged and their rebellion intensified, in spite of the heavy use of force and the outlawing of the Arab Higher Committee.'[13]

In 1939, just before the outbreak of the Second World War, the Arab rebellion faded away with the arrival in Palestine of large numbers of British troops. At the same time another British White Paper recommended that the number of new Jewish immigrants to Palestine should be restricted to 75,000 over the following five years. Within 10 years, the White Paper said, a Palestine state should be set up – with, the implication was, an Arab majority. But this attempt to mollify the Arabs failed, while the Jews, predictably, were enraged.

During the Second World War Gaza was occupied by British and Australian forces. Palestine did not become part of the theatre of conflict as it had done during the First World War, despite some air raids on Haifa. Gaza remained quiet. But preparations had been made, just in case. Sir Gawain Bell, who was running the Palestine Police Camel Gendarmerie at Beersheba, remembered that when 'Italy came into the war it was evident that we would have to do something. The likelihood was that there would be air raids on Palestine from Italy, and at that period the Australian troops had not yet taken over responsibility for security in Gaza. I went to Gaza to discuss the matter with Rushdi Bey Shawa, the mayor, and other people.

The British Road to Disaster

We formed a "security council". There were no air raid precautions of any sort in Gaza, no sirens and no means of informing the people if we heard that hostile enemy aircraft were approaching. So we decided that if we heard that enemy aircraft were coming, the *muezzins* should go up to the minarets and cry out with a loud voice that enemy aircraft were quite close and everyone should take precautions. We also decided that to reinforce this and make it appear that it was a matter of some importance the *Ramadan* gun should be fired; and for this purpose we ordered 50 pounds of black powder. But there was never a raid on Gaza.[14]

Tala'at Ibrahim recalled life in Gaza during the Second World War. He said he hadn't felt oppressed by the presence of the Allied troops. Mr Ibrahim remembered 'the dresses [traditional kilts] of the Scottish soldiers', as well as seeing lots of Australian troops. 'Because there were so many foreign troops here we felt that there was a war going on, but it was not happening here in Gaza. At that period, Gaza city was confined to the Shuja'iya and Zaitoun area. The area from Palestine Square to the sea was like a jungle, with sand and trees. It was so dense and wild that it was dangerous to go at night to the sea.'

Majid al-Hussaini was a boy in Gaza in the post Second World War years. He remembers that Palestine Square was the centre of Gaza, with Umar al-Mukhtar street the only major thoroughfare. During the British mandate his father had a job transporting meat and other food from Gaza to Sarafand. As far as the general impressions of British rule are concerned, Mr Hussaini, like many others, sets his memories against the experience of living under the more recent Israeli occupation. As far as he can remember, and going on what his elders said, the Palestinians did not feel that the British were occupiers in the sense that the Israelis were in later decades. 'For one thing, the British tended to keep their soldiers in their camps, except at times of trouble. We had complete freedom to come and go. You could make a living as best you could. It was not really an occupation, it didn't feel that way – it was more a case of protective custody.'

Mr Hussaini said that in the pre-1948 days the mass of people 'didn't care much about politics. They didn't question why things were happening as much as they did later on. And, anyway, the British limited the amount of education the people could get. It was a different matter for the very rich who could afford to go to private schools or to go abroad. For the mass of the population, the British limited education to the seventh grade.' I asked Mr Hussaini why he thought the British wanted to restrict the Palestinians in this way. 'I think they hoped to stay in Palestine for ever and didn't want the Palestinian self-awareness to develop too much. The British had made the Jews a promise many decades earlier in the Balfour Declaration, and they needed to keep us down to enable them to fulfil the promise.'

Like the overwhelming majority of Palestinians in Gaza and elsewhere, any thoughts Mr Hussaini had about the presence of the British during the mandate era, regardless of whether those sentiments were positive or not, are overwhelmed by hostility felt towards the British government for its decision to pull out of Palestine in 1948, thus allowing the creation of Israel. 'Britain did not leave Palestine until they saw that Israel was able to settle the country. We can never forget that,' Mr Hussaini said.[15]

In the early 1940s the British faced pressures from a number of directions. For a start, tens of thousands of Jews who had fled from the atrocities being committed by the Nazis in Europe were homeless and wanted to travel to Palestine. Attempts to restrict immigration were bitterly denounced by the United States and others in the international community. At the same time the Jewish underground groups were becoming stronger and targeting British troops and police, while

The British Road to Disaster

continuing to encourage the expansion of Jewish control on land and property.

In August 1947 a United Nations commission recommended the partition of Palestine into Arab and Jewish states. Under this scheme, the Jewish state would have acquired 55 per cent of Arab Palestine, even though the Jews constituted about one third of the total population of 1.9 million. The Arabs rejected the plan and the mufti of Jerusalem proclaimed a *jihad* or holy war against the Jewish settlers in Palestine. In September Britain announced that it would be relinquishing its mandate the following year; and in November the United Nations General Assembly endorsed the partition plan.

As the day approached when Britain was to pull out of Palestine the violence intensified still further, reaching the level of civil war. The Jewish underground groups adopted a policy of forcing as many Arab Palestinians as possible out of their homes, or causing them to flee in terror. The massacre of up to 120 Palestinians in the village of Deir Yassin near Jerusalem in April 1948 did more than anything else to terrorise the Arabs.

The end of the British mandate came on 14 May 1948; on the same day David Ben Gurion proclaimed the establishment of a Jewish state in Palestine. The next day the Egyptian army followed the route taken by military men from that country for three millennia and passed through Gaza to the north. The aim, in coordination with other Arab armies, was to defeat the new Jewish state and raise the Arab flag over Palestine. But the result was summed up in one Arabic word *nakba* – disaster. Not only were the Arab armies defeated, but hundreds of thousands of Palestinians joined those who had already fled their homes. Many came to the Gaza area, signalling the start of a new era in the life of the city and its surroundings.

The refugees have never forgotten and will never forget their last moments in their home towns and villages. Ali Hassan Ali had lived with his family in the village of Karatya, east of

Life at the Crossroads

Ashqelon. The villagers, he says, were able to hold out for 11 days. Only when the Israelis started to come into the village did they flee, leaving themselves no time to collect together any of their clothes or possessions. 'Everyone scattered, into the countryside, into other villages. Some were killed, some were injured. We tried to get into Falluja where the Egyptian army was in control. But unfortunately they thought we were Israeli agents or something and fired to stop us getting in. So we headed west on foot towards Ashqelon. My family got split up at this point, but we eventually came together again at the village of Herbya.'

Ali Hassan Ali and his mother, father and brother spent two months in Herbya, wondering what was happening and what they should do. After two months, they went on foot to Gaza. They settled in a small empty building, two metres by three metres, with no window. 'Back home we had had chickens, sheep, goats. We weren't rich, but by comparison with the way we ended up, we had been living like kings. We stayed in that building in Gaza which was unfit for chickens to live in for six years. My father and his second wife died in it.'

The family were then given a tent in the Shati (Beach) refugee camp. 'The weather that winter was so severe that one night the wind took the tents from where they were pitched and blew them way down the coast. From that terrible winter I'm still suffering in my eyes and in my kidneys.' Finally, after six months in Beach camp the family were moved into a unit in Jabaliya where they have been ever since. 'I have become in a sense a temporary Gaza citizen; but I want to go home. I don't always want to be an object to be moved around. It's a matter both of land and dignity.'[16]

Hassan Muhammad Dabbour is the owner of a textiles shop in the town of Khan Younis. His father had a similar business in Ashqelon, and he was a kitchen worker for the British and Australian armies. In 1948 the area where his family lived came under attack. 'My father refused to move, and we stayed for about 18 days. Then we left home and took shelter on the beach. We hoped the fighting would stop and we would be able to go home. We decided to go back and have a look; but we found that only a handful of Arabs were left, and the Egyptian army positions were empty. So we realised we couldn't stay.'

The Dabbour family took what possessions they could carry and headed for a nearby village. There, for five Palestinian pounds, they bought a camel and headed south to Gaza. They spent one night in a mosque in Gaza city, and after searching in vain for a home, they headed further south to Khan Younis. Here they found the Egyptian army distributing tents. They lived in a tent near the centre of the town.

'After 10 days the Quakers came and helped us, bringing blankets and other things we needed - and cigarettes.' The family put the materials they had been able to bring with them from Ashqelon in front of a deserted shop, and gradually started the long process of trying to build up a business from nothing in a new era. Mr Dabbour is still in that shop today, selling textiles as his father used to do.[17]

Mousa Saba was living with his family in Beersheba when fighting broke out in 1948. He was aged 19 at the time. 'The Jewish fighters surrounded the town, shelled it and occupied it the next day. All Arabs that remained were sent out. There was no chance to stay. But the Jews kept back 200-300 men – they kept them in a mosque which has since been turned into a museum and made them work every day. Eventually one of them led a protest, and in the end they too were sent out. So none of us was allowed to stay.'

The Saba family 'put as much furniture as we could, plus our clothing, into a truck and headed for Gaza. Others set off by foot to the east in the direction of Hebron. My father was originally from Gaza, so he had family. We moved in with them. But most people were living in tents distributed by the Red

Life at the Crossroads

Cross and the Quakers.'[18]

The chaotic circumstances of 1948 left the Palestinians little time to ponder over the course of events – beginning with the Balfour Declaration – which had led up to the establishment of the state of Israel. But they have since had more than half a century to brood over and analyze what happened; and for better or worse the inhabitants of Gaza and all other Palestinians continue to lay the blame for their disastrous fate at the feet of the former mandate power.

The aftermath of the disaster opened another chapter of outside rule in Gaza. Once again, as had been the case so often over the centuries, Egypt was the power in the land.

Notes

[1] Jacob M Landau, part of *Handbooks to the Modern World – The Middle East*, edited by Michael Adams, London, 1988, p. 396.
[2] A H Hourani, *A Vision of History: Near Eastern and Other Essays*, Beirut, 1961, p. 94
[3] Bruce Westrate, *The Arab Bureau: British Policy in the Middle East*, Pennsylvania, 1992, p.176.
[4] Mansfield, *op. cit.*, p. 204 .
[5] Interviewed by the author, 1994.
[6] Interviewed by the author, 1994.
[7] *Boston Globe*, 1 November 1925.
[8] Mansfield, *op. cit.*, p. 204.
[9] *Ibid.*, p. 204.
[10] Ibrahim Khalil Sakkik, *Ghazzah 'Abr al-Ta'rikh*, Gaza, 1982, p. 114.
[11] Interviewed by the author, 1994.
[12] Interviewed by the author, 1994.
[13] Mansfield, *op. cit.*, p. 206.
[14] Interviewed by the author, 1994.
[15] Interviewed by the author, 1994.
[16] Interviewed by the author, 1994.
[17] Interviewed by the author, 1994.
[18] Interviewed by the author, 1994.

CHAPTER 12

Egyptian Rule and the First Israeli Occupation

Ali Hassan Ali sits for hours each day outside the tiny shelter provided for him and his family by the United Nations Relief and Works Agency (UNRWA) in the Jebaliya refugee camp in the Gaza Strip. Young men come and sit with him from time to time to help him pass the empty hours. Ali Hassan Ali, at around 60 years of age, was waiting, as he had been each day since 1948, for a sign that he could go back to his village of Karatya (inside Israel).

He talked a lot about the past. 'It is vital that we keep our memories of our land and our villages, so that we can pass them on to our children. We must always believe that one day we will go home. Our children must believe that as well.'

Most of Ali Hassan Ali's memories of his early days in Gaza when he and his family arrived on foot are of hardship and poverty. Mousa Saba, another refugee from 1948, also said that his overwhelming memory of Gaza at that time was of 'poverty, great poverty. All the people had were the things they had been able to bring with them in the rush of leaving their towns and villages. And most of the people arriving in Gaza were poor to start with. Ninety per cent of them were from small villages in the Gaza area or from further north around Jaffa – agricultural areas. They were peasants, they had been working on their land. They had nothing in the way of possessions or savings. They had to depend on rations and handouts from the Quakers to survive.'

As part of armistice arrangements worked out by a UN mediator in February 1949 (following the humiliating defeat of the Arabs in the war with Israel which began in May 1948 and continued until the opening of the following year), the Gaza Strip had been assigned to Egyptian administration; but the government in Cairo was in no position to provide food and accommodation for the 200,000 homeless and destitute people seeking shelter there.

UNRWA was created by a resolution passed in the United Nations General Assembly in December 1949, and the agency began operations on 1 May 1950. The idea was that its function would be only temporary, with the prospect at the time that some refugees would soon be allowed back to their homes and that others would be absorbed by neighbouring Arab countries. But in the absence of a solution to the Palestine refugee problem, the General Assembly has repeatedly renewed UNRWA's mandate. The new body replaced an earlier *ad hoc* agency, the United Nations Relief for Palestine Refugees. This had been set up in November 1948, but it had lacked staff and work 'was done at its request on a voluntary basis by the Red Cross, several religious societies, and the American Friends Service Committee [the Quakers].'[1] UNRWA inherited a list of 950,000 persons from these predecessor agencies. In the first four months of operations it reduced this list to 860,000 persons by what it described as 'painstaking census efforts', the elimination of 'fraudulent claims' and the removal of 'undeserving names' from the relief role. The 1948-registered refugees and their descendants now number more than 4.6 million.

As UNRWA was getting established in the Middle East, living conditions throughout the Gaza Strip were appalling. Tala'at Ibrahim spoke of the big change in atmosphere, with the Gaza region suddenly cut off from the rest of Palestine. 'It was a very difficult period. Gaza is very small and thousands and thousands of people took refuge here. To begin with there was no choice but to make them temporary homes wherever we could. So they settled in schools and in mosques, in private houses and in any buildings where there was room. Only gradually was the United Nations able to make arrangements for temporary accommodation. And they're still living in it all these years and decades later. The refugee problem changed Gaza. But we became accustomed to it. It's reality.'

In the winter of 1950, Sir Ronald Storrs, who had been the first British Military Governor of Jerusalem after its capture from the Turks by General Allenby's army in 1917, made several public appeals, written and broadcast, in Britain for clothing to be donated to UNRWA through the Red Cross. In one pamphlet he quoted an account written by a UN official who had visited the Middle East to highlight the appalling suffering of the homeless Palestinians. 'We went to see the refugees – thousands of men and women exposing their suffering in a mood of utter despair beneath a grey winter sky. Children by the hundred, most of them half-naked – shoeless, shivering – conveyed the depths of their misery in gestures that were more eloquent than words. The parents showed us the camp, they showed us the holes in the ground – deep, like wells – where the children were living in total darkness, piled one on top of the other on the icy rock.' Early in January 1951, in a radio broadcast, Sir Ronald reminded listeners of how 'about a million outcasts – three quarters of the then Arab population of Palestine (nearly half a million of them children – 48,000 under 12 months old) – fled from their homes of more than 1,000 years,' with some 200,000 refugees finding themselves in 'the so-called Gaza Strip where only 80,000 Arabs lived formerly.'[2]

The plight of the Palestinian refugees in Gaza was clearly desperate. But that of the 80,000 indigenous Gazans was also appalling. As Sir Ronald Storrs's radio appeal was being broadcast, the UNRWA Chief District Officer in Gaza, D C Stephen, was sending to his superior in Beirut a graphic description of the suffering of the inhabitants of Gaza. Apart from the sudden strain on the severely limited resources of the area, many farmers had lost the use of land which lay under Israeli control. In a great many cases the inhabitants of Gaza, ironically, ended up being worse off by far than the refugees. 'The increasingly desperate plight of the Gaza residents,' Stephen wrote, 'cannot continue to be ignored, but must be attended to in the nearest future if the women and children are to survive the winter. Daily appeals made by groups of these people to various local bodies receive the identical neutral response of: "We can do nothing for you." The orderly, but dull and listless manner in which they make their appeals best indicate their own realization of the hopelessness of their situation. As they do not demand money, but simply food for their children, the request should conceivably gain the sympathy of any humanitarian body. However they are not considered as refugees because they have not lost their homes in addition to their livelihoods. Before declaring a person not to be a refugee the particular circumstances should be judged, and those existing in Gaza are possibly unequalled anywhere. A unique situation prevails here, incomparable to that in other areas, which becomes apparent only after sojourning in Gaza.'

Stephen pointed out that 'before this tragedy occurred, these people led a day-to-day existence, entirely depending on agricultural work which, though seasonal, was sufficient to

Egyptian Rule and the First Israeli Occupation

grant them a fair livelihood according to standards generally accepted in the Middle East. This did not, however, enable them to accumulate any savings for such an emergency as now exists... They are of a proud race and it is as degrading to them as it would be for us to be in their present position. The vast majority of them do not understand much else of their plight except that they have been divorced from their own simple livelihood. The setting of the present boundary by the "Powers that be" means that the people of Gaza have completely lost their only means of existence.'

Stephen warned that unless urgent action was taken, starvation would result. 'UNICEF,' he wrote, 'is contributing milk which we are distributing to Gaza children and to certain categories of women, with a promise of a small quantity of cheese to come in about two months time. How can a people exist on milk and promises?'[3]

On the basis of the above report, the UNRWA Chief Medical Officer, Dr Jerome Peterson, was dispatched to Gaza. He sent back a report which, in the words of one of his superiors, showed that 'the non-refugees are in a very bad way.' The report does, indeed, make grim reading. In the homes in poor districts of Gaza City visited by Peterson, 'overcrowding was evident, with four to 10 people said to be living in a room no larger than 12 feet by 12 feet. Only one family admitted to earning any money, and that was a woman who cleans wool and earns 8 piastres for 10 days' work. The children are said to spend most of their time begging around the town, or collecting manure for use as fuel. Practically all these people claimed that their only diet was bread, occasionally with red pepper and salt for flavouring. They denied having had meat for years, and no fruits, vegetables or even onions for a long time... It was claimed that food was obtained either by begging or by sale of possessions, and indeed the houses were extremely bare. The last of the possessions to be sold would be the doors and windows. In one instance a man had sold the timber from the roof of one room and the family had moved into the other room.'

Visiting shops, Peterson noticed that 'commodities such as flour, pulses, rice, sardines and a few vegetables were there. The shopkeepers, however, said their sales were to the refugees and not to the locals.'

He made the following summary of his findings in Gaza City: 'The appearance of the locals in their homes from a medical point of view was more or less that of a low grade chronic malnutrition. There is no evidence as yet of deaths from starvation, but these people in their homes looked gaunt and thin and of poor colour. The children under two years of age were particularly poorly.'[4]

The question of who should help the non-refugees of Gaza became an international political issue. The British government, for one, believed that it was the responsibility of Egypt, as the occupying and administering power in Gaza, to care for its inhabitants, not that of UNRWA. A British Foreign Office telegram sent to the UN in New York in January 1951 said 'we do not (repeat not) consider that the Agency should, at least at this stage, offer to meet the cost of relief, even on a temporary basis. In our view, the Agency should be immediately authorized to make an emergency loan (repeat loan) of food supplies. They should insist on repayment in cash or kind by the Egyptian government, and no (repeat no) hope of finance either from the Agency itself or from other sources should be held out. We agree. . . that relief should be administered by the Egyptian authorities.'

The Foreign Office was also not prepared to support the idea that the inhabitants of Gaza should qualify as refugees. Replying to a suggestion to this effect coming from the British embassy in Cairo, the Foreign Office said on 3 February 1951, that UNRWA was 'already desperately short of funds and could only finance the Gaza programme at the expense of the refugees.

Egyptian Rule and the First Israeli Occupation

The inhabitants of the Gaza Strip are still living in their own homes and are not refugees. As we see it, their present plight is probably due more to their being cut off from the hinterland than to the presence of the refugees who are being cared for by the Agency. In fact there is some evidence that the inhabitants benefit indirectly from the refugees and the Agency supplies which the latter receive.'[5]

While the suffering both of refugees and the local population continued to be the subject of political wrangling, Egypt was establishing administrative control over the Gaza Strip. But before this came about Gaza was the centre of a brief attempt to establish a Palestinian government. The move came about in large part to counter the efforts of King Abdullah of Jordan to use the Arab Legion to make himself master of Arab Palestine in the aftermath of the 1948 war with Israel. The king was arguing, too, that Jordanians rather than members of the Palestinian Arab Higher Committee supported by the Mufti of Jerusalem, al-Hajj Amin al-Hussaini (who was in exile), should represent the Palestinians in the Arab League.

On 22 September 1948 (in a lull in the war between Israel and its Arab neighbours) the Arab Higher Council, based in Gaza, issued a communiqué announcing the formation of a Palestine government. The announcement stated that 'the inhabitants of Palestine, by virtue of their natural right to self-determination and in accordance with the resolutions of the Arab League, have decided to declare Palestine in its entirety... as an independent state under a government known as the All-Palestine Government which is based on democratic principles.' When the Mufti of Jerusalem 'who had been living in Cairo, the most recent stop in his eleven-year exile, defied the Egyptian authorities and turned up in Gaza, he was welcomed by local inhabitants in a display of great excitement and jubilation... During the first week of its life in Gaza, the All-Palestine Government revived the Holy War Army, the Mufti's irregular forces which had played a major part during the unofficial phase of the Palestine war, and began to mobilize with the declared aim of liberating Palestine.'⁶

But the new government could not convert rhetoric into action. For a start it had no money and 'even in the small enclave around the town of Gaza its writ ran only by the grace of the Egyptian authorities. Taking advantage of the new government's dependence on them for funds and protection, the Egyptian paymasters manipulated it to undermine Abdullah's claim to represent the Palestinians in the Arab League and in international forums. Ostensibly the embryo for an independent Palestinian state, the new government, from the moment of its inception, was thus reduced to the unhappy role of a shuttlecock in the ongoing power struggle between Cairo and Amman. Within a few months, the new government had evaporated – as had the prospect of Gaza at that time becoming the centre of Palestinian political power.'

One factor that helped to kill off the new government was the resumption of fighting between Egypt and Israel, and the ultimate defeat of the Egyptians. The outcome of the war had a significant effect on the fate of Egypt – and, by extension, on Gaza – in the 1950s. This was because of the presence of one army officer, Gemal Abd al-Nasser, later to become president of Egypt.

In 1948 Nasser had travelled by train to Gaza (on the line put down by the British during their battles with the Turks in 1917) on his way to the front as part of the army sent to confront the new state of Israel. In the early days of fighting, the Arabs made good progress. Units of the Egyptian army 'reached Hebron and Bethlehem; the Iraqi army was a mere eight miles from the Mediterranean and cutting Israel into two. The Arab Legion [the British-commanded Jordanian army] had surrounded Jerusalem, and some Israelis spoke of surrendering the holy city to the Arabs. Suddenly, on June 14, 1948, the Arab

Egyptian Rule and the First Israeli Occupation

governments – in the case of Egypt and Jordan, without soliciting the opinions of their field commanders – buckled under Western pressure and accepted a UN call for a truce... For Nasser and other officers it was a simple case of betrayal.'[7] When the fighting resumed one month later, the initiative had swung to Israel.

During a second truce, in August 1948, Nasser's unit found itself cut off by the Israelis from the rest of the army in the town of Falluja (north of Gaza). The Falluja pocket held out bravely for several weeks until a negotiated end to the siege was agreed. Falluja was swapped for the village of Beit Hanoun (on the northern edge of the Gaza Strip today) which was under Israeli control. As part of the armistice agreement, 'the Falluja garrison was allowed to march out with the honours of war, carrying its arms and with its colours flying, in recognition of brave resistance.'[8]

The Egyptian troops passed through Gaza on their way back home, and crowds turned out to greet them as heroes. Majid al-Hussaini remembers being taken out of school to stand by the roadside to cheer the convoy as it passed down the main highway towards Rafah and the Egyptian border. 'I was a 10-year old boy,' he said, 'and I stood near the police station in Gaza City to wave. They were in military lorries – each officer with his troops and their guns. I remember in particular seeing Nasser.'

Gaza, for Nasser and the other officers with him represented on that day a crossroads of a particular kind. Aside from what they perceived as the betrayal of their government, their experience in the war with Israel had shown up the inadequacies of military planning and preparation. For example, when Nasser's unit had arrived first in Gaza by train on the way to the front, 'no provisions were made for any hot meals for the troops' and Nasser himself was given money 'to buy local cheese and olives for the rations.'[9] The young officers decided, on the basis of what they had witnessed in that war – high level corruption as well as incompetence – that the British-supported monarchy in Egypt had to be overthrown. So their passage through Gaza represented the first step on the road to revolution in Egypt.

While the officers were planning their anti-royalist coup, Gaza's strategic location was causing it to be the subject of secret speculation and debate thousands of miles away, in London. The British government was considering whether it might be able to use the Gaza Strip as a military base. Foreign Office documents of February 1951, marked 'Top Secret', discuss the possibility of the territory being used as 'the location for a striking force' to defend the Suez Canal. Correspondence between Cairo and London centred on whether or not Britain had the legal right to station troops there, given that 'the status of the Gaza Strip is somewhat obscure.'[10] In the end, the plan came to nothing; but it showed that Gaza's traditional strategic importance continued to be recognised in the middle of the 20th century, despite all the upheavals which had been taking place there. (Gaza, incidentally, had been linked to another scheme relating to the Suez Canal in the 1940s. A British writer visiting Palestine at the time noted that 'if British control of the Suez Canal is lost, there is already talk of an alternative canal across Palestinian territory from Gaza to Aqaba.'[11] Had that scheme come to fruition, Gaza's role as a crossroad would have been assured for many more decades.)

The revolution in Egypt in 1952 which overthrew the monarchy and spelt the beginning of the end of British influence in the country also led to a greater concentration of Egyptian effort in developing the Gaza Strip. For the people of Gaza certain aspects of life under Egyptian administration changed for the better, when compared with the era under British rule. In the view of Tala'at Ibrahim, 'the best change at this time was the way in which the Egyptians started to interest people in education. The British had discouraged the Palestinians from

Egyptian Rule and the First Israeli Occupation

pursuing education beyond a fairly basic level. With the Egyptians in control we suddenly had the opportunity of sending young people to study in Cairo and elsewhere. And they opened schools here in Gaza.' Majid al-Hussaini also noticed this change. 'The schools which the Egyptians set up were open to everyone. This meant that proper education was available to all, not just to the rich as had been the case under the British. That meant that in a few years we were producing our own engineers, doctors, lawyers, and so on. It opened up all aspects of life for the first time. We appeared on the map, you could say, and became better educated than we had been at any time under the British. It was an era when we developed self-confidence and there was a sense of the possibility, at least, of self-fulfilment.'

Mousa Saba, a refugee of 1948 from Beersheba who runs the YMCA in Gaza, agreed that 'Egypt played a very important role in education. The Egyptians encouraged people to go and study at university; and they paid for it all. They gave students a monthly grant of 6 Egyptians Pounds to cover their expenses, and out of that some of them were able to send money home. Later the grant was raised to 10 pounds.'

Amin Dabbour, taking a wider view of the Egyptian era, said the Palestinians of Gaza had no choice but to adjust their horizons to the new post-1948 reality: 'When the Palestinians lost the land, they had to change the way in which they invested their money and energy. So instead of investing all this in the land, they invested it in the education of their young people – to make them doctors or whatever. I am one of 16 children. My father was an agricultural worker. Yet he gave everything to ensure that his sons and daughters would get the best education. And I'm doing the same for my own children.'[12]

One of the secondary schools founded in Gaza by the Egyptians soon after they took over the administration of the area was the Princess Firyal school for girls. After the revolution in Egypt its name was changed to remove the association with the overthrown royal family to al-Zahra'. The school occupies the large, solid building of the Mamluk period in the centre of Gaza City which was used by British police and administrators. Today the school has 1,200 pupils who attend either morning or afternoon classes.

The era of Egyptian administration saw other changes in Gaza. Money was put into the development of the city centre. Majid al-Shawa remembers the Egyptian deputy governor of Gaza, General Khaffaja, announcing plans in 1949 or 1950 for the opening of two of the boulevards which still form major east-west arteries serving the city today, Thalaathin and Wahda streets. 'I remember,' Majid al-Shawa said, 'the general informing people of the plans, and offering owners of land where the roads would go compensation either in land or in money.'[13]

Given the fact that Gazans, who are Palestinians, were being administered by Egyptians, I wondered whether the era was thought of as another period of foreign occupation. 'The Egyptians did not feel like occupiers or conquerors,' Hussaini said. 'There were sometimes differences with the government in Cairo, and with the intelligence services. But you have to keep a distinction between governments and people. Between the two peoples there were no problems. There was intermarriage. It was as if we were part of the same country. And Egypt opened up its borders for us; no one was forbidden to cross; and this was our only free window on to the world outside.' (During the time of Egyptian administrative control, the people of Gaza were issued with *laissez-passer* documents, but not passports. Many Gazans still travel on these today. Some years after the Israeli occupation began, Jordan agreed to a request from the mayor, Rashad al-Shawa, to issue passports to inhabitants of Gaza; but these passports are valid only for two years, although renewable.)

Shuhada Qudaih, *mukhtar* of the village of Khuza'a,

Egyptian Rule and the First Israeli Occupation

retained his title when Egypt took over the administration of the Gaza Strip, maintaining similar relations with the new authorities as he had done with the past. But there was a difference. 'When I compare the Egyptians with the British, I have to say that I prefer the Egyptians because at least they were Arabs. And under them, despite all the traumas and all the difficulties caused by 1948 – the terrible suffering of the refugees – things did start to get better. The Egyptians opened up possibilities for Gazans that had not existed before. For example, they took around 3,000 teachers from Gaza and found jobs for them in Egypt and elsewhere – in the Gulf and other places.'

Another big development during the Egyptian period was the beginning of the military conflict with Israel which led eventually to full-scale wars, as well as to frequent cross-border clashes. These were sparked off by *fedayeen* (guerrilla commando) raids from the Gaza Strip into Israel which increased as Egypt's relations with Western states deteriorated and Cairo started developing close ties with East bloc countries. The cross-border raids prompted ruthless retaliation from the Jewish state, and involved Gaza closely in the Palestinians' military struggle against Israel which lasted into the 1990s. In the view of one Western political scientist, 'Israel's thunderous attacks across the armistice lines included the assault on the Buraij refugee camp on August 28, 1953, when more than seventy civilians were killed or wounded, most of them women and children.'[14]

In early February 1955 President Nasser made a brief visit to Gaza to assure the population that all possible would be done to defend the territory from Israeli reprisal attacks. He met notables in the Zahra' school. While demanding better protection for the territory, Gazan dignitaries presented President Nasser with a map of Palestine with black around the edges. The Egyptian leader promised not to remain silent in the face of Israeli aggression, adding that he had given orders for aggression to be answered in kind.

The pattern of *fedayeen* attacks inside Israel followed by disproportionately strong Israeli retaliation continued. On 28 February 1955 an Israeli armoured column pushed its way into the Gaza Strip as far as Gaza City, attacking an Egyptian army position at the railway station. Fourteen Egyptian soldiers and one civilian were killed. At the same time, further south, the Israelis ambushed a military truck with Egyptian officers and Palestinian volunteers on board. Twenty-two Arabs were killed in that attack. Eight Israelis were killed and nine were wounded in the fighting – the most serious incident since the armistice of 1949. Before the Israelis withdrew they 'destroyed buildings, bridges, and a pumping station that supplied a third of the town's water. Infuriated Palestinians rioted outside UN offices, stoned Egyptian soldiers, and demanded to be given arms.'[15] Slogans read: 'If you want to save us, arm us.' Mousa Saba took part in the demonstrations organised by two underground groups, the Communists and the Muslim Brotherhood. 'We denounced the Nasser regime, the United Nations, the West, everyone. The Egyptian authorities responded by detaining all the political leaders.'

But the government in Cairo also took steps to help the people of Gaza. Yasser Arafat, who had led a student demonstration in the Egyptian capital, was given permission by the Egyptian authorities to go to Gaza to draw up a report on arming the Palestinians. Two days after the raid had taken place the military leadership in Cairo decided to reinforce Gaza with 10 battalions of National Guards, for which Palestinians were recruited under Egyptian officers. A *fedayeen* battalion was also set up, with a number of men who had been imprisoned for illegal infiltration across the border being brought out of jail to join it. The battalion, which ended up with 700 trained men, carried out hit-and-run raids against Israel.[16]

The pattern of attacks and retaliation continued. Three

days after the Israelis had once again crossed into the Gaza Strip in August 1955 guerrillas penetrated deep into Israel, killing five soldiers and 10 civilians. Israel responded with another 'large-scale assault on Gaza.'[17] So angered was the Israeli government of the day by the *fedayeen* raids that Prime Minister David Ben Gurion 'pushed hard for the seizure of the entire Gaza Strip and the expulsion of the refugees into the Egyptian hinterland.'[18] His proposal was voted down.

In April 1956 the people of Gaza experienced yet another atrocity when mortars fell on Gaza City on market day. Sixty-three civilians were killed, 31 of them women and children. Mousa Saba remembers the mortars hitting 'the area from the Palestine Bank in the centre down to the market areas to the west. All the ministry areas were hit. Many people were killed and injured. The attack came from outside the Gaza Strip to the east.'

As Israeli retaliation bombardments intensified, major changes were under way in Egypt. In July 1956, President Nasser shocked the world by announcing the nationalization of the Anglo-French Suez Canal Company. The move served to increase still further tension between Egypt and Israel. Egypt strengthened further its military presence in the Gaza Strip and Sinai region. The main concentration near Gaza City was at Rafah, with only about 5,000 troops, mostly Palestinian or National Guards, deployed north of there.[19]

President Nasser and his advisers were unaware of the secret plot hatched by Britain, France and Israel, under which the Israelis would seek a confrontation with the Egyptians in the canal zone in order to give the British the excuse they wanted to invade Egypt. All the Egyptian leadership knew was that on 29 October, as the diplomatic crisis with Britain over the canal issue was reaching its climax, their forces came under attack at the Mitla Pass, about 40 miles south of the southern end of the Suez Canal. As the fighting spread, on the evening of 31 October

Life at the Crossroads

President Nasser 'ordered a general withdrawal of all Egyptian forces from Sinai. The forces in the Gaza Strip were told to surrender at a suitable moment to avoid casualties to the large civilian population there. In the event, part of the Gaza Strip garrison, the Palestinian brigade at Khan Younis, refused to surrender and was overwhelmed by an Israeli attack with tanks and aircraft.[20] Israeli troops spread out over the Gaza Strip, and by the evening of 2 November, the whole area was under occupation.

Gaza's fate then became entangled with the Suez crisis. On 5 November British and French paratroops landed at Port Said and Port Fouad at the northern end of the Suez canal. At the same time the two Western powers were roundly condemned by the international community. Britain could ignore most of the hostile comment, but it had to take notice of strong criticism from the United States; and by 22 December the Anglo-French force had been pulled out of Egypt.

In January 1957, the Israelis withdrew from most of the land they occupied, allowing a United Nations Emergency Force (UNEF) to take up positions in their wake. But Israel still held on to Gaza. The Israelis wanted assurances that the strip would not return to Egyptian control, but would come under the umbrella of the UNEF. When the Israelis finally withdrew from Gaza on 7 March 1957, UNEF troops took over. But the move led to 'demonstrations by the local Arab population and by the refugees demanding the return of the Egyptians. UNEF troops had to use tear-gas and fire over the heads of the crowds.'[21] President Nasser responded to the popular mood in Gaza by appointing an Administrative Governor and other officials to the territory. To the anger of the Israelis, the UN force withdrew, leaving the Gaza Strip once again under Egyptian administrative control. But the Egyptian army did not return, and UN troops patrolled the Gaza-Israel border.

In 1958, the Egyptians permitted the creation of an

executive council in Gaza, together with a legislative council, the members of which were indirectly elected. They were allowed to stand on the ticket of the Arab Socialist Union, the only party allowed in Egypt. The council was chaired by Dr Haidar Abdul-Shafi, and while it had limited powers, it gave the notables of Gaza experience in political organisation which was useful in later years when opposition to Israeli occupation began to take shape.

While Gaza's links with Egypt remained strong in the 1960s, the people of the region could not erase the memory of the events of 1956-57, their first experience of being under intense Israeli attack and living under Israeli military occupation. The Palestinians of Gaza, inhabitants and refugees, were dazed by these experiences; but they toughened the Gazan people and gave them a realistic view of what support they could expect from the Arab world. The refugees had been forced to suffer the indignity of living under the guns of the nation which had set up a state on their land; and they had seen the Egyptian army wasting no time in surrendering as the Israelis advanced. No other Arab state made a move to help them. This seemed, correctly as it turned out, to be an ominous sign for the future. Exactly 10 years after Israel had pulled its army out of Gaza in the wake of the Suez crisis, the territory was once again coming under Israeli occupation, this time for a lot longer than four months.

Notes
[1] Milton Viorst, *Reaching for the Olive Brunch — UNRWA and Peace in the Middle East*, Washington, 1989, p. 34.
[2] PRO 371 91406.
[3] *Ibid.*
[4] *Ibid.*

[5] *Ibid.*
[6] Avi Shlaim, 'The Rise and Fall of the All-Palestine Government in Gaza', *Journal of Palestine Studies*, California, autumn 1990, p. 42.
[7] Said K Aburish, *Nasser: The Last Arab*, London, 2005, p. 25.
[8] Robert Stephens, *Nasser – A Political Biography*, London, 1971, p. 82.
[9] *Ibid.*, p. 78.
[10] PRO 371 90163.
[11] Bernard Newman, *Middle Eastern Journey*, London, 1947, p. 155.
[12] Interviewed by the author, 1994.
[13] Interviewed by the author, 1994.
[14] Jeremy Salt, *The Unmaking of the Middle East: A History of Western Disorder in Arab Lands*, California, 2008, p. 170.
[15] *Ibid.*, p. 171.
[16] Keith Kyle, *Suez*, London, 1991, p. 64.
[17] *Ibid.*, p. 171.
[18] *Ibid.*, pp. 171-172.
[19] *Ibid.*, pp. 225.
[20] *Ibid.*, pp. 231.

[21] *Ibid.*, pp. 243.

CHAPTER 13

Arab Defeat and Israeli Occupation

For a few months after the 1967 defeat we were traumatised, we were in shock.' The words of a Gaza school administrator, Mahmoud Ashour,[1] 30 years after the event, might have been spoken by any of the inhabitants of the territory who lived through that period, the most traumatic in the recent history of Gaza.

The occupation of Gaza and the West Bank, after the June 1967 Middle East War, represented the end of an era in the Arab world. The late 1950s and 1960s had been dominated by the statements and actions of President Nasser of Egypt. It was a period when the Egyptian leader put the Arabs firmly on the map, giving them self-confidence and self-esteem after decades of European domination.

But for most of this period President Nasser was not greatly concerned with the Arab- Israeli problem or the plight of the Palestinian refugees. The Egyptian leader was eager to establish his country as the key player in efforts to foster secular, pan- Arab nationalism. In 1958, for example, a union was proclaimed between Egypt and Syria. The new state was called the United Arab Republic, with President Nasser its first leader. Until the early 1960s 'it seemed that Nasser had done nothing concrete to help the Palestinians regain their lost lands. Nasser had concentrated on his Philosophy of Revolution, on making Cairo the capital of the Arab world and, failing that, the centre of Black Africa. This was his personal mission. Initially it might have seemed to him that Arab unity under Cairo was essential before anything could be done about Israel. Nasser did his best to ensure that the Palestinian refugees in Gaza were comfortable, but deliberately avoided conflict with Israel and tried to see that other Arab countries did the same.'[2]

The refugee camps had been integrated by this time into the Gaza landscape, with UNRWA as involved as ever in its vital role as organiser of welfare and education programmes. While Egypt, too, was helping the inhabitants of Gaza in education and other spheres of life, the economy of the territory was stagnating. A large percentage of the population was without work and depended on UNRWA for food and other essentials. The Way of the Sea, the ancient coastal highway that for centuries had brought traders as well as invading armies to Gaza, was blocked to the north. For the Palestinians of Gaza, refugees and inhabitants alike, there was a growing sense of being abandoned to their miserable fate. Not only had the world at large apparently forgotten about them, but the Arab world, too, seemed to be indifferent to their cause. Young Palestinians leaders began to think that they would have to take matters into their own hands rather than wait for joint Arab action to help them.

The Palestinians were heartened in the first half of the 1960s when Arab attention was directed once again on to the struggle against Israel. In January 1964 Arab leaders met in Cairo to discuss the diversion by Israel of the waters of the River Jordan from the Sea of Galilee. At this meeting recognition was

Arab Defeat and Israeli Occupation

given to the importance of the Palestine question, but no action was proposed. So the Palestinians began the process which has continued into the 21st century of taking action themselves to achieve their goal of self-determination. In May 1964, a Palestine National Congress met in Jerusalem under the chairmanship of Ahmad al-Shuqairi. A National Charter was drawn up, and there were calls for the creation of a liberation organisation to train fighters for the struggle against Israel.

In September the same year, Arab leaders held another summit - in Alexandria. It was agreed that a new body, the Palestine Liberation Organisation (PLO), should be set up, along with a Palestine Liberation Army (PLA). The new organisations, with their headquarters in the Gaza Strip, were to be financed from contributions through the Arab League from several Arab states. The government in exile would also be headquartered in Gaza. Thus the city and the surrounding area was, from the very first, the focus of the organised political and armed struggle of the Palestinians against Israel. But the development of Palestinian institutions in Gaza were carefully monitored by Egypt. The Egyptian government 'allowed Palestinians to set up affiliated trade, women's, and military units in the Strip. But autonomous movements such as Fatah [the group led by Yasser Arafat which became dominant within the PLO] the Communists, and the Muslim Brotherhood continued to be harassed.'[3]

In its early years, with UNEF still deployed along the Egypt/Gaza border with Israel, the PLO carried out most of its operations against Israel from bases inside Syria and Jordan. In November 1966, the Israelis responded to a landmine attack on a military vehicle in which three soldiers were killed by carrying out a brutal retaliatory raid against Jordan. An army brigade with tanks, artillery and aircraft attacked the West Bank village of Sammu near Hebron and virtually razed it to the ground.[4] The stage was being set for much more serious fighting that would

Arab Defeat and Israeli Occupation

deeply affect Gaza.

The aftermath of the Sammu raid, in which 18 Jordanian troops were killed and 125 houses were destroyed, was a period of anger and recrimination in the Arab world. Jordan criticised Egypt and other Arab countries for failing to support it; in particular, it accused President Nasser of shrinking from confrontation with Israel by hiding behind the UNEF presence.

In the early months of 1967, stung by these taunts, President Nasser's oratory became increasingly bellicose, and he promised the Arab people that victory over Israel, when the moment came, was assured. Tension rose throughout the Middle East. On 13 May 1967 the Soviet Union confirmed Egyptian and Syrian intelligence reports that Israel was preparing for an imminent attack on Syria. Three days later President Nasser asked the UNEF to withdraw some units on the border between Sinai and Israel, but not those in Gaza or Sharm al-Shaikh. But the UNEF said that if some units were to pulled out, they would all have to go. The Egyptian leader, in the warlike atmosphere of the day to which he himself had greatly contributed, had no choice but to agree. The Egyptian army began deploying in areas vacated by the UN force. But time was running out, and Gaza was effectively at the mercy of its giant and powerful enemy to the north.

The danger of war was growing fast; and the Arab people, hanging on every word spoken by President Nasser, were confident of victory. On 25 May the Egyptian leader declared that the Straits of Tiran (the entrance to the Gulf of Aqaba) were closed to Israeli shipping. War was then inevitable. On 30 May, Egypt and Jordan patched up their dispute and signed a defence pact. But when war broke out on 5 June, the Arabs immediately faced disaster. All 17 air bases in Egypt were attacked by the Israelis and within hours 309 of the Egyptian air force's total fleet of 340 planes had been destroyed. Without air cover, the Egyptian army found itself in a hopeless position.

The main thrust of the first Israeli army offensive was towards Rafah, 'the hinge between the Gaza Strip and Egypt proper... By the end of the first day the Israelis had almost destroyed the Egyptian Seventh Division in the Rafah area. They had cut off the Gaza Strip and captured the key supply base and road and rail junction of EI-Arish.'[5]

There was intense fighting on the outskirts of Gaza, but ultimately the inhabitants of the city and the surrounding towns and villages were left to their fate as Egyptian troops either were killed, surrendered or fled. Ismail Qudaih, now a lawyer in Khan Younis, was a 12-year-old schoolboy in Khuza'a village southeast of the town in 1967. 'I remember,' he said, 'seeing the Israeli army coming eastwards towards Gaza. There was a huge number of tanks and other vehicles because I remember there was a lot of dust from them. People in the village were rushing around getting things together and getting ready to run like they did in 1948. Also, unfortunately, I saw the Egyptian soldiers taking off their boots and uniforms and escaping with the civilians, instead of fighting.' Ismail Qudaih said that a few young men in the village who had arms wanted to stay and fight. But the others dissuaded them, saying they would have no chance of inflicting damage or surviving, fighting tanks with pistols.

Ismail Qudaih remembers rushing away with his family towards nearby orchards. 'We hid among the fruit trees for about a week, then we went back to our homes. Everything there was the same, the Israeli army had only passed through the village, nothing else.'

Khuza'a escaped lightly. Elsewhere in Gaza Palestinians have grim memories of the start of the Israeli occupation. Majid al-Hussaini, a resident of Gaza City, said the Israelis 'behaved like a wild animal which hasn't eaten for two or three years. They took everything and didn't leave a thing. It was as though they wanted to destroy the Palestinian people, to wipe us off the map. Such action builds hatred on both sides.'

Hassan Muhammad Dabbour was in his textiles shop in the centre of Khan Younis on June 1967. 'I heard a lot of noise. I opened my door and saw tanks flying Iraqi flags coming down the street. I was standing just here outside my shop watching them. I thought that as they were Iraqis I would get some water and cigarettes for them. But as the tanks got closer I realised that in fact they were Israeli. So I hurriedly locked the shop and walked away fast. I'd got about 20 metres when firing started. The Egyptians had their tanks near the centre of the town, and when they, too, realised that the approaching vehicles were Israeli, a battle started. But the Israelis defeated them and what were left of them headed back towards Egypt.'

Amin Dabbour, whose family lived in the Jabaliya refugee camp, remembers everyone being ordered by the Israelis to assemble around the Abu Rashid pool, a stagnant pond which doubled both as an open sewer and a play area for children of the refugees. 'We stood there for about 14 hours while they checked our identity, and so on. They were also searching our houses. And they pointed guns at us from over the buildings around the pool as we stood there. They tried to frighten and intimidate us. They wanted us to tell them where our weapons were and so on.'

The Israelis, in the days and weeks that followed, started assembling the machinery of occupation, appointing a military governor. The security of the region was also tightened with the setting up of road blocks, military camps with watchtowers, and street patrols. Amin Dabbour noticed that the Israelis had destroyed the statue of the Unknown Soldier which had been put up jointly by the Palestinians and the Egyptians a few years before on a plinth outside the Legislative Council building in Gaza. 'I remember it, because for the previous two years I had marched by it as part of a Boy Scout group. The march was to celebrate the end of the Israeli occupation of Gaza after the Suez crisis of 1956. Now the statue had gone and we were under occupation once more.'

It took the Palestinians of Gaza several months to start recovering from the shock of losing their links with the Arab world. The Way of the Sea was now effectively blocked to the south as well as the north. Gradually, as the Israeli forces established tighter and tighter control over the Gaza Strip, the people began to organise resistance to the occupation. Organisation was difficult to achieve because, even under the Egyptians, the scope for political activity had been narrow. According to one assessment, 'when Israel occupied the Strip in June 1967, civic institutions were still weak, dominated by the landowning elite, and carefully circumscribed by Egypt. Nonetheless, the Strip was heavily armed. PLA units and underground groups had light arms and rudimentary military training. Within months they turned to guerrilla tactics against Israeli control. Guerrillas hid in orange groves and congested quarters of the towns and camps. They lobbed grenades at Israeli military vehicles, burned buses... and attacked the banks, post offices, and markets that symbolized a return to normal life in the Strip.'[6]

Mahmoud Ashour remembered that the first act committed by resistance fighters was against a train on the railway that once ran from Kantara to Jerusalem, passing through Gaza. 'Immediately,' he said, 'the Israelis imposed a curfew and arrested dozens of people and took them to a school for interrogation.' A short time later there was an attack on an Israeli military vehicle.

Most of the attacks on the Israelis were carried out in Gaza and the main towns where the perpetrators could escape into narrow and crowded streets and alleyways. Growing up during this period in the village of Khuza'a, Ismail Qudaih was not as acutely aware as his contemporaries in the towns of the daily effects of occupation. But, like every Palestinian in Gaza, he has memories of people being detained and arrested. He said he first became aware of the full implications of the occupation while taking part in a demonstration in 1970 to mark the death of President Nasser of Egypt. 'Three times on that day the Israelis tried to catch me, but I managed to escape. Then once when I was at school the army came in and started beating pupils. They beat me on the leg. That evening they came to our home and searched. By then I knew what occupation meant.'

Popular anger towards Israel soon began to grow in the aftermath of the occupation. But popular resistance did not start for another 20 years. Also, with the PLO hierarchy far away in Jordan – and after the conflict there in 1970, in Lebanon – there was little in the way of broad-based political and military leadership in Gaza at this time. 'Palestinian nationalism, though germinating for some decades under Arab rule, had not yet passed into an aggressive stage. Although the military administration in both the West Bank and Gaza Strip had to contend with some *fedayeen* who identified with the PLO, popular support for them was still thin. For a decade or so, until the rightward shift in the majority in the Knesset, Israelis and Palestinians lived in sullen and generally calm coexistence.'[7]

The *fedayeen*, members of Fatah and the Popular Front for the Liberation of Palestine (PFLP), drew their support from the refugee camps where 'Israeli soldiers patrolled during the day but at night the guerrillas ruled.' When the civilian population took action to express their anger at the Israeli occupation it usually came in the form of civil disobedience. 'Students demonstrated and struck on national days, teachers protested against changes in the curriculum and soldiers' violation of school grounds, and lawyers boycotted the military courts.'[8]

This early spell of anti-Israeli violence and civil disobedience, a precursor of the first full-scale uprising which began in 1987, caused concern within the Israeli government. In January 1971 the occupation authorities dismissed the mayor and councillors of Gaza City, and in the spring the head of the Israeli army's Southern Command, Major General Ariel Sharon, personally organised a ruthless campaign, using overwhelming force, to eliminate the organised Palestinian resistance to the occupation. The military arrested 'dozens of activist professionals and detained some 12,000 relatives of wanted guerrillas. Sharon's forces placed the refugee camps under lengthy curfews during which the army searched houses, smashed belongings, and forcibly removed thousands of residents. Roads bulldozed through the camps broke up the rabbit-warren of alleys and facilitated military control. After last-ditch gun battles in mid-1971, Sharon broke the resistance movement. The guerrillas lost their sanctuaries, ran out of arms and ammunition, and the last PFLP commanders were killed.'[9]

The 1970s thereafter was a period of relative calm in Gaza. Businessmen in Gaza were keen to exploit the new markets in Israel, and when the position of mayor was restored by the Israeli authorities, a prominent local establishment figure, Rashad al-Shawa, filled the post with public backing. His appointment marked the start of the last period in Gaza's history in which leading families of the old landowning social order dominated the territory. Rashad al-Shawa, through his Benevolent Society, was able to extend charity and thereby win patronage and control. A close relative 'headed the Palestine Bank – the only non-Israeli bank – and other members of the municipal council owned light industries and land. The traditional social order was based on family influence, education, wealth, and patron-client relations. That order seemed legitimate and natural to the elite.'[10] Only at the end of the 1980s was the old order forced to accept a role for a younger generation who had become impatient at their elders' acceptance, albeit reluctant, of Israeli occupation.

At the start of the 1970s, then, the Israelis felt themselves in the comfortable position, thanks to the work of General

Arab Defeat and Israeli Occupation

Sharon's army, of having 'cowed the refugee camps. Given the relatively low level of political organisation and sophistication among the residents at that time, the failure of the violent revolt led to apathy and despair. Residents were terrified of the consequences of opposing the occupying power and concentrated on basic survival.'[11]

The struggle to survive led to a considerable amount of contact between the people of Gaza and the Israelis because after 1967 workers from the territory were allowed to travel each day to Tel Aviv and other cities to look for work. While the jobs available to them were invariably at the bottom end of the market – as labourers on building sites, as fruit pickers and so on – the chance to find work at least reduced the dependency of refugees and others on United Nations or charity hand-outs. About half the labour force in Gaza started to find work in Israel and the Israeli shekel, alongside the Jordanian dinar, became the common currency for Gazans.

The economy of Gaza became tied to Israel in other ways. Palestinians paid taxes of various kinds to Israel. Most imported goods and produce came from or via the Jewish state; while goods and produce from Gaza had to find markets in Israel or else be handled by Israeli agents if they were to be exported further. Gaza lacked the easy access to Jordan that the West Bank enjoyed. Even today Gazan exports have to travel via Israel.

The people of Gaza also came into frequent contact with Israelis in administrative matters – in such trivial day-to-day tasks as applying for a driving licence, an identity card, or a *laissez-passer* to travel abroad.

A third physical way in which Palestinians encountered Israelis was through the presence of Jewish settlements on Arab land occupied in 1967, in Gaza as well as in the West Bank. Even though the land of the Gaza Strip does not have the same religious significance for Jews as that of the West Bank (with the

Life at the Crossroads

ancient tribes of Israel never having succeeded in capturing the coastal plain from the Philistines) colonies of Jewish families were settled there, with one third of the territory confiscated for their use. Their presence in the vicinity of Arab towns, village and refugee camps – often on rich agricultural land with good water resources – contributed greatly to the sullen anger felt towards Israel by the Palestinian community.

As the Gazans adjusted to life under occupation in the 1970s they felt isolated from the outside world. They also realised that the Palestinian leadership's inability to have a voice in the territory meant that Gaza could easily become hostage to plans hatched by other Arab leaders or outside powers. Alarm was expressed in Gaza at the beginning of the decade, for example, when the United States Secretary of State, William Rogers put forward a plan aimed at breaking the deadlock in the Arab-Israeli conflict. Under the scheme the status of Gaza was left open to negotiation, and the Gazans realised right away that they would not be party to those discussions. Towards the end of the decade a momentous event occurred in the Middle East – the visit of President Sadat of Egypt to Jerusalem in 1977, the first time that an Arab leader had set foot on Israeli soil. The leading state in the Arab world (and Gaza's former protector) had taken the first step towards a peace treaty with Israel. Refugees in Gaza were left in despair. They saw the chances of Arab states supporting their demand to be allowed back to their homes receding fast. Furthermore, the people of Gaza noticed once again that outside powers, in this case Egypt and Israel, had decided on how their fate should be settled. Under the Camp David accord Egypt and Israel agreed that Gaza and the West Bank should be the subject of talks leading eventually to autonomy in the two regions. The people of Gaza had not been consulted over the matter.

So, at the beginning of the 1980s the need for Palestinians to take action themselves to control their fate was felt even more

Arab Defeat and Israeli Occupation

acutely than it had been in the 60s. According to Ismail Qudaih, 'from the 1980s onwards we started to organise parties again and the momentum began to build up. The number of people in prison increased substantially. Suddenly, everyone seemed to have a member of his family in prison. It was all building towards something, though we didn't know what.'

A new and largely unknown factor in Gaza at this time was the Islamic movement. In the early 1970s, in a move to weaken the influence of the secularly-minded PLO and the communists, the Israelis had encouraged Islamic charitable organisations to establish themselves in the Gaza Strip. Since the 7th century the overwhelming majority of the population of Gaza had been Muslim and these organisations, the Islamic Charitable League, and the Islamic Society (founded by a leading Islamic cleric, Shaikh Ahmad Yassin in 1973), enjoyed immediate success. While the organisations concentrated on charitable work they also carried out religious instruction and, with support and inspiration from the Muslim Brotherhood in Egypt, advocated the idea of a pan-Islamic revival in the Middle East to defeat Israel. At the same time they denounced the ideals of Palestinian nationalism. Many member of the Muslim Brotherhood in Egypt moved to Gaza after repeated crackdowns on the organisation by the Egyptian authorities. The Islamic University of Gaza became a major centre for Muslim Brotherhood activities.

The Israeli tactic of divide and rule enjoyed early success: in January 1980, a group of 500 people marched from a mosque in Gaza City to attack the Red Crescent Society. They also destroyed shops and restaurants selling alcoholic drinks, and set fire to cinemas. The Israeli army did nothing to restrain the crowd.

While tension between secular and Islamic groups continued for some years, popular enthusiasm for the latter was diminished by the support they enjoyed from Israel and by their anti-nationalist stance. As the 1980s progressed, however, the Islamic groups gradually adopted ideals of Palestinian nationalism without losing any of their religious zeal. This trend, springing out of the charitable groups in Gaza encouraged originally by the Israelis, spawned Islamic Jihad and Hamas – two radical Islamic groups which later played leading roles in the struggle against Israeli occupation. (Hamas means 'zeal' in Arabic, but is also an acronym for *Harakat al Muqawama al-Islamiya* – Islamic resistance movement.)

A major change in public attitudes in Gaza towards the Israeli occupation came in November 1981, one month after the assassination of President Sadat by Islamic fundamentalists. A strike was called in Gaza to protest against new taxes levied by the Israeli military government and against new administrative restrictions. 'This time, urban professionals rather than refugees led the movement. Doctors, dentists, veterinarians, pharmacists, lawyers, and engineers struck for two weeks... Merchants and the Gaza municipality supported the strike. The effort indicated the emergence of a self-conscious group of middle-class intelligentsia, whose professional concerns merged with nationalism in the strike.'[12] The Israelis carried out many arrests and imposed heavy fines. The strike, in essence, failed in its objectives. But it 'coincided with the introduction of the Israeli civil administration, designed to provide a facade of non-military rule. Palestinians viewed the change as a step toward absorbing the territories into Israel.' The municipality in Gaza, like those in the West Bank, refused to cooperate with the new body. As a result, in July 1982, Rashad al-Shawa was removed from the post of mayor.[13]

The Israeli decision to take over the municipality in Gaza and dismiss the old guard meant that the traditional elite of the city were out of power. The middle class professionals, in their strike of November 1981, had shown that anti-Israeli feelings were building up fast and were beginning to surface in public.

But neither the traditional elite, nor the middle class was able to provide the leadership necessary to mobilise the people of Gaza as a whole by converting pockets of simmering anger into a united movement to oppose the Israeli occupation. That leadership came from an unexpected quarter: from the generation of young men born under occupation, the *shabaab* as they were called. They were shackled neither by respect for their elders nor for the traditional Gazan elite. They were not intimidated, either, by the Israeli army. So it was the *shabaab* who led the way into the first battle against occupation.

Notes

[1] Interviewed by the author, 1994.
[2] Ritchie Ovendale, *The Origins of the Arab-Israeli Wars*, London, 1984, p. 170.
[3] Ann M Lesch, 'Prelude to the Uprising in the Gaza Strip', published in *Journal of Palestine Studies*, California, autumn 1990.
[4] *Ibid.*, p. 463.
[5] *Ibid.*, pp. 495-496.
[6] Lesch, *op. cit.*, p. 3.
[7] Viorst, *op. cit.*, p. 41.
[8] Lesch, *op. cit.*, p. 3.
[9] *Ibid.*, p. 3.
[10] *Ibid.*, p. 6.
[11] *Ibid.*, p. 4.
[12] *Ibid.*, p. 4.
[13] *Ibid.*, p. 4.

CHAPTER 14

The First *Intifada* – 'A Mass Expression of Outrage'

The Mahbouh family – about 40 of them, men, women and children – had assembled their possessions in a half-finished building close to the Jabaliya Refugee Camp and were preparing a meal. The children were playing around the outside of the building while some of the men sat on the roof watching the activity of Israeli soldiers at the family house which stood on a slight hill several hundred metres away. The family were whiling away the time waiting for the Israeli army to blow up their house. The Mahbouhs were being punished collectively because of the alleged activity of one of the brothers. He had been accused of killing an Israeli soldier. He was never caught, but for weeks the Israeli army harassed the family, believing that they were hiding him. On one occasion the whole family was put into an army truck and told they were being deported to Lebanon. For hours they were driven around, only to be deposited eventually back home. In the end, it turned out that the brother had fled the country. But the army decided that

213

the family still deserved punishment.

What was striking, observing the family in the hours before the house was demolished, was the sense of calm resignation. The men were smiling as they told me the family's story. 'The Israelis,' one of them said, 'think that by blowing up our house they will break our determination. They think that we are like them, that if we lose something we will get upset. But for us it is of no great importance. Allah teaches us that we must be patient. Patience is part of our faith.'[1]

The incident involving the Mahbouh family's house occurred in 1989, more than a year after the first *intifada* – uprising – against Israeli occupation had begun in the Gaza Strip and the West Bank. It showed how, for many Palestinians – especially those in the Gaza Strip – the belief in Islam had become an integral part of the popular struggle. It showed too how the population as a whole, across the span of generations, had passed what could be called the fear threshold. The contempt and hatred of the Israeli occupiers felt by Palestinians, led by the younger generation but followed soon by their elders, was now matched by fearlessness.

There is general agreement on when and where the first *intifada* began: 8 December 1987 at the Jabaliya refugee camp. But it is harder to determine when the people of Gaza overcame their fear sufficiently to begin the revolution.

Raji Sourani, a lawyer in Gaza, has described the *intifada* as 'a mass expression of that feeling of outrage against the Israeli occupation by those who were directly suffering beneath it.'[2] Ending the occupation, which began in 1967, was clearly the primary aim of the 'mass expression' of feeling. But the uprising produced an explosion of anger which had been building up in Gaza for at least two decades before Israel occupied the territory. The people of Gaza have clear memories of events just before and just after May 1948, when destitute and heartbroken families straggled into the city having been terrorised or driven

The First Intifada – 'A Mass Expression of Outrage'

out of their homes by the Israeli army. This was the period when an UNRWA doctor had described the citizens of Gaza as looking 'gaunt and thin and of poor colour – having the appearance of' a low grade chronic malnutrition.' The Gazans remember the Israeli reprisal raids on their towns and villages in the 1950s leading to the brief occupation in 1956-57, to be followed 10 years later by the catastrophic disaster of the Arab-Israeli war.

These experiences in turn compounded the collective experience of a people who had earlier been living under British and Ottoman rule. There should have been no surprise, therefore, that the *intifada* began in Gaza and was joined with such venom. The people of Gaza felt fearless and reckless: after all they had been through, there was nothing to lose. While the explosion began on a particular day in December 1987, the spirit of fearlessness among young Gazans had started to develop several years earlier. Gaza was not a place one went for a relaxed excursion. A tourist guide book to Israel researched in 1985 warned that 'the threat of unrest [in Gaza] makes visits inadvisable.'

The first signs of serious trouble had appeared in April 1982 after a Jewish militant had attacked Muslim worshippers outside al-Aqsa mosque in Jerusalem, the second most sacred site in Islam. Students at the Islamic University in Gaza (which had opened in 1978) held a demonstration, and there were similar protests at mosques in the city. The Israeli army beat up some of the protesters (female as well as male) and shot into one of the mosques, killing a youth and wounding other worshippers. Thereafter during the 1980s there were sporadic clashes, mainly involving Palestinian students and the Israeli army. In December 1986 the occupation authorities ordered the arrest of the leader of Shabiba, the youth wing of Fatah. His deportation the following month led to a large protest demonstration at the main mosque in Khan Younis. Israeli troops opened fire, killing one person and wounding others.

Another significant event that contributed indirectly to the start of the *intifada* was a spectacular escape from prison in Gaza in May 1987 of six members of Islamic Jihad, the radical Islamic group which was attracting more and more attention in the territory. In August one of the escapees shot dead at close range the commander of the Israeli military police. He was sitting in an army jeep at the time, stuck in traffic in the centre of Gaza city close to al-Umari Mosque. In reaction to the killing the Israeli authorities sealed off the Gaza Strip for three days, preventing people getting to work and blocking trade, a method of collective punishment that has been employed frequently, and for much longer periods, ever since.

Despite the continued pattern of army searches and mass arrests, the Israelis could not intimidate the people of Gaza. Throughout August and September, 'violent attacks continued: a firebomb thrown at an Israeli vehicle in the Gaza market; a nighttime attack on an Israeli soldier near Jabaliya camp; remote control bombs in Gaza town. Each attack led to lengthy curfews and house-to-house searches.'[3] In this period there were also a number of incidents involving Israeli settlers in the Gaza Strip. Their cars were frequently stoned as they drove to and from their homes; and on occasions the settlers vented their anger by beating Palestinians with clubs and gun butts, and smashing their property.

While the violence in the Gaza Strip was continuing, two unrelated events away from the territory contributed to the determination felt by Palestinians there. Towards the end of November 1987 a Palestinian gunman attached himself to a powered hang-glider and flew through Israel's sophisticated border defence system into northern Galilee. The presence of the unidentified object crossing the border was noted and all settlements in northern Israel were put on alert. Despite this, the gunman landed and made his way to an army base. When he opened fire, the guard on duty ran away. The soldiers inside

The First Intifada – 'A Mass Expression of Outrage'

were watching television and were caught unprepared. The gunman killed six soldiers before being killed. Palestinians in Gaza saw in this incident evidence that Israel, the all-powerful occupying power, was not invincible in the face of a determined attack.

If the hang-gliding incident gave the Gazans courage, events in the Jordanian capital, Amman, in the opening days of December fuelled their anger. An Arab summit was being held there; and to the fury of the people of Gaza, the question of the Palestinians living under occupation was ignored. Furthermore, the PLO Chairman, Yasser Arafat, had been snubbed by King Hussain on arrival in Amman, and Egypt, in isolation after signing a peace treaty with Israel, was again represented in the summit. Not for the first time since the creation of Israel, the Palestinians of Gaza felt abandoned by the Arab world. As in the past, they came to the conclusion that they would have to take matters into their own hands.

These outside developments formed the backcloth for the violent events that sparked off the uprising. An Israeli settler was stabbed to death in the centre of Gaza city on 6 December. Two days later an Israeli army tank-transporting lorry ploughed into a line of vehicles in the territory. Four Palestinians were killed. The Israelis described the incident as an accident; but in the Gaza Strip it was seen as a deliberate act of retaliation for the murder of the settler. In the evening, when the funerals were held in the Jabaliya camp for the four dead men, mass anger overflowed. Mourners swarmed through the camp attacking Israeli positions. Soldiers fired live ammunition, killing a 24-year-old man. That single bullet, it can be said, started the *intifada*.

Within hours, violence spread throughout the Gaza Strip. Israeli soldiers and their positions were attacked fearlessly by Palestinians throwing stones and fire-bombs. Curfews were imposed; but after a few days, when the violence had spread to the occupied West Bank, the Israelis realised that what they had on their hands was not another isolated period of serious unrest but a popular revolution. With the young men, the *shabaab*, leading the way, Gazans of all ages and backgrounds joined the struggle.

Ismail Qudaih worked as a lawyer in Khan Younis during the *intifada*, monitoring, recording and following up the many incidents which took place. He was impressed by the degree to which the whole of Gazan society became involved. 'All sections of the community played a part. This was not just the work of a minority of activists. In the early months, it was a 100 per cent success; everyone obeyed the orders of the leadership to strike or to boycott Israeli goods or whatever. And when someone was killed or was injured, as happened all the time, then the whole of Gaza considered it like a death in the family.[4] In the first six weeks of the uprising 27 Palestinians were killed by the Israeli army and more than 200 were injured. The many years of underground work by Fatah and other Palestinian organisations finally began to bear results.

As a news correspondent in those days it was astonishing to see young and old women coming out of houses to join the men in street protests or supporting them in one way or another. On one occasion, from inside the Shifa hospital in Gaza city, I watched a crowd of young men who were pelting an Israeli army unit with stones. The soldiers were trying to get inside to arrest some of the Palestinians who had been injured in clashes earlier in the morning. Girls and women had formed a human chain to keep the *shabaab* at the front line, the faces of the young men masked by *keffiyehs*, supplied with small rocks and pieces of jagged masonry. As tear-gas was fired into the hospital older women provided raw onion to help ease the stinging pain.

Arriving in the Gaza Strip at the Erez checkpoint in the opening weeks of the uprising was to step into a dangerous world of chaos and mayhem. The road south (the ancient Way of

The First Intifada – 'A Mass Expression of Outrage'

the Sea) was strewn with smouldering car tyres and debris of various kinds. Often, looking over to the right towards the sea, thick black smoke from burning tyres was rising from the Jabaliya refugee camp or from Beach camp. I recall one day in 1988 standing by the Dallour petrol station, just south of Gaza city where the road from the city joins the highway heading south. The scene was medieval, swirling smoke from dozens of burning tyres obliterating the sun. For a few moments that day, as on many others, the Israelis had lost control. The main road was blocked by rocks and burning tyres; and many of the side roads were blocked in a similar way. Palestinian flags, which were banned by the Israelis in those days, hung from telegraph wires. The *shabaab* controlled the streets. Finally, Israeli vehicles with bulldozer blades came through the smoke to try to reopen the road; youths with their faces half covered with *keffiyehs* appeared from alleys and doorways as the vehicle ran a gauntlet of stones, bottles and fire bombs. The response was a series of thumps and more puffs of smoke as tear gas grenades were fired. And the air became a choking cocktail of the fumes of urban warfare. On that occasion the blood of the *shabaab* was boiling and they were ready to set upon any vehicle that did not have the recognisable white Gaza plates. The only way our car, which had blue West Bank plates, could get out of the Gaza Strip that day was by securing the services of one of the youths who sat on the bonnet of the car and gave us safe passage through the stone-throwers.

Even though Fatah and other underground groups had worked hard for many years outside the occupied territory to organise resistance to the Israeli presence, the sudden eruption of the violence and spirit of defiance in Gaza came as a shock to the Israelis and the rest of the world. While the uprising started as a spontaneous reaction to decades of frustration and anger, a local leadership emerged, bringing together secular and religious groups (Hamas was formed at the start of the *intifada*) under a unified command. This operated in little cells within different districts of towns or different areas of refugee camps, later using clandestinely printed leaflets to spread information. The cells also helped families in need; during lengthy curfews they organised, surreptitiously by cover of darkness, the provision and distribution of food. All the while, attacks on the increasingly nervous Israeli army continued. 'I remember the Israelis were so nervous at night,' a resident of the Jabaliya camp told me, 'that they would shoot at anything that moved. Each morning we would find cats and dogs that had been killed.' One particular area of the camp, 'B' block, was notorious for the ambushes carried out on the occupying troops and became known locally by both Palestinians and Israelis as Vietnam.

The initial fire of the uprising became less intense after the first year for another reason: the majority of the population of Gaza was extremely poor, and 46 per cent of the workforce (85,000 people) depended on finding work inside Israel in order to feed their families. For purely practical reasons, whatever their inner thoughts and emotions, Gazans needed periods of calm in order to earn money. While Ismail Qudaih was working as a lawyer in Khan Younis during the *intifada*, one of his elderly relatives, Shehadah Qudaih, was watching developments from the village of Khuza'a. 'In many ways things here were much like in the towns. Israelis would come in as they did there, applying the same heavy-handed policy, smashing houses and arresting people on the basis of rumours. The other difficulty was making a living. Since 1967, when the Israelis took much of our land, a lot of young people had no choice but to go to Israel each day in search of work. And with all the curfews and closures of the crossings during the *intifada* period this was not easy.'

Severe disruption to education was another price the people of Gaza paid for their determination to end Israeli rule. Ina'am Mahmoud, headmistress of al-Zahra' secondary school

The First Intifada – 'A Mass Expression of Outrage'

for girls in Gaza city, said that she and her staff 'were more like guards than teachers much of the time, trying to stop the Israeli army from coming into the school and trying to keep them away from our pupils. The students were getting involved in activity away from the school. But as far as I was concerned, school itself was a sacred place for learning. Because of this, many of the students and teachers used to come to school even on strike days, even when they had to walk through streets full of trouble to get there. Education is so important. I would say to them: the Israelis are still learning today, so we must learn as well.'

But there were enormous pressures on the schoolchildren. 'Pupils would go home and go to sleep. Then in the middle of the night. Bang, bang, bang. Soldiers were coming into the house. "We want your brother. Where is he?" Students would come to school shaken because their brother had been taken away in the night. I had one student whose two brothers were killed. I just encouraged her to go on studying. But there was always this psychological pressure. Then during the classes there would be disturbances and shooting outside. It was very difficult to carry on classes under those circumstances, but I insisted that we should. We were determined that the Israelis should not destroy the school or destroy education.'[5]

While Mrs Mahmoud said her pupils responded to her appeals to separate political activity from school attendance, she said her pupils were frequently provoked. 'Israeli troops would grab youths as the girls were coming into school and hope to incite them to get involved in the trouble.'

The task of helping the 460,000 registered Palestinian refugees in the Gaza Strip during the first *intifada* – as at all other times since its creation in the early 1950s – fell to UNRWA. The uprising presented new challenges and new strains, putting both staff and resources under unprecedented stress. The UNRWA spokesman in Gaza, Isa al-Qarra, said the biggest practical difficulty came from the frequent imposition of curfews by the Israeli occupying authorities, combined with the constant clashes between the army and the Palestinian civilian population. 'UNRWA had to cope with the changing circumstances by expanding its mission and carrying out emergency health and welfare programmes. For example, health care centres had to be open around the clock to deal with casualties coming in during the night. And we had to establish special physiotherapy units to cope with *intifada*-related injuries.'[6]

Statistics involving humans in scenes of conflict can seem cold and impersonal; they camouflage the experiences and emotions of the individual. But UNRWA casualty statistics on their own give a strong indication of the impact of the *intifada* on a small corner of the occupied territories. In the Gaza Strip between 1987 and 1993 at least 500 people were killed, and 50,000 injured. (Not all the deaths were caused by the Israeli army. The start of the uprising was a signal for the hunting down and killing of dozens of Palestinians who were alleged to have collaborated with the Israeli intelligence services. Despite appeals from the leadership inside and outside the territories, these inter-Palestinian killings continued.)

Other hospitals and clinics, aside from those operated by UNRWA, were also busy around the clock during the *intifada* treating the injured after clashes with the Israelis. The Ahli Arab Hospital (the successor of the British Church Missionary Society hospital set up at the end of the 19th century) in Gaza city treated 13,000 cases during that period. Records show that one third of those were aged 15 or less, indicating the degree to which young people – sometimes very young – took the lead in the uprising against the Israelis. According to Samira Farah, one of the senior administrators at the hospital, 'the majority of the injuries were caused by live, plastic or rubber bullets.' Plastic bullets (small pointed pellets, up to 1.5 centimetres in length) were frequently fired at demonstrators. Despite their size they could inflict serious injuries (fractures, bleeding or internal wounds) or, in some cases, fatal ones. 'I remember,' Samira Farah said, 'a 14-year-old girl being brought in with two plastic bullet injuries, one each side of the chest, and she died.'[7]

Injuries and fatalities were also caused by the irresponsible use of teargas. Israeli soldiers and police were often seen by Gazans and by foreign observers firing teargas canisters into dense crowds and into buildings. The instructions on the side of the canisters point out the dangers of the gas being used in this way. There is a clearly worded and explicit warning on the MK II 560-CS 150 Yard Long Range Projectile (manufactured in Pennsylvania in the USA) used by the Israeli security forces: 'Must not be fired directly at persons as death or injury may result. FOR OUTDOOR USE ONLY.' Staff at the Ahli hospital say that misuse of teargas resulted in many pregnancies being aborted, in burns and in serious respiratory problems.

Dealing with emergencies under circumstances of great stress was hard enough. But the job of medical staff was made more difficult by the restrictions frequently placed on freedom of movement within Gaza and between the territory and the outside. During periods of prolonged curfew, for example, staff had difficulty getting to work. Medicines, which had to be brought in through Israel, frequently were in short supply when the crossing points between the two territories were closed. And routine maintenance work often could not be carried out because of a shortage of parts.

More serious than all this was the fact that there were sometimes problems getting serious cases out of Gaza for specialist treatment in Israel or in a better-equipped Arab hospital in Jerusalem. 'Transferring seriously injured patients in this atmosphere,' Samira Farah said, 'and trying to get permission from all the various authorities and so on, was very stressful.' Sometimes the Israelis came into the hospital 'saying they were chasing someone who they'd seen throwing stones or something. They'd come charging in and we'd run behind trying to stop them, asking what they wanted. They would just ignore us. But we had some foreign members of staff, from America and Europe, and they were a great help to us on such occasions.'

Stress affected every Palestinian in Gaza during the first *intifada*. 'I never felt any kind of security,' said Laila, a mother of four from Gaza city. 'I was worried when my children were out of my sight, wondering what might be happening to them at school or on their way there or back. And when they were here I was worrying, too. Worrying that soldiers would come. Sometimes they'd beat their way in at three or four in the morning and make my sons come out and paint over the slogans on the walls, or put out a fire, or take down a Palestinian flag. At three in the morning.'

Curfews became a part of daily life. 'When the Israelis imposed curfews,' Laila said, 'they were punishing the whole Palestinian community. It was like keeping us in a big prison. We would have to be ready all the time, trying to keep basic food in supply in case. Which was all right for us, but what about those with no jobs and no money?'[8]

But Laila is convinced that the Israeli tactics back-fired. 'Prisoners do not come out of prison loving their captors. That's one thing. Secondly, the new generation born under occupation like my sons simply reject all that has happened to us up to now. They have much more courage than we had, and they are prepared to fight fearlessly to get their freedom. And that's what they did in the *intifada*.'

Pictures of violent confrontation, particularly in the early months of the uprising that began in 1987, appeared on television screens and newspapers all around the world. This was the period in which Gaza became a household word, synonymous with violence and squalor. Gaza's image in the world had not been brilliant before the *intifada*. Those people in the West who knew the name probably associated it more with a novel by Aldous Huxley (*Eyeless in Gaza*) than with the place in the late 20th century. The common perception of Gaza prior to this had been of a remote and largely forgotten outpost of Egypt, and before that a southern and not particularly significant part of British and Ottoman controlled Palestine.

Gaza's moment centre stage (albeit for reasons that did nothing to revive memories of its rich history) was relatively brief on this occasion. As the protests and the Israeli response continued month after month, events in the occupied territories were no longer guaranteed front page treatment. But the violence continued, becoming almost as routine as the outside reaction to it. The human rights organisation, Middle East Watch, in a report published in 1990 catalogued, in a list of killings carried out by the Israeli army, that of a youth, Khalid al-Atawneh. The killing in May 1989, the report said, 'attracted no more than one paragraph in the newspapers the following day and received no subsequent publicity. It appears to be a rather ordinary case – a killing that occurred during clashes between youths and soldiers in the tense Jabaliya Refugee Camp, during which 12 other Palestinians were injured, according to camp residents, and five soldiers were slightly wounded by stones, according to the IDF [Israel Defence Forces].'[9]

The circumstances of the incident were typical of many. According to an UNRWA employee in Jabaliya a van carrying soldiers in civilian clothes drove into the camp. Residents thought they were settlers and started pelting the van with stones. The soldiers got out and began shooting. Reinforcements were brought in. Troops raided a boys' school in the camp, believing that stones were thrown from there. A youth who was with Khalid al-Atawneh said the two of them had been in an orchard near the school. When they saw a uniformed soldier 10 metres away they turned to flee. The soldier opened fire, fatally wounding Khalid al-Atawneh in the chest, and wounding his friend in the back. There was no indication that either youth had been engaged in acts of violence at the time of the shooting.

Such incidents served continually to convert the despair of the people of Gaza that had been gathering since 1948 into determination to end the Israeli occupation. At the Jabaliya camp, where the uprising began, Ali Hassan Ali, reflected on what the *intifada* achieved. 'Even though it was difficult, I prefer the *intifada* period to any other since 1948 because I feel that there was a strong sense of hope and purpose, through the use of stones against guns. Israeli bullets did not distinguish between Christians and Muslims, secular and religious, men and women, or even adults and children. There was national unity like never before. A lot of youths fell in the fighting. That was the price we paid.'

The *intifada* continued, with occasional outbursts of sustained protests and mass punishment making the headlines from time to time, up to and beyond the opening of the Middle East peace process in Madrid in October 1991. The uprising in the occupied territory was credited as having been a major factor in bringing about the change of atmosphere that made the start of the process possible. Few Palestinians in Gaza believed that the process itself would end the occupation. Even when it emerged that the PLO and Israel had been holding secret talks leading to an agreement on limited self-rule in Gaza, there was still widespread scepticism. The international community hailed the agreement signed on 4 May 1994 in Cairo by Arafat and the Israeli Prime Minister, Yitzhak Rabin, as a triumph. Gaza was headline news once more as television cameras recorded the departure of Israeli troops from the centre of Gaza city in the early hours of 18 May. 'Israeli troops leave Gaza', the headlines around the world said. But the people of Gaza were not fooled. The troops had left Jabaliya and other refugee camps, just as they had left Gaza city and other population centres. But Israeli settlements and Israeli troops remained in place in large areas of the territory. It soon became clear that the 'mass expression of outrage would not die away until the last Israeli settler and soldier had left the Strip.

Notes
[1] Interviewed by the author, 1989.
[2] *Ibid.*, 1994.
[3] Lesch, *op. cit.*, p. 16.
[4] Interviewed by the author, 1994.
[5] Interviewed by the author, 1994.
[6] Interviewed by the author, 1994.
[7] Interviewed by the author, 1994.
[8] Interviewed by the author, 1994.
[9] 'The Israeli Army and the Intifada – Policies that contribute to the killings', Middle East Watch, New York, August 1990, p. 200.

CHAPTER 15

Optimism and Countdown to War

Throughout its history, despite the succession of wars and occupation, Gaza has enjoyed periods of peace and optimism. One occurred in the mid-to-late 1990s, after the Oslo Accords[1] had been signed and the first *intifada* had petered out. 'History, beauty and warm hospitality: That's Gaza,' declared a brochure published by the city's municipality ('Partners In Progress'). The cover was illustrated by a montage of images: waves breaking on a sandy beach, a palm tree-lined boulevard and a mosque gateway. 'After years of Israeli occupation,' the brochure said, 'Gazans are now fighting in rebuilding their city. A lot has already been done and one can enjoy the beautiful seashore and wonderful hospitality of the Gazans. Like the Phoenix, symbol of Gaza, the city is born again from its ashes and is taking on a new lease of life.'

Many Palestinians, too, believed that a new page in their history had been turned. For Gazans, the absence of Israeli troops, the presence of armed Palestinian police and the establishment of the Palestine National Authority (PNA) on their territory seemed together to point towards a more hopeful future. 'The history of Gaza entered a new phase on 18 May 1994, at about 2.00 am, as the last Israeli troops left military headquarters in the centre of Gaza city.' The speaker was a Gaza lawyer, Raji Sourani, addressing a seminar in the city the following September called to study human rights in the territory following the establishment of a Palestinian self-rule authority. To the west of the city, overlooking public gardens and the plinth where the statue to the Unknown Soldier once stood is the former legislative council building established by the Egyptians in the late 1950s. It has the look of a small-scale parliament building with wide steps leading up to the main door, and a domed roof. The Israeli military governor took it over after the 1967 occupation. Despite its modest appearance, the council building has represented authority in Gaza for several decades. 'We watched the Israelis pull out from various places in Gaza early in 1994,' one Palestinian said. 'But only when we saw them quit this building did we really believe that they were going properly.'

Given the history and symbolic importance of the building it was appropriate that Yasser Arafat, on his return to Gaza in July 1994, should have made his first public speech from that spot, his words frequently drowned by cheering from the vast crowd in front of it and by the celebratory firing of thousands of rounds of bullets into the air. The people of Gaza who greeted Yasser Arafat that day hoped that the Middle East peace process of the early 1990s, despite the initial misgivings expressed by many, would represent a step towards eventually re-attaching the Gaza Strip to those parts of Palestine outside the borders of Israel: the West Bank and east Jerusalem. The arrival of the PLO leader, the international symbol of the Palestinians' struggle for independence, seemed to herald a better future at last.

Optimism and Countdown to War

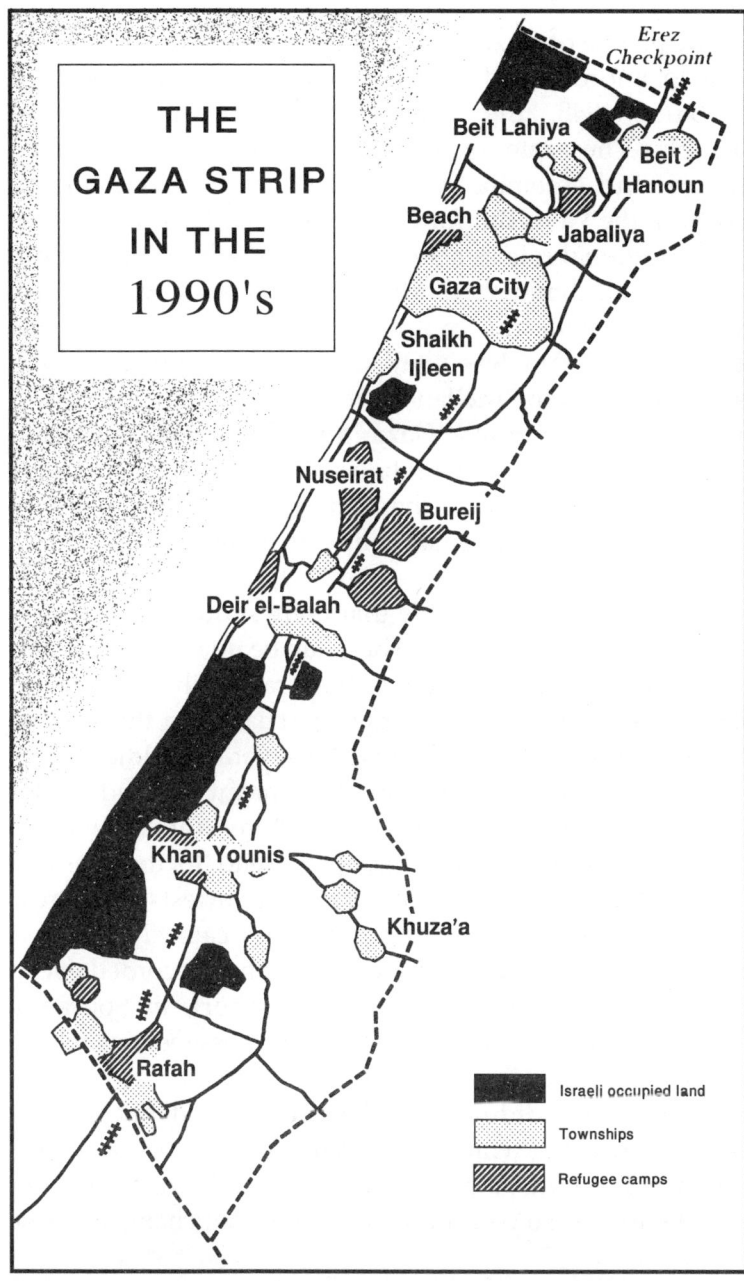

Life at the Crossroads

The people of Gaza were hungry for signs that life might be about to improve and devoured the crumbs of hope they found. Since 1948, the land of Palestine had changed considerably. The state of Israel had enjoyed international recognition and seemingly unlimited and unquestioning support from the West. But for Gaza, these had been wilderness years. Its traditional role as a strategic crossroads on the Middle Eastern map had diminished. Modern methods of warfare and communication made the control of the land access between Africa and the Levant less vital. Gaza was no longer, in the words of one historian, 'the land bridge and meeting place and battlefield of great Empires.' Gaza in the 1990s felt unwanted, even by its closest Arab neighbours. Modern transport and production methods had also changed radically, and Gaza was no longer a thriving commercial centre as it had been for many centuries.

So it was understandable that there should have been a mood of optimism in July 1994. 'There can be no doubt,' Sourani said, 'that after the redeployment of the Israeli military from the population centres there was a dramatic change in the lives of Palestinians in Gaza, simply because those Israeli soldiers were no longer there.' In practical terms this meant 'an end to the curfew which the people of Gaza had endured for some seven years [since the start of the *intifada*]; the end to the massive military attacks and house demolitions; fewer arrests; and a real reduction in the level of deaths and injuries caused by Israeli soldiers with appalling regularity which we had recorded every month for the previous seven years.' In short, in Sourani's words, 'Gaza came alive, and was able to express feelings which it had not expressed for two generations.'

The euphoria did not last long. The inhabitants of Gaza realised gradually that while the PNA had been established and Palestinian police had taken the place of Israeli troops on the streets of the towns, some aspects of life had not changed. Most important of all, the withdrawal of Israeli troops from population centres had simply been part of a redeployment of forces within the territory, rather than a complete withdrawal. The arrangement, furthermore, had been sanctioned by the PLO in agreements signed with Israel. This meant that while the world was blandly talking about the pull-out of the Israeli army from Gaza, up to 5,000 soldiers were still deployed there, with another 10,000 engaged in the overall security of the area. The citizens of the Gaza, in other words, still had to pass Israeli military checkpoints on Gazan territory and pass beneath Israeli gun positions, even – at one point in the middle of the territory – on the main Rafah-Jaffa road.

Raji Sourani acknowledged that the redeployment of the army 'involved the consolidation of military camps, and the building of new camps and checkpoints. This involved the confiscation of more Palestinian land or interference in it.' Towards the end of 1994, Mr Sourani counted more than 50 Israeli military installations in the Gaza Strip. Ali Hassan Ali, a resident of the Jabaliya refugee camp since 1948 was baffled, like thousands of other Palestinians, by how the PLO could have signed an agreement which allowed the Israeli military deployment on Gazan soil to continue. 'In this period our future is not clear. Our minds are frozen. We still don't have total independence. Our officers are still operating under Israeli guns. Therefore, to my way of thinking the occupation still exists. The occupation is veiled in something mysterious and strange. We won't feel real independence until we can match the Israelis at every level them on one side of the border, us on the other. At the moment I have eaten a piece of bread, but I am still hungry.'

The major purpose of the Israeli military presence in Gaza towards the end of 1994 was to guard Jewish settlements and the roads leading to them. With the Palestinian flag flying without restriction over the whole of Gaza and with Palestinian police in control, the sight of the settlements seemed more anomalous than ever. At the northern edge of the strip the Nissanit settlement looked like a slice of suburban Europe or north America placed incongruously in the Arab world – white-painted villas and cottages with sloping tiled roofs in neat rows along the ridge of the dunes and among the sand.

Most striking of all was the Israeli presence in the centre of the strip, at Kfar Darom by the side of the main north-south highway. Behind an earth wall and high wire and barbed-wire fences children wearing *kippas* (the skullcaps which are obligatory for observant Jews) played in the gardens after being brought home by cars bearing Israeli number plates by their mothers. Across the road, under the gaze of Israeli troops in well fortified gun positions, Palestinian children played in their schoolyard. But their parents were not allowed to drive their cars to the school to pick them up - because the Israeli troops would not allow vehicles to stop next to the settlement. Similarly on the road west towards the coast and the huge Gush Katif settlement, Palestinian drivers still had to pass through Israeli checkpoints. More than 5,000 Israeli settlers were still living in the Gaza strip in 16 settlements which covered up to 30 per cent of the land.

The continued presence of the settlements, as the euphoria of May 1994 receded, was a constant reminder of how the Gaza Strip after so many years of occupation, was still attached securely to Israel. At the most basic level, Israel controlled access to and from the territory; and it continued to exercise its power to seal off the Gaza Strip as a collective punishment even after the establishment of the PNA and the redeployment of the Israeli army.

Nevertheless, money was being invested in new industries and building projects. Gaza had its own port and international airport, 40 kilometres south of Gaza city, close to the border with Egypt. One notable arrival at the airport during this period of optimism – in December 1998 – was that of

Optimism and Countdown to War

President Bill Clinton – the first visit by an American president to an area under Palestinian control. Moreover, in a speech to the Palestine National Council he appeared to acknowledge the validity of Palestinian grievances and aspirations as never before, saying that the Palestinians 'have behind you a history of dispossession and dispersal, before you the opportunity to shape a new Palestinian future on your own land.' The US leader expressed understanding 'for your concerns about settlement activity, land confiscations and home demolitions,' and acknowledged that 'neither side has a monopoly on pain or virtue.' Clinton declared that 'Israel must recognise the right of the Palestinians to aspire to live free today, tomorrow and forever.'

But by the time of the Clinton visit the shortcomings in the Oslo agreement were apparent. It was an accord that Yasser Arafat accepted from a position of weakness. Official peace talks that began after the 1991 Gulf war made little progress, and that was not a satisfactory state of affairs for Arafat. His authority had been dented by a number of factors. The outbreak of the *intifada* in December 1987 had 'heralded a rapid growth in the influence of Hamas and, to a lesser extent, Islamic Jihad, both at the expense of the PLO, whose nationalist rhetoric had previously dominated the Palestinian discourse.'[2] Furthermore, Arafat's ill-judged decision to support Saddam Hussain in the build-up to the 1991 war resulted in the Arab Gulf states cutting off funds to the PLO and expelling many thousands of Palestinians. A third factor was that with the collapse of the Soviet Union, the sole superpower was the United States, a strong ally and supporter of Israel. So, the conditions of a Middle East peace deal 'were worked out at a time when Yasser Arafat's organization was politically and financially weakened. Arafat's Palestinian Authority, which at the outset was to be based in Gaza, gave the impression of being subjugated to the political whims of the ruling majority in Israel.'[3]

235

The late Edward Said, a formidable Palestinian intellectual and trenchant critic of the Oslo process, interviewed in 1999, also pointed to the 1991 war as the turning point for Yasser Arafat: 'My sense of his downfall begins with the Gulf War. He was already quite isolated. It was quite clear that the *intifada* had nothing to do with him. It broke out and I think it surprised him. He tried as any leader would to capitalise on it. But I think his position in the Gulf War has brought upon us this tremendous disaster of Oslo. The Oslo agreement wasn't, in my opinion, a solution to the Palestinian problem, it was a solution to Arafat's problem. It was a question of his survival. And that came before anything. My feeling at the time, and I said it publicly, was it was a bad agreement. He had got himself into this process, and if he had been a real leader he would have had the courage to put it before the people in referendum, saying, "This is what the agreement really entails, and if you don't like it I will resign." He could have done that. But he lied to himself. Abu Mazen [Mahmoud Abbas] says it took a year after the signing of the first agreement in 1993 to convince Arafat that he wouldn't get a state.'[4]

There were other disappointments, too. The PLO leadership arrived in Gaza from their exile in Tunisia and rode roughshod over the indigenous authorities who had remained in the territory throughout the years of Israeli occupation. The PNA gained a reputation for corruption in the awarding of major construction projects and in their scant respect for human rights. Bassem Eid, a Palestinian human rights activist, spoke in 1999 about the disappointment felt throughout the West Bank and Gaza Strip: 'When we heard about the peace process and the coming of the Palestinian leadership to the territories there were many expectations and dreams of the Palestinian people that after more than 30 years of occupation we would receive an authority which would go in to protect our violated rights from the Israelis. Unfortunately when the leadership came they started acting in the same way as the occupying forces had. We are talking about death in custody, hundreds of cases of torture inside the Palestinian Authority jails, hundreds of political prisoners subject to arbitrary arrest. Most of these people spent over three years in the Palestinian jails without charges, without trials.'[5]

Another serious development that gradually undermined the optimism in Gaza during the 1990s was the worsening of relations between the PLO-dominated PNA and Hamas. As early in the decade as November 1994, Palestinian police opened fire outside a Gaza mosque, killing 16 demonstrators. PNA officials claimed that outside instigators were behind the incident. Whatever the case, the killings raised the stakes in the rivalry between the PLO/PNA and Hamas and threatened to polarise Palestinian opinion to a potentially dangerous degree. Hamas accused Mr Arafat of 'collaborating with the Americans and Zionists to liquidate the virtuous heroes in our movement and ultimately quash the whole group together' and pledged that 'we will confront the Authority the same way we have confronted the Zionist enemy throughout the years.' The Qassam Brigades (Hamas's military wing)[6] threatened to 'respond to the massacre at the right time... it will be a bitter revenge' unless the PNA removed a number of officials (including its police chief and justice minister). The opening shots had been fired in a war that would last well into the next century and become one of the factors ensuring that the Gazans' yearning for peace and prosperity would remain unfulfilled.

Tension between the PNA and Hamas increased during 1995, as did the suffering of the people of Gaza, with frequent periods when workers were unable to cross into Israel to seek a day's work. The PNA, meanwhile, 'improved its capacity for repressing Hamas, by jailing several thousand Islamist leaders and militants. He [Arafat] dismantled their networks, interrupted their external sources of finance, and placed their mosques under surveillance.'[7] Hamas's decision to boycott parliamentary and presidential elections in January 1996 resulted in a resounding endorsement for Yasser Arafat and Fatah. But Hamas was by no means out of the picture. In November 1995, Israeli Prime Minister Yitzhak Rabin had been assassinated by a right-wing religious Jew. In the nervous and uncertain atmosphere in Israel following the killing, Hamas stepped up suicide bomb attacks. In January 1996, Israeli intelligence forces assassinated Hamas's main bombmaker and Qassam Brigades leader, Yahya Ayyash. Despite this killing and the election victory of hardline Likud leader Benjamin Netanyahu, sporadic Hamas suicide bombings continued throughout 1996 and 1997, leading to harsh Israeli retaliation against institutions and individuals in the Gaza Strip.

As conditions deteriorated in Gaza, efforts were continuing to promote peace talks between the Palestinians and the Israelis. But the Oslo peace process had 'reached a stalemate. Mounting frustration on both sides impeded any progress in the Israeli-Palestinian negotiations under President Bill Clinton, then in the last month of his tenure.'[8] Talks at Camp David in the United States between Israeli Prime Minister Ehud Barak and Yasser Arafat in July 2000 ended in failure. With Arafat's security forces unable to contain the Islamist suicide bombers from Gaza, there was a growing sense that a major conflagration between Israel and the Palestinians was likely. (One leading expert on contemporary Islam described suicide bombing as 'a gesture of rage and despair at the failure of the Oslo peace process and the continuing and systematic humiliation of the Palestinian people by the Israeli army.'[9]) A strong possibility seemed to be that the flare-up would come when Israel decided to retake some of the territory that it relinquished in 1994.

In the event, the spark for the second *intifada* was lighted in Jerusalem on 27 September 2000 when Likud leader Ariel

Optimism and Countdown to War

Sharon visited the Haram al-Sharif, the site of the Dome of the Rock and al-Aqsa mosque – sacred Islamic shrines. He was accompanied by 1,000 heavily armed riot police, in what was widely assumed to have been a gesture designed to ignite Palestinian violence and thus increase Sharon's chances of being elected prime minister. Clashes erupted immediately across the West Bank and Gaza Strip. The al-Aqsa *intifada*, as it came to be called, had begun; and it was a much more deadly confrontation than the previous uprising. Young Palestinians in 1987 had attacked Israeli troops with rocks and stones. In 2000, they had rifles and pistols, most of which had been issued to the Palestinian police. They also had suicide bombers. But Israel had at its disposal tanks, jets and a large army. It could also use a number of sophisticated methods to assassinate Palestinian leaders. The people of Gaza, as ever, became trapped in the middle of the conflict and suffered the greatest number of casualties. Reports on how many people died in those early years of the second *intifada* vary. But most estimate that between 2000 and 2005, more than 3,000 Palestinians were killed, and around 1,000 Israelis lost their lives.

Three days after the start of the al-Aqsa *intifada*, with fighting raging across the Gaza Strip, one image captured the terror and helplessness of the civilians trapped in the middle. It showed 12-year-old Muhammad al-Durrah caught in the crossfire. Muhammad and his father, Jamal, cowered behind a small metal barrel. Jamal was trying to shield his son from the shower of bullets, while waving in despair at Israeli soldiers nearby. Muhammad was hit four times and died. His father was critically injured.

The nature of conflict as a whole and its wider ramifications were well summarised by French academic and expert on Islam, Gilles Kepel:

'By mid-2001, Arafat was losing ground to the radicals,

both Islamists and younger Fatah activists who believed that violence, not merely tension, was the only strategy capable of achieving the desired political outcome. Suicide bombers became the main symbols of this second *intifada*. They blew themselves to death in Israeli pizzerias and bus stations, killing as many Jews as they could, while Islamist religious authorities called for *jihad*. They claimed that Israeli civilians, including women, were legitimate targets because Israel was a military society where everybody, regardless of gender, performed military service. Lebanese Hezbollah had forced Israel to leave Lebanon by using suicide bombers; the same tactics would now be applied in the Al Aqsa *intifada*.

'But this time, Israeli retaliation was severe. Sophisticated weaponry guided by intelligence reports targeted with precision many leaders of radical movements, while Arafat was pressured into taking extreme action against the terrorists. Gradually, Israeli military action destroyed with a vengeance the infrastructure supporting his political power. Images of this unnamed Arab-Israeli war of attrition shocked the Arab and Muslim world. The suicide bombers became heroes of the youth and of a wide segment of the populace – a development that put pressure on pro-West Arab governments. This demonstration of Israeli military might provoked rage and frustration, as it became only too obvious that no Arab army could match the Israeli Defense Forces and take up its challenge in the future.'[10]

Among the prominent Palestinians in Gaza who were assassinated by the Israelis during this period (in March 2004) was Shaikh Ahmad Yassin, the wheel-chair-bound spiritual

Optimism and Countdown to War

leader of Hamas and Abdel Aziz Rantisi, the new Hamas leader (the following month).

The intensity of the violence diminished somewhat in 2005. In January that year, Mahmoud Abbas was elected President of the PNA, in succession to Yasser Arafat who had died in November 2004. Talks between Abbas and Israeli Prime Minister Ariel Sharon led to the two sides agreeing to a truce. Hamas and other groups agreed to observe it. This marked an unofficial end to the second *intifada*. But the ending of one phase of violence was a cue for the start of a build-up to the next one – the war on Gaza in 2008-09. By July 2005 the truce had been broken by a bombing inside Israel, prompting major raids into the West Bank. Hamas, in turn, retaliated by firing rockets into Israel from the Gaza Strip.

These truce infringements did not change Israeli plans to withdraw all Jewish settlers from the Gaza Strip in August 2005 and to demolish the settlements. A month later the last military positions inside the territory were removed. But the Israeli army's grip on the Gaza Strip from the outside remained as tight as ever. For the people of Gaza, years of peace talks between the PNA and Israel had failed to deliver either peace or security. The PNA, furthermore, was deemed as being even more corrupt than it had been in the 1990s. Against this background Hamas won parliamentary elections in January 2006, taking control of the Palestinian Legislative Council. It was as much a protest vote against Fatah as an expression of support for Hamas. In any event, because of Hamas's refusal to recognise Israel, the international community decided to boycott the new government – even though the elections were accepted to have been free and fair. With Hamas in power but politically and diplomatically in isolation, the stage was set for a confrontation between the two wings of the Palestinian community.

Midway through 2006, Palestinian militants killed two Israeli soldiers and abducted another, Corporal Gilad Shalit, from a town in southern Israel. They took Shalit to the Gaza Strip. Three days later, on 28 June, Israel sent troops into the northern and southern ends of the territory, backed by helicopter gunships and fighter jets. The aim was twofold: to release Shalit and stop Hamas firing rockets into Israel. The Israelis attack also targeted the Ministry of Interior and other buildings in Gaza City, as well as the territory's power station.

As has been the case over the centuries, the number of innocent Gazans killed in this particular confrontation is uncertain. But innocent lives were lost. Nabil Abu Salmiah, his wife Salwa, two sons and five daughters were killed when a 550lb Israeli bomb landed on their house in July 2006. Two other sons had lucky escapes. They were saved because they had gone out onto the balcony to see what was happening after being woken by the sound of aircraft overhead. One son was thrown from the balcony, the other trapped – but not killed – by falling masonry. The Israeli army said it did not know there was a family in the house at the time. The army insisted that its aim was to target a group of Hamas militants lead by Muhammad Deif.[11]

Before the end of 2006, the Israeli forces had withdrawn from Gaza, without securing the release of Shalit or putting a stop to the firing of rockets into Israel. But the Gazans had another pressing concern: a further rise in tension between Hamas and Fatah, leading to street clashes and abductions. Each faction blamed the other for a failure to form a joint government. Not until February 2007, after talks in Mecca, Saudi Arabia, was agreement reached on forming a National Unity Government, headed by Hamas's leader, Ismail Haniya. But from the day the announcement was made the signs did not look good. President Mahmoud Abbas called on the new administration 'to respect international law and agreements signed by the PLO.' Hamas had no intention whatsoever of complying with the second condition. The government itself, finally established in March,

Optimism and Countdown to War

was not expected to last long.

In June, heavy fighting erupted on the streets of Gaza between Hamas and Fatah. It ended after six days in an outright victory for Hamas, the dissolution of the National Union Government, and the establishment of competing Palestinian authorities in the West Bank and Gaza Strip. Hamas took control of all military and government institutions in Gaza. Abbas reacted to Hamas's victory with a statement on 14 June dismissing Haniya and 'declaring a state of emergency in all the lands of the Palestinian Authority... and establishing a government authorised with implementing the regulations and instructions of the state of emergency.' He also indicated that he intended to hold elections 'as soon as the situation on the ground allows us to do so.'[12]

The intensity of the hatred in that week of inter-Palestinian fighting was revealed in a Human Rights Watch report which spoke of armed groups having 'committed serious violations of international humanitarian law, in some cases amounting to war crimes.' It added that 'both Fatah and Hamas military forces have summarily executed captives, killed people not involved in hostilities, and engaged in gun battles with one another inside and near Palestinian hospitals.' In one instance Hamas military forces captured 28-year-old Muhammad Swairki, a cook for President Mahmoud Abbas's presidential guard, and executed him by throwing him to his death, with his hands and legs tied, from a 15-storey apartment building in Gaza City. Later that night, Fatah military forces shot and captured Muhammad al-Ra'fati, a Hamas supporter and mosque preacher, and threw him from a high-rise apartment building. On another occasion, Hamas military forces attacked the home in Beit Lahiya of Jamal Abu al-Jadiyan, a senior Fatah official, captured him, and executed him on the street with multiple gunshots.[13] This must have been one of the blackest periods in Gaza's long history – Palestinians cruelly taking the lives of fellow Palestinians because of differences over how to deal with their common enemy.

Through the first half of 2008 Hamas fighters and Israeli forces exchanged fire on a number of occasions, and rockets were fired from the Gaza Strip. In June, the two sides agreed to a six-month truce brokered by Egypt, as part of which Israel agreed to ease the economic blockade it had imposed when Hamas took power. The blockade was taking its toll. 'Impoverished Palestinians on the Gaza Strip are being forced to scavenge for food on rubbish dumps to survive as Israel's economic blockade risks causing irreversible damage, according to international observers,' the London *Observer* reported in December 2008, just before Israel's war on Gaza began. UNRWA figures showed that 51.8% – an 'unprecedentedly high' number of Gaza's 1.5 million population – were living below the poverty line. While there was some easing of the blockade after June 2008, before the end of the year it was strictly enforced again. The Israeli army in November said it had discovered a cross-border tunnel used by Hamas to smuggle arms into the Gaza Strip and launched a military operation to block it. Hamas said this amounted to a violation of the truce. Israel, for its part, accused Hamas of breaking the truce by firing more rockets into southern Israel.

The upshot was that on 18 December Hamas declared the end of the ceasefire. It was followed by an outbreak of heavy fighting across the border. On 24 December, there was a sharp increase in rocket fire towards Israel. The Israeli government snapped and in effect declared war on Gaza. In the course of Saturday 27 December 2008, the start of Operation Solid Lead, at least 229 Palestinians were killed in massive Israeli air strikes on the territory. Three days into the new year, the Israelis launched a ground invasion.

The war brought the Arab world to a halt. People stayed for hours in front of their televisions, transfixed with horror and anger. Here, in their homes, were live images of a conflict of such intensity that it will be bracketed in Arab minds with the other decisive wars in the region in the modern era – in 1948, 1956, 1967, 1973 and 1982. The coverage on *al-Jazeera* television – with footage often supplied by the Gaza-based *Ramattan News Agency and Media Services* – was relentless around the clock, and the pictures were frequently far more gruesome than those considered acceptable for Western audiences. The cameras showed the bodies of babies and young children, very often with mutilated limbs, being carried into ambulances, the air inevitably filled with smoke. A close-up of a vehicle that had been targeted by an Israeli helicopter gunship revealed part of a charred human torso. A massive bomb that was dropped on the house where a senior Hamas leader, Nizar Rayyan, was staying left a crater the size of a giant empty swimming pool. Men were seen rushing to the scene and scrabbling with their hands through the rubble in the search for survivors. In the smoke-filled pandemonium, a man ran towards the camera carrying a flat wooden box containing a severed human leg.

The footage showed fear on the faces of men, women and children. By night, the skies over Gaza were illuminated by flares as the bombardments continued. The Roman Catholic parish priest of Gaza, Fr Manuel Musallam, said 'there is extreme fear everywhere here. The bombs the Israelis are dropping are literally cutting through people and through homes. Night and day the sound of children crying is everywhere. The people here don't sleep, they have lost everything.' Hassan Shamri, an engineer in Gaza City spoke of 'living in a nightmare' as the Israeli forces inched their way into crowded urban areas. 'It was bad all along. Now the gunmen are retreating up on to the roof of apartments to fire at the Israelis. So now we are all targets.'

The whine of ambulance sirens mingled with the explosions, the drone of helicopter gunships and the roar of

Israeli jets. Hospitals, with diminishing supplies of medicaments and exhausted staff, were stretched to the limited. The Ahli Arab hospital, for example, was receiving up to 40 new patients each day, including those that the main al-Shifa hospital and other health centres could not cope with because of the increasing number of casualties. A statement from the hospital gave a graphic account of the acute shortages and the desperate attempts at improvisation: 'The hospital is short of fuel which is required to continue operating the electrical generator because little electricity is available in Gaza. Glass in windows and doors at the hospital was shattered by nearby rocket and missile strikes. Glass is unavailable in Gaza at the present time for permanent repair, so the windows are temporarily covered with plastic rubbish bags until plastic sheeting becomes available for better protection from the cold.' At the same time, 'food is in increasingly desperate need. Our efforts at this time are focused on providing nutritional supplements for the most vulnerable people: for example, children and nursing mothers.'

A truce ended the hostilities on 18 January. According to Human Rights Watch, some 1,300 Palestinians were killed and more than 5,000 wounded, 40 per cent of them women and children. In addition, the casualties included an undetermined number of male civilians not taking part in the hostilities. Over the same period, Palestinian rocket fire killed three Israeli civilians and wounded more than 80. Ten Israeli soldiers were killed. Human Rights Watch called for an impartial international investigation into allegations of serious violations of the laws of war by Israel and Hamas.[14]

* * *

The descent from the brief years of optimism to the war of 2008-09 was steep. The human cost, year by year, was appalling and unacceptable. But in the aftermath of the war there was no obvious winner, and no suggestion that the Palestinians of Gaza would escape further blockades and attacks, of the kind their

Optimism and Countdown to War

ancestors experienced from the time of Alexander the Great in 332 BC onwards. Gazans today have inherited the stubbornness that has allowed the city and the territory to survive so long and under such overwhelming odds. 'Let Israel kill four members of Hamas's leadership,' a spokesman for the group said during the war in 2009, 'and it will have recruited 400 new members. Kill 400 and the number of recruits will rise to 4,000. And so on.'

The Arab states were paralysed and powerless to help during the war. 'Where are you, Arabs? Where are you,' a Gazan woman shouted in front of an *al-Jazeera* television camera. But Arab governments were diplomatically impotent, and unwilling to risk a military confrontation with Israel. Egypt and Saudi Arabia suggested that Hamas had inflicted the suffering on the Palestinians of Gaza by not renewing the truce with Israel. They went on to say that Hamas could have stopped the firing of rockets and renewed the truce at any time, in order to have saved innocent lives. But the sentiments of the Egyptian and Saudi governments were out of line with the public mood in the Arab world. Anti-Israel demonstrations in Arab cities voiced condemnation of Cairo and Riyadh.

Arab anger and indignation were not in short supply. But in the end, Gaza was left to face Israel's overwhelmingly superior military machine alone. Never had the world witnessed a war in which the pathetically weak party was prepared to endure so many civilian casualties for so long. Seldom can a territory have felt so abandoned in the face of such an onslaught. During the three British attacks on Gaza in 1917, most of the civilian population were able to flee while the city was wrecked, first by the Turks in search of timber for the trenches, and then by the Allied bombardment. In 2008-09, Gazans had nowhere to go. The degree to which 1.3 million people are trapped in a vast open prison was presented clearly to the world. The fact that this open prison lies on what was for three millennia the Way of the Sea merely emphasises how it has lost its traditional role and is living in suspension, waiting for its fate to be decided.

Gazans' aspiration to be part of a free and independent Palestinian state is as strong as ever. But their experience since 1948 has been so different from that of Palestinians in the West Bank and elsewhere that reintegration could be difficult. As early as 1991, Edward Said, during a visit to Gaza, commented on the resentment felt by the Palestinians there towards the inhabitants of the West Bank. 'There was a lot of anger. The phrase I kept hearing was *mawt bati'*, slow death. There seemed to be considerable animus against West Bankers, who were variously described by Gazans as spoiled, or privileged, or insensitive. "We are forgotten," they all said.'[15]

Denied the unrestricted contact with the world that other peoples take for granted, and living under difficult social and economic conditions, life in Gaza has become increasingly oppressive – especially for women. Normal social and economic development is impossible. Andalib Adwan, who works in a women's centre in Gaza said that 'even in the last few years we have seen regression. Whenever we speak of our rights we are told we women will have to wait until we get liberation from Israel. But it is not only independence from occupation that we want. It's independence from all kinds of restrictions.'

In Gaza, she added, 'it's a very difficult to be a woman and a refugee. The traditions and social norms are strong and stamp the life of the women strongly. The majority of the people are under the poverty line. They are very poor. This causes a lot of problems, and it's the women who have to handle the effects of them. If there is not enough money to finance the education for both the boys and the girls, then the woman is required to find money to educate just the boys, not the girls.' The shortage of money has also forced families to marry their daughters as soon as possible. 'The occupation is one strong reason behind the high level of early marriages in the Gaza Strip. Because of all the closures of the crossings into Israel, men have not been able

Optimism and Countdown to War

to work. They are poor and have no future. So they marry off their daughters when they are just young girls, because it means one less mouth to feed.'[16]

Then there is the psychological effect of the years of violence – experiences again that, among Palestinians, are unique to those in Gaza. During the 2008-09 war, many children watched their parents or other members of their families killed or maimed. Often ambulances were not able to reach them for hours, even days. BBC Middle East Editor Jeremy Bowen reported on the experiences of, Ahmad, a 16-year-old boy. When the building in which he and 90 members of his extended family was bombed, 29 people were killed, including his mother. 'Three of my brothers died next to me,' the boy said. 'I had been lying next to my brother Ismail. My head was half a metre from his. My brother Yaqoub was hurt. There was a hole in his stomach that you could have put a coffee cup into.' Ahmad stayed next to the dead bodies of his family until members of the International Committee of the Red Cross were able to reach the ruins of the building 48 hours later. Ahmad's face was a blank mask. All he could talk about were the family's animals that had been killed – his way of coping the trauma.

The psychological effects of living in Gaza are many and complex. Over the years, young Gazans have witnessed occasions when their elders – their fathers in particular – have been unable to protect their families or even provide for them. This, psychologists say, has contributed to a crisis of authority – when children regard their parents as impotent, lacking the means to protect or care for them. The long-term consequences of this trend are serious.

Looking back over three millennia of history it is hard to think of when the people of Gaza were in a more desperate state than after the 2009 war. They were forced to deal with deaths and injuries that left few families untouched, with psychological scars, and with massive damage to homes, offices and infrastructure. At the same time there was no prospect of chronic economic conditions improving, and no indication that their isolation – from fellow Palestinians in the West Bank, from the Arab world and the international community – was about to end. Despite the war, Israel failed to destroy Hamas or the latter's ability to fire rocket, and failed to free its missing serviceman. Hamas won supporters in the Arab world, but failed to win diplomatic recognition in the region. So there appeared to be much unfinished business.

The battles and blockades, the loss of life and the destruction that Gazans have endured in the past century have shaped their character in a way that has made them tougher and more determined than other Palestinians. They have had to be. The longer that Gazans live separated from the West Bank and the wider Palestinian community, the more likely it is that they will become something akin to a race apart – on territory steeped in history, but with a long experience of war.

* * *

From 'Silence for Gaza' by the late Mahmoud Darwish:

> The only value for the occupied is the extent of his resistance to occupation. That is the only competition there. Gaza has been addicted to knowing this cruel, noble value. It did not learn it from books, hasty school seminars, loud propaganda megaphones, or songs. It learned it through experience alone and through work that is not done for advertisement and image.
>
> Gaza has no throat. Its pores are the ones that speak in sweat, blood, and fires. Hence the enemy hates it to death and fears it to criminality, and tries to sink it into the sea, the desert, or blood. And hence its relatives and friends love it with a coyness that amounts to jealousy and fear

at times, because Gaza is the brutal lesson and the shining example for enemies and friends alike.

Gaza is not the most beautiful city.

Its shore is not bluer than the shores of Arab cities.

Its oranges are not the most beautiful
in the Mediterranean basin.

Gaza is not the richest city.
It is not the most elegant or the biggest, but it equals the history of an entire homeland, because it is more ugly, impoverished, miserable, and vicious in the eyes of enemies. Because it is the most capable, among us, of disturbing the enemy's mood and his comfort. Because it is his nightmare. Because it is mined oranges, children without a childhood, old men without old age and women without desires. Because of all this it is the most beautiful, the purest and richest among us and the one most worthy of love.

From 'Hayrat al-A'id – The Returnee's Perplexity, translated by Sinan Antoon. (Riyad al-Rayyis, Beirut, 2007)

Notes
[1] The Oslo Accords were the results of secret negotiations in Norway between Israel and representatives of the PLO – at a time when another PLO delegation was involved in public talks with Israel in Washington. On 13 September 1993, in the presence of President Bill Clinton, Israel and the PLO signed the 'Declaration of Principles On Interim Self-Government Arrangements'. This envisaged a five-year interim period of Palestinian self-rule. Permanent

status issues were to be the subject of further negotiations, to begin no later than the third year of the interim period. It was agreed that self-rule would be introduced first in Jericho and Gaza. An agreement on an Israeli withdrawal from these two areas was signed in Cairo on 4 May 1994.

[2] Gilles Kepel, *Jihad: The Trail of Political Islam*, London, 2002, p. 323.

[3] *Ibid.*, p. 324.

[4] Interviewed by the author, 1999.

[5] Interviewed by the author, 1999.

[6] The Izz al-Din al-Qassam Brigades was established in 1991. It is named after a Syrian-Palestinian killed in a clash with the British army in Palestine in 1935.

[7] Kepel, *op. cit.*, p. 330.

[8] *Ibid.*, p. 332.

[9] Malise Ruthven, *A Fury for God: The Islamist Attack on America*, London, 2002, p. 102.

[10] Kepel, *op. cit.*, p. 332.

[11] *The Guardian*, 13 July 2006.

[12] *Middle East Economic Survey*, 18 June 2007.

[13] Human Rights Watch, 12 June 2007.

[14] *Ibid.*, 27 January 2009.

[15] Edward Said, *The Politics of Dispossession: The Struggle for Palestinian Self-Determination 1969-1994*, London, 1995, p. 195.

[16] Interviewed by the author, 2002.

Bibliography

Aburish, Said K, *Nasser: The Last Arab*, London, 2005

Allenby, General, Letters of, to his wife Mabel, 1917, Liddell Hart Centre for Military Archives, King's College, London, reference: 1/8/16

Antonius, George, *The Arab Awakening*, London, 1945

Anchor Bible Dictionary, volume 2, New York, 1992

Archaeology, January-February 1983

Biblical Archaeologist, vol XXIX 1963

Biblical Archaeologist, March 1989

Boston Globe, 1 November 1925

Bosworth, A A, *Conquest and Empire – The Reign of Alexander The Great*, Cambridge, 1988

Bowder, Diana, *The Age of Constantine and Julian*, London, 1978

Bridge, Anthony, *The Crusades*, London, 1980

Bright, John, *A History of Israel*, Philadelphia, 1981

al-Dabbagh, Mustafa, *The History of Gaza and Palestine*, vols. I-II, Beirut, 1964-66

Daily Chronicle, 10.9.17

Life at the Crossroads

Downey, J D, *Gaza in the Early 6th Century*, 1963

Drawer, Margaret S, *Sir Flinders Petrie – A Life in Archaeology*, London, 1985

Fodor's *Israel 1986*, London

Fregosi, Paul, *Dreams of Empire*, London, 1989

Gardiner, Sir Alan, *Egypt of the Pharaohs*, Oxford, 1961

Grant, Michael, *History of Ancient Israel*, London, 1984

Green, Peter, *Alexander of Macedon 356-323 BC – An Historical Biography*, California, 1974

Hadawi, Sami, Bitter *Harvest: Palestine between 1914 and 1979*, New York, 1983

Hughes, C E, *Above and Beyond Palestine*, London, 1929

Ibn Battuta, *Travels*, Beirut, 1992

Jarvis, Major C S, *Desert and Delta*, London, 1938

Kepel, Gilles, *Jihad: The Trail of Political Islam*, London, 2002

Kinross, Lord, *The Ottoman Centuries: The Rise and Fall of the Turkish Empire*, New York, 1977

Kyle, Keith, *Suez*, London, 1991

Landau, Jacob M, in *Handbooks to the Modern World – The Middle East*, edited by Michael Adams, London, 1988

Lawrence, T E, *Seven Pillars of Wisdom*, London, 1935

Le Strange, Guy, *Palestine under the Moslems. A Description of Syria and the Holy Land from AD 630 to 1500*, London, 1890

Lesch, Ann M, 'Prelude to the Uprising in the Gaza Strip', in *Journal of Palestine Studies, California*, autumn 1990

Lewis, Bernard, *The Arabs in History*, London, 1968

Maalouf, Amin, *The Crusades Through Arab Eyes*, London, 1984

MacInnes, Rennie, *Notes for Travellers by Road and Rail in Palestine and Syria*, London, 1933

Mansfield, Peter, *A History of the Middle East*, London, 1991

Marlowe, John, *The Seat of Pilate: An Account of the Palestine Mandate*, London, 1959

Mayer, Martin, *The History of Gaza*, New York, 1960

Middle East Economic Survey, 18 June 2007

Middle East Watch, 'The Israeli Army and the Intifada - Policies that contribute to the killings', New York, August 1990

Newby, P H, *Warrior Pharaohs – The Rise and Fall of the Egyptian Empire*, London, 1980

Newman, Bernard, *Middle Eastern Journey*, London, 1947

Ovendale, Ritchie, *The Origins of the Arab-Israeli Wars*, London, 1984

Prawer, Joshua, *The Latin Kingdom of Jerusalem*, London, 1972

Roberts, J M, *The Penguin History of the World*, London, 1990

Robertson, William, Papers of, Liddell Hart Centre for Military Archives, King's College, London, July 1917, reference: 1/32/62

Rodinson, Maxime, *Israel and the Arabs*, New York, 1982

Runciman, Steven, *A History of the Crusades*, Cambridge, 1962

Ruthven, Malise, *A Fury for God: The Islamist Attack on America*, London, 2002

Said, Edward, *The Politics of Dispossession: The Struggle for Palestinian Self-Determination 1969-1994*

Sakkik, Ibrahim Khalil, *Ghazzah 'Abr al- Ta'rikh*, Gaza, 1982

Salt, Jeremy, *The Unmaking of the Middle East: A History of Western Disorder in Arab Lands*, California, 2008

al-Sarraf, Faraj, "Christianity in Gaza", *Christians in the Holy Land*, London, 1994

Shaban, M A, *Islamic History AD 600-750 (AH /32): A New Interpretation*, Cambridge, 1971

Shlaim, Avi, 'The Rise and Fall of the All-Palestine Government in Gaza, *Journal of Palestine Studies*, California, autumn 1990

Sivan, Hagith, *Palestine in Late Antiquity*, Oxford, 2008

Stephens, Robert, *Nasser – A Political Biography*, London, 1971
Storrs, Ronald, *Orientations*, London, 1939

Bibliography

The Times Concise Atlas of the Bible, London, 1991

The Times, History and Encyclopaedia of the War, Part 187, Volume 15, March 19 1918

Viorst, Milton, *Reaching for the Olive Branch: UNRWA and Peace in the Middle East*, Washington, 1989

Wilkinson, John, *Jerusalem Pilgrims before the Crusades*, Jerusalem, 1977

Wilson, Trevor, *The Myriad Faces of War*, London, 1986

INDEX*

A

Abbas, Mahmoud (*see also* Abu Mazen) 241-3
Abbasids 101, 106, 119
AbdulShafi, Dr Haidar 195
Abu Mazen (Mahmoud Abbas) 236; *see also* Abbas, Mahmoud
Abu Salmiah, Nabil and Salwa 242
Adwan, Andalib 248
Ahli Arab Hospital 141, 222-3, 246
Ainuni raisins 104
al-Arish 55, 61, 133, 135, 137, 146
al-Dimashqi 130
al-Hussaini
    Fahmi Bey 170
    Majid 173, 187, 189, 202
    Mufti al-Hajj Amin 166, 171, 185
al-Jazeera television 245, 247
Al-Mas'udi 103
al-Mukhtar, Umar 17-8, 124, 170, 173
al-Muqaddasi 101-5
al-Nasser, Gemal Abd 186-7, 191-4, 197-8, 201, 205
al-Shafi'i, Imam 101
al-Shawa
    Ala-Eddine 13
    al-Hajj Said 166
    Majid 190
    Rashad 190, 206, 210
Aleppo 18, 131-3
Alexander 9-10, 66-9, 72-5, 81, 134, 247
Alexander's army 67-8
Alexandria 72-3, 76, 85, 92, 135, 200
Ali, Hassan 175-6, 179, 226, 233
All-Palestine Government in Gaza 185
Allenby, General Sir Edmund 9, 150-5, 157-8, 164, 168, 181

Amarna letters 30-3
Amman 18, 186, 217
Amon 34-5, 48, 50
Amr ibn al-As 98-9
Anglo-French Suez Canal Company 193-4
Anthedon 74-5, 77, 79
Antiochus 72-3
Antony 76
Apollodotus 74
Apostle Philip 83
Arab Christians 111
Arab conquest of Gaza 99
Arab League 185-6, 200
Arab Legion 185-6
Arab population of Palestine 181
Arabs of Gaza 133
Arafat, Yasser 11-2, 17, 192, 200, 217, 226, 230, 235-41
Arsa 58
Ashdod 42, 44-5, 48, 60, 106
Ashqelon 42, 45, 61, 86, 106, 112-17, 130, 176-7
Assyria 24, 26, 31, 53-7, 59
Assyrian invasions 54
Assyrians 53-5, 57, 59
Ayyash, Yahya 238
Ayyubids 116, 119

B

Babylon 31, 57, 60-1, 69, 72
Babylonia 24, 26, 59, 60
Babylonians 53, 59-61
Baghdad 18, 101, 106, 119, 135
Baibars 129-30, 135
Bait Lahya 103
Baldwin 9, 111, 113-16
Balfour Declaration 165-6, 174, 178

259

Bar Kokhba 80
Barak, Ehud 238
Batis 68-9
Bedouins 112
Beersheba 140, 146, 152-3, 155, 172, 177, 189
Beirut 14, 87, 133, 140, 182, 251,
Ben Gurion, David 175, 193
Bowen, Jeremy 249
Britain 65, 136-7, 139, 141, 145-6, 159-60, 164-5, 169, 172, 174-5, 181, 188, 193-4
British 9, 62, 70, 83, 125, 135-8, 140-53, 155-8, 160, 163-76, 181, 184, 186-91, 193, 215,222,225
British and Commonwealth War Cemetery in Gaza 128
British attacks on Gaza 247
British High Commissioner in Palestine 159
Brook of Egypt 55, 60
Byblos 43, 54
Byzantine empire 106-7, 133
Byzantine Gaza 92
Byzantines 93, 96, 100-1, 106, 112

C
Caesar, Julius 76
Cairo 14, 22, 116-17, 129-33, 135-9, 141, 145-6, 158, 180, 184-6, 188-92, 198, 226, 247
Caliph Umar Ibn al-Khattab 99, 104
Camp David 208, 238
Canaan 26-8, 30-7, 40, 42
Canaanites 27, 33, 44, 46
Carthage 73, 75, 93
Christian holy sites 107
Christianity 23, 81, 83-7, 92-3, 97, 99, 110, 156
Christianity in Gaza 83, 85, 87
Christians 23, 83-4, 90, 99, 100-2, 110-12, 118-19, 133, 226
Church Missionary Society (CMS)

140, 156
Cleopatra 74, 76-7
Clinton, President Bill 12, 235, 238, 251
Constantinople 85, 87, 110, 133-4, 137-9, 145
Crete 40, 43, 75
Crusader army in Gaza 110
Crusaders 86, 106, 109, 111-17, 119-20, 130, 143
Crusades 112, 115, 120-1, 131, 135, 156
Cyprus 28, 33, 40, 43, 74-5, 86
Cyrus, King 61

D
Dabbour, Amin 189, 203
Dagon 44, 47-8
Damascus 14, 18, 56, 98, 100-2, 104, 115, 129, 131-3
Darwish, Mahmoud 250
David 49-50
Deif, Muhammad 242
Deir al-Balah 21, 33, 85, 114, 146-7, 150, 157-8
Deir Yassin 175
Delilah 47
Duri raisins 104

E
East Indies and Egypt Seaplane Squadron 152
Egypt
  ancient 26, 29
  borders of 50, 56, 74
Egypt/Gaza border 200
Egyptian administration 180, 188, 190
Egyptian army in Gaza 119
Egyptian army positions 177
Egyptian Mamluks 119
Egyptian pharaoh Sethos 34-6, 40, 148
Eid, Bassem 236
Ekron 42, 45

Index

Empress Eudoxia 87-8
Esarhaddon 57-9
Eudoxiana church 88-90

F
Falluja 176, 187
Farah, Samira 222-3
Fatah 200, 205, 215, 218-19, 238, 240-3
Father Waggett 9, 18, 156-8
Fatimids 106, 112-13, 116
Filastin 51, 104-6
First Battle of Gaza, 1917 149
First World War 3, 18, 141, 145, 158, 163-5, 167-8, 172
France 107, 117, 138-9, 145-6, 159, 164, 193
Franj 111, 120
frankincense 66-7, 71
Franks 112, 118, 130
French occupation of Egypt 134

G
Gaza
  attacked, 1917 155
  captured, 734 BC 55, 66
  conquered, 350 BC 63
  conquest of, 1580 BC 28, 69, 99
  destruction of, 1917 156, 159
  isolated, 100-99 BC 74
  occupied, 618 98
Gaza City 12, 16, 19, 21, 25, 33, 39, 58, 75, 86, 88, 95-6, 109-10, 129, 140, 149, 152, 155, 166, 168, 171, 173, 177, 183-4, 187, 190, 192-3, 202, 206, 209, 216-19, 221-2, 224, 226, 230, 234, 242-3, 245
Gaza military prison 163
Gaza Museum 33
Gaza port 15, 17, 106
Gaza railway station 125
Genghis Khan 118-19
Grand al-Umari Mosque in Gaza City 109, 114, 156
Gulf War 235-6

H
Habiri 32-3
Haifa 171-2
Hamas 13-14, 210, 219, 235, 237-8, 241-7, 250
Hammam al-Samarra 88-9
Hanun 54-6
Hanun of Gaza 55-6
Hasmonaeans 74-5
Hatshepsut 29, 30
Hattin, Horns of 116-17
Hejaz 98-9, 146
Hellenistic cities 72-3
Heraclius 93
Herbya 176
Herod 9, 76-8
Hittites 32, 36, 40, 46
Human Rights Watch 243, 246
Hyksos pharaohs 28

I
Ibrahim, Tala'at 171, 173, 181, 188
indigenous Gazans 182
Intifada 10-12, 15, 22, 214-26, 229, 232, 235-6, 238-41
  al-Aqsa 239
Islamic conquest of Gaza 99
Islamic University of Gaza 209
Israeli agents 176, 207
Israeli army in Gaza, 2008 244
Israeli attack, 2008 195
Israeli settlement of Darom 114
Israeli troops leave Gaza 226
Israeli war on Gaza, 2008-09 10
Israelite supremacy 49-50
Israelite tribes 45, 48
Israelites 44-50

J
Jabaliya Refugee Camp 148, 176, 203,

261

213-14, 216-17, 219-20, 225-6, 233
Jannaeus 74
Jemal Pasha 145
Jewish settlements 21, 207, 233
Jewish settlers 170, 175, 216, 241
Jewish underground groups 174-5
Jihad 175, 210, 216, 235, 240
Jordan 16, 22, 57, 88, 98, 185-6, 190, 198, 200-1, 205, 207
Judaea 72, 75-6, 80

K
Kantara 29, 34, 167-8, 204
Karnak 35, 50
Khan Younis 21, 129, 135, 146-7, 152, 167, 176-7, 194, 202-3, 215, 218, 220
Khuza'a 166, 190, 202, 204, 220
King Abdullah of Jordan 185
King Baldwin 115-16
Knights Templar 114
Kressenstein, Kress von 145, 155

L
Latin Kingdom of Jerusalem 112-13
Latin kingdoms 111, 113
Lawrence, T.E. 149, 160, 255
Ludd (Lydda) 103

M
Macedonia 66-7, 69, 75
MacInnes, Bishop Rennie 147, 158, 160-1, 255
Maioumas 17, 85-6, 90-1, 104, 106
Makka 96
Mamluks 9, 119, 129-30, 132-4
Mark Antony 76
Marnas 86-7
Marneion 87-8
Mary, mother of Jesus 78, 90
Mark Antony 96-8, 110, 146, 164, 242
Middle East Watch 225

Mongols 118-19, 129
Mosul 58-9, 113
Murray, Sir Archibald 146-50, 158
Musallam, Fr Manuel 245
Museum, Israel 27, 33, 44, 90-1, 101
Muslim Brotherhood in Egypt 209

N
Nabataeans 77, 91
Napoleon 9, 29, 134-8, 167
Nasir 18
Negev 25, 51, 91, 112
Netanyahu, Benjamin 238
Nineveh 58-60

O
Octavian 76-7
Oslo agreement 235-6
Ottoman army 9, 133, 137-9, 158
Ottoman control 139-40, 225
Ottoman Empire 79, 135, 138, 141, 164

P
Palestine Liberation Army (PLA) 200
Palestine National Congress 200
Palestine Police 167, 172
Palestine Square 17-8, 114, 141, 173
Palestinian National Authority, *see* PNA
Palestinian refugees 20, 197
Palestinian refugees in Gaza 182, 198, 221
Palestinian state, independent 5, 12, 186, 248
Persia 24, 61, 63, 68, 93, 98, 106, 118-19
Persian occupation of Palestine 62
Peterson, Dr Jerome 183-4
Petrie, Sir Flinders 70, 139-40
PFLP (Popular Front for the Liberation of Palestine) 205-6
Philistia 21, 40, 42, 50, 53-62, 104

Index

Philistine cities 53, 57, 59
Philistine city states 42, 45, 50
Piacenza pilgrim 89-90
PLO (Palestine Liberation Organization) 11, 200, 205, 209, 226, 230, 233, 235-6, 242, 251
PNA (Palestinian National Authority) 13, 230, 232, 234, 236-7, 241
Pompey 9, 75-6
Pope 110-11
Porphyry 87-8, 91, 99
Portuguese 132
Procopius of Gaza 89
Prophet Muhammad 95-7, 102, 157
Ptolemaic period Gaza 72
Ptolemies 9, 71-2, 76

Q

Qassam Brigades 237-8
Quakers 177-8, 180
Qudaih
  Ismail 202, 204, 209, 218, 220
  Shuhadah 166-7, 190, 220

R

Rabin, Yitzhak 226, 238
Rafah 12, 18, 19, 21, 35, 51, 56, 72, 75, 104-5, 127, 146, 187, 193, 202, 233
railway, Egypt to Gaza 25, 147, 154, 157-8, 167-8, 171, 192, 204
Ramattan News Agency and Media Services 245
Ramlah 103
Rantisi, Abdel Aziz 241
Richard, King, Coeur de Lion 117
Rimal, district of Gaza City 17-8

S

Saba, Mousa 177, 179, 189, 192-3
Sabra, district of Gaza City 18
Sadat, President of Egypt 208, 210

Said, Edward 236, 248
Salah al-Din 115-17, 119, 120, 135
Salha Sycamore 78-9
Samaria 56
Samson 44, 46-8, 51, 156
Samuel, Sir Herbert 159, 164, 166, 169
Sargon 56-7
Sea People 40, 42, 44
Second World War 172-3
Seleucids 69, 72, 74-5
Seljuq 106-7, 110-11, 113, 130, 133
Sethos 34-6, 40, 148
shabaab 211, 218-19
Shalit, Corporal Gilad 241-2
Sharon, Major General Ariel 206-7, 239, 241
Sheikh Radwan, district of Gaza City 18
Shifa hospital in Gaza City 218, 246
Shishak 50-1
Shuja'iya 18, 95, 173
Sidon 27, 54, 60, 133
Simirra 55-6
Sinai 27, 29, 34-5, 133, 140, 146, 193-4, 201
Solomon 50, 114
Sourani, Raji 214, 230, 232-3
Storrs, Sir Ronald 158, 181-2
Suez Canal 29, 145, 188, 193-4
Suez crisis 22, 194-5
suicide bombers 12, 238-40

T

Tell al-Ajjul 27-8
Tell Jemmeh 25-6, 33, 44, 57-8, 61-2, 148
Tiglath Pileser 54-6
Tuffah 18
Tuthmosis 28-30, 33-5, 43, 135-6
Tyre 54, 60, 67-8, 117

U
Umayyads 100
UNEF (United Nations Emergency Force) 194, 200-1
United Nations 20, 175, 179-81, 192, 194, 207
United Nations Emergency Force, *see* UNEF
United Nations Relief and Works Agency, *see* UNRWA
Unknown Soldier Memorial in Gaza 127
UNRWA (United Nations Relief and Works Agency) 179-84, 184, 198, 215, 221-2, 225, 244

W
Wadi Ghazzah 25, 27, 33, 36-7, 44, 148, 152
Wen Amun 43

Y
tiri 31-2
Yaqut 114
Yassin, Shaikh Ahmad 209, 240

Z
Zaitoun 18, 173